World and Environment

World and Environment

Odil Hannes Steck

Biblical Encounters Series

ABINGDON
Nashville

WELT UND UMWELT

Copyright © 1978 Verlag W. Kohlhammer GmbH
WORLD AND ENVIRONMENT

Translation Copyright © 1980 by Abingdon

Library of Congress Cataloging in Publication Data

STECK, ODIL HANNES.
   World and environment.
   (Biblical encounters series)
   Translation of Welt und umwelt.
   Bibliography: p.
   1. Creation—Biblical teaching—Addresses, essays, lectures. 2. Na-
   ture (Theology)—Biblical teaching—Addresses, essays, lectures.
   3. Human ecology—Moral and religious aspects—Addresses,
   essays, lectures.
   I. Title. II. Series.
   BS651.S79313   231.7′6   80-12683

   ISBN 0-687-46240-1

MANUFACTURED BY THE PARTHENON PRESS AT
NASHVILLE, TENNESSEE, UNITED STATES OF AMERICA

THE NATURAL WORLD
AND LIFE

From the time I was about nine years old, I spent every summer on my father's estate, and when I was fourteen I moved from my grandfather's house to my father's house in the town.

My father's influence on my mental development was of a different kind from that of my grandparents. It did not really come from the intellect, properly speaking, at all.

In his youth my father had had strong intellectual interests. He had thought seriously about the questions raised by books such as Darwin's *Origin of Species* and Renan's *Life of Jesus;* but quite early he began to devote himself to farming, and he gave himself up to it more and more as time went on. Soon he became an example for landowners in eastern Galicia.

When I was still a child he brought from the Paris Exhibition a great package of hatching eggs from a kind of chicken that was still unknown in east Germany. He had held this parcel on his knees during the whole journey, so that none of the eggs should be damaged. He worked for thirty-six years with all kinds of fertilizers, trying out their specific effects exactingly, in order to increase the productivity of his land.

He had mastered the techniques of his time in his own field. But I realized what his real concern was as I stood beside him in the middle of a herd of splendid horses and watched how he greeted one animal after another, not simply kindly, but positively personally; or when I drove through the ripening fields with him and watched him stop the carriage, get out, and bend over the ears of corn, again and again, until he finally broke one open and sampled the grains carefully and reflectively. What this utterly unsentimental and completely unromantic man was concerned about was a truly humane contact with nature, a contact that was active and responsible. Accompanying him like this from time to time, the growing boy came to realize something he had never learned from all the many writers whose books he had read.

This relationship of my father's to nature came to light in its own way in his relationship to the sphere that is generally called the social one. The way he participated in the life of all the people who were dependent on him in one way or another—the laborers in the cottages, built according to his design, which were grouped round the farm buildings; the small tenant farmers, who served him under conditions he had worked out with the strictest justice; his concern about their family circumstances, the upbringing and education of their children, the sickness and old age of all of them—all this was not "on principle"; it was welfare work, not in the usual sense, but in the personal one. In town, my father behaved in just the same way. He was fiercely opposed to blind charity. He understood no help except the help of person to person, and that was the help he practiced. Even when he was old, he allowed himself to be elected to the charity committee of the Jewish congregation in Lemberg, and went tirelessly from house to house, in order to discover the truly needy and what their real needs were. How else could that have been done except through genuine contact?

From: Martin Buber,
Begegnung. Autobiographische Fragmente

March 1978, television news: The oil tanker "Amoco-Cadiz" has run aground, and 230,000 tons of crude oil are in the sea. The oil slick. The oil on the coast of Brittany. Miles of it. We are shown a seabird in the surf, its feathers covered with oil. It beats with its wings in its struggle for life, tires, sinks. The child beside me cries, "Why doesn't anyone help? Help it!" and begins to weep.

We are visiting the Senckenberg Natural History Museum in Frankfurt and have an upsetting experience. On one of the walls there are specimens showing the stages of growth of the human embryo. We and our children are marveling over the miracle of the way human life grows in the mother's womb. A young woman comes over to the wall and calls to her companion: "Look! Here you can see the beasts grow."

Contents

CONTENTS

CONTENTS

CONTENTS

CONTENTS

CONTENTS

To my Bavarian homeland
and the powers of its life

Preface

From the very beginning, creation was intended to be the subject of this volume in the Biblical Encounters Series. However, the title *World and Environment* was finally chosen, so as to give a name to the challenge of our time with which the ancient biblical statements about creation are today confronted. In this volume, accordingly, we shall be discussing the *natural* world and environment.

Our whole outlook on the world and the environment, and especially the realm of nature, is a live issue today, and one that is vital for our survival. But readers will not expect the book to be a handy aid to argument or the source of patent solutions drawn from the Old and New Testament; the challenges of the twentieth century were not the challenges of the biblical period. But what readers *are* invited to do in their search for the perspectives of knowledge and action offered today in the relationship between man and nature, is to look at, to learn, and to think actively about what the Old and New Testaments disclose in the way of orientations and impulses. The center of gravity of this account is the tracing of biblical findings, while considering our contemporary theme of world and environment. Our goal is to encourage theology and faith in the face of a survival crisis in our time and to pursue the path for ascertaining the true Christian position. In our present book, the Bible and the present start out together.

To encounter the Bible with the present in this way, to let ancient texts have their say on new questions, is an unusual undertaking, at least for someone concerned with the historical exegesis of the Bible. To do justice to the circle of readers in such a wide field as world and environment, without doing injustice to the specialists, pushes the writer into new territory—the explorer begins hesitantly and is often tempted to turn back. It is impossible to see everything in an undertaking of this kind—impossible to think of everything—impossible to take everything into account. Whether we arrive at our goal is for the reader to decide. It seems to me that in our situation today the risk of trying to make a contribution, as a biblical scholar, to a theology that is responsible to the present is more important than the need to secure one's position in the guild of historical specialists.

The book's dedication is intended to express my gratitude to the world that molded me. Gratitude for my Bavarian home, its landscape, its people, its feeling for elemental values and for moderation. I am more conscious today than ever of how much in experience and outlook I owe to this background—and not least for my work on this book.

While I was living in Hamburg, I was able to have numerous discussions with Udo Krolzik about questions in the field of science and systematic theology, and later discussions with scientists at the University of Mainz have given me both criticism and help from the scientific point of view. I should like to express my thanks to all these discussion partners, as well as to my assistant Susanne Krüger, for her intelligent cooperation in reading the proofs, and to Maria-Theresia Küchenmeister, for typing the manuscript.

ODIL HANNES STECK

Haibach/Aschaffenburg
March 1978

Introduction

Four Essential Conditions for an Encounter Between the Bible and Our World and Environment

The biblical texts grew up in a preindustrial world. Two to three thousand years lie between us and their formulation. But the subject of the world and the environment, as we are all talking about it today, is a modern problem. *Pollution, ecological crisis, environmental protection, energy problem, raw materials depletion,* and *over-population* are quite recent terms. They represent phenomena belonging to the world of today. They are the components of the dangerous threat to our survival which has grown up as a result of the technical possibilities and qualitative claims of modern industrial society. Consequently, they do not occur at all in express form in the biblical texts. A biblical encounter with the subject of the world and the environment therefore has its own difficulties, because such a confrontation means putting questions to the Bible in the context of problems of which the Bible knows nothing. If our confrontation is not to be impaired by this immense historical difference; and if it is to produce more than the conclusion that in earlier times everything was simply different and that every age has its own problems, then we must take these difficulties into account in the course of the encounter itself. We must come to terms with the essential conditions under which our undertaking has to be carried out; and these conditions must take account of the special circumstances surrounding our subject.

The first and most fundamental condition: We must define the whole complex of the world and the environment in such a way that biblical statements and contemporary questions can be usefully related to one another. But what are these contemporary questions?

The second essential condition: We must delve into the important aspects of the present world and environment, even if historical interpretations of biblical texts only convey these with naive oversimplification. A confrontation can, after all, only come into being if the biblical texts are not merely unfolded in the light of historical questions raised by current exegetical discussions among specialists. Rather, we must have in front of us an outline of our present problems, so that the biblical texts can reveal their character as something unique and different in relation to these present-day questions.

The aim of this encounter is to lead us to the biblical texts in a manner that opens up their critical power and their continuing stimulus for our own time. This cannot come about in any simple and direct way, as if we had only to set the unique historical character of the biblical statements against the background of modern questions in order to gain direct solutions and specific directions for our present challenges. This would simply mean leaving out the difficulties we mentioned at the beginning or drawing a veil over them. If the unique character of the biblical statements and the unique character of the modern world are both to be preserved, we must take a different approach to biblical exegesis. That approach is the starting point for a *third essential condition:* We must make clear what can and cannot be said about our topical subject in the framework of this exegetical book.

A fourth and final condition: We must explain the plan for this book.

Let us now develop these four essential conditions.

1. The Natural World and Environment as the Common Field of Reference for Our Encounter

a. The problem of approach

Let me first of all draw two demarcation lines, in the negative sense.

One—The concept of creation is not suited to act as a guiding thematic term or starting point when we confront the

Bible with the present, under the heading world and environment. The statement that God made the world and man—that he made me—is undoubtedly anchored in the biblical texts. But if we want to address today's problems and experience, then we can no longer begin with the concept of creation, because in our scientific world, molded as it is by scientific, technical, and economic processes, no empirically demonstrated knowledge and no independent, self-sustaining experience corresponds to that concept.[1] In the street or at school, and on into the discussions that shape scientific and political opinion, the creation perspective no longer has the binding force of something viewed as a matter of course. The philosopher Karl Löwith said years ago: "The post-Christian world is a creation without a creator and an era which—for lack of a religious perspective—can no longer even be called profane [literally, "outside the temple," and therefore what is not sacred]; it is simply worldly."[2]

Two—On the other hand, the paired concepts world and environment do not provide an adequate approach either. The words certainly have the advantage of describing aspects of our reality that are open to experience and investigation—even if the ambiguous term world needs closer definition because it only acquires a clearly defined content through the concept environment; and they are words used in our own contemporary language. But at once a new difficulty emerges. On the basis of these concepts, no corresponding facts can be drawn from the Bible. Needless to say, the modern concept of the environment does not occur in either the Old or the New Testament. Only late and scattered terms such as kol ("the universe," "everything") or ôlam ("the world") can be found in the Old Testament to correspond with the total concept world.[3] The New Testament does offer the comparable terms kosmos and aion; but these words are parallel to the description of a total view of things, which includes nature, and they are used in connection with the world of man and mankind. Or they may designate a spatial and temporal sphere of power belonging to this earthly time, which is coming to an end in order to be replaced by a future time.[4] These concepts are not therefore

entirely reconcilable with our contemporary use of the word
world, especially when it is linked with the concept of the
environment.

b. World and environment as a total view of things

If in considering the subject of the world and the
environment we want to bring the Bible face to face with the
present, we cannot do so simply on the level of using common
terms. The field of reference necessary for the confrontation is
only valid when the theme involves *a common view of the facts*,
under which both the biblical statements and our contemporary conditions can be investigated and brought into a
relationship of confrontation. What can this all-embracing
viewpoint be?

I would recommend beginning with the term borrowed
from biology which stands for environment in the ecological
sense. In biology, the environment is the *milieu*, the elemental
aspects of natural life (as distinct from the social environment);[5]
it means "the surroundings, living and nonliving, that affect an
organism,"[6] with the totality of the elemental factors that
determine existence. Or, picking up the difference between
surroundings and environment, we may be more precise and
say that the environment is "that, and only that, in the
surroundings of a living thing which is of direct importance for
itself."[7] The essential thing about this viewpoint for the
framework of our encounter is that here living things are not
seen in isolation as individual subjects. They are viewed from
the very beginning *in the elemental and vitally decisive complex
of the surrounding natural conditions that are essential for
their existence*.

F. W. Dahmen has impressively described, even for the
nonbiologist, the presuppositions, factors, and processes in this
whole complex.[8] In what follows we shall be adhering to his
viewpoint. Our subject, the environment, will cover the milieu
of constitutive, natural living conditions as these affect the
living being which is related to them. In this sense, therefore,
the environment is not only the habitat, or living space, which is

of decisive importance for the life of the organism, it is the connection between habitat and the living thing itself. This connection presents itself in a different form for different kinds of organisms. As the different habitats (or biotopes) show, minute organisms have a different habitat from the bee, and a deer's is different from that of man.

In this sense, the concept of environment is isolationist because it is directed toward the vital conditions of existence for only one kind of living thing in a given class. Nevertheless, taking a broader look at life's phenomena, environments are found to be interpenetrating, with different kinds of living things existing together in biozenotic communities. Consequently, our viewpoint must be developed further to cover the phenomenon of the ecosystem. By an ecosystem "we understand highly varying, widespread sections of the earth's surface in which several—it may be a few, it may be very many—kinds of living things always live together and are linked with one another and with their milieu through numerous relationships."[9] In an ecosystem, stable conditions of life develop through the reciprocal effects of surroundings and living things, and through active shaping and control on the part of the living things themselves. These stable conditions can also be endangered, however, if they are overtaxed.[10] In a total viewpoint covering organisms as a whole, the ecosystem—that is to say, "the cohesion of effects between different living things and the conditions in which they live, or the complex of living communities and their living space"[11] can and must be seen as the surrounding milieu of constitutive conditions of existence for all living things. The ecosystem is therefore really the whole terrestrial globe, including the atmosphere as biosphere and the heavenly bodies with their effects on life.[12] In what follows we shall sum up this phenomenon of ecosystems on earth, as well as the ecosystem of the earth itself—as the milieu of constitutive natural living conditions in connection with all the living beings related to it in their totality—gathering it together under the heading *world*.

In combining the concepts of world and environment, then, we are starting out with a certain perspective of the facts.

It implies a view and examination of the connection between all living beings, together with the surrounding milieu of all their constitutive, natural living conditions (the world), as well as the particular aspect of this connection for an individual species (the environment); and this is all to be viewed in the context of an ecosystem—on the level of the elemental preconditions, factors, and processes that determine existence.

c. Explanations and definitions

This connecting viewpoint needs further explanation and definition.

It is characteristic of this perspective that, in accordance with our ecological starting point, everything that lives and the factors determining their existence are, from the beginning, seen in conjunction with one another; this viewpoint is neither confined to man, nor does it exclude him. A further characteristic of this perspective is that it takes into account living things, together with the milieu of their elemental living conditions, i.e., their habitat and the living and nonliving elements of that habitat—weather, food, reproduction, etc. In this way it takes account of the vital basic equipment required by the living thing. Inherent in this basic equipment is quality: what is given with the habitat, what is the precondition or basis for life that it offers, and what is the possibility of achieving life in each specific case. Note that the acquiring of this equipment is not, ultimately, within the power of the living thing, but is always its already existing presupposition and accompaniment, insofar as it lives at all.

This does not exclude the fact that a living thing can and must adjust itself to this already existing basic equipment (adaptation); and that it always actively forms or reforms its sphere of existence by means of instinctive reactions or deliberate activity. We have only to think of eating, for example, or of building nests or cultivating fields, and also of metabolism—the conversion of energy, the giving-off of heat, and the excretion of waste products.[13] World and environment must therefore, in our sense, include the natural world as a given datum and foundation, together with the way the living thing uses and shapes it in order to secure the elements necessary for its life. The viewpoint that we have worked out is accordingly not an artificial, theoretical one that sets the particular living thing apart from the elemental factors necessary for its existence. On the contrary, in its approach it is primarily a phenomenological viewpoint—one which takes account of the particular character and the totality of conditions that are of elemental importance for the living thing; which perceives the active use of this equipment, as reality shows it; and which thereby penetrates farther, grasping the given, essential presuppositions that make the achievement of life and the utilization of life's equipment possible in the first place.

Finally, since this elemental perspective is oriented toward living things in general, and penetrates into given elemental conditions in the special case of man, what it does not include is man's self-formed, anthropogenic (or "human") milieu. That is to say, it does not cover man's milieu in the sense of the social, political, and historical conditions and activities that exist between people—although these factors certainly belong to those that determine existence and quality of life, and they undoubtedly determine human interventions in the world and the environment (seen as life's given, elemental equipment) and always mold life's elemental milieu in the form in which man meets it. Yet, man's self-formed milieu, as we find it in the manifestations we have mentioned (social, political, etc.), always has as a presupposition and foundation the given fact of the elemental basic equipment linking human beings with other living things, and also the use and shaping of it by man and every living thing for the purpose of securing the elements necessary for life. Consequently, in what follows we shall only be discussing man's self-formed milieu insofar as its connection with the basic perspectives of our subject require it.

If the subject world and environment is related in this book to the elemental, pragmatic perspective of the living thing in the milieu of its constitutive, natural conditions of existence, then the reader may well ask why this subject is not simply called nature? It is true that if nature is defined in the usual sense, then the viewpoint we have worked out has undoubtedly to do with nature, particularly in its orientation toward the world and the environment in the sense of what is of elemental importance for life. In order to contrast this fundamental, given world of life (including its life-securing use and shaping by every living thing) with the world and environment built up by social, cultural, and historical conditions, we shall call our viewpoint the natural world and environment.

However, it would not be advisable to change over to the term "nature" in describing this viewpoint, because this would constitute a serious shift in perspective; for the modern concept of nature,[14] with its prevailing confrontation between nature and man, would have to be taken over as well. For us, on the contrary, the important thing is to find an approach that takes life and milieu together, the milieu being the presupposition, together with the vital use made of it and the form given to it. Such a viewpoint comprehends everything living to an equal degree, and yet it comprehends man's unique nature. If, in accordance with a widespread concept of nature, we were to set nature apart as being untouched by all the phenomena which have come about through human intervention and modification, then this guiding concept would inevitably lead to the loss of our viewpoint. For where can untouched, unmodified nature as the milieu of living things be found? Even more decisive are the consequences that the modern concept of nature would have for our approach to today's challenges. We are accustomed to understand nature as a physical world of phenomena that surrenders to the scientifically inquiring human subject, as an arsenal of logical, mathematical laws in a countless number of individual sectors, and as a potential source of material for industrial and economic exploitation. Is this classical scientific concept of nature adapted to comprehend, separately and in totality, our viewpoint of the specifically existing cohesion of living things, including man, with the elemental world in which he lives? Today critical voices cannot fail to be heard; so for the moment, we shall do better to dispense with the concept of nature as symbol for our view of things.

We have already said that our viewpoint of the world and

environment aims to be a phenomenological one, notwithstanding its link with ecological insights; i.e., it is not
intended merely as a specific question put by biology, which
in the biblical sphere would at most bring to light ancient
insights relevant for the history of science. As a phenomenological perspective it has many strata. Seen in this way, the
connection of the living thing with the elemental world in
which it lives (in totality and in its separate parts) includes the
selective scientific questions about laws and constituents in
origin and process. But the essential thing is that our
viewpoint of the world and environment includes considerably more. It covers the observation of the whole of this
complex as such, together with its reciprocal relationships;
questions about its meaning and value, the existence of its
given facts, and its preservation or modification in the process
of time; questions about its openness to human experience;
questions about human responsibility; and questions about
connections with the political and social organization of man,
who makes the living space of the world the stage of his own
history.

In this study of the connection and reciprocal effects of
living things and their natural world—a connection which is
constitutive for life—the subject world and environment is
elemental and is formulated in total and fundamental terms so
that it can effectively act as the common perspective in our
confrontation between the Bible and the present.

2. Some Problematic Aspects of the Natural World and Environment Today

The historical scholar feels passionately responsible in his
advocacy of the unique character, original meaning, and
historical difference of the biblical texts, which lie so far back in
time. But even this activity of his, devoted though it is to a life
that is past and gone, is practiced in the present and is therefore
inevitably related to contemporary circumstances that are

certainly not the same but are at least equivalent. If the interpretative scholar were to disregard his own historical place and the historical position of his activity, he would be hindering the impact and interpretation of biblical statements in our time. For he would be avoiding the question of how the unique historical character of biblical facts appears in respect to our own present, and he would thereby be avoiding his duty and the service he can render in keeping biblical and historical pointers and impulses open for contemporary challenges.[15] Consequently, we must now satisfy ourselves, even if only provisionally and incompletely, about some important aspects of today's problem in the field of the world and the environment.

a. *Common present-day experience*

If we pursue the viewpoint world and environment today with the eyes of an average mid-European, we find ourselves in a strangely ambiguous situation.

On the one hand, we still find in the scope of our daily experience that the components of the ecosystem, as these affect our natural milieu, unquestionably continue to function. The reciprocal play of climate, weather, soil-constitution, usable water, and stocks of animals and plants, together with proven and continually more effective utilization techniques, seem to be evidence that admits of no problem. Worldwide economic relations meet every demand for both necessities and luxuries in the sectors of foodstuffs, raw materials, and energy. True, there are breakdowns: unusual climactic conditions, storms, droughts, earthquakes, insect plagues, but these are local and temporary. Immediate measures and counter-measures through the appropriate channels can be expected to bring relief and help to the people affected. The protection of whales, seals, storks and sea eagles, alpine plants, marshes, moorland and mud flats, simply for their own sakes is more or less accepted; and so is aid to improve natural living conditions in other parts of the world. But, when all is said and done, there is diminished enthusiasm; for these are not the living conditions in which people around about us have to live. Deficiencies in man's natural surroundings, however, appear to be locally confined, unavoidable, and compensable. After all, even if rivers are very seriously threatened as natural habitats, there is enough usable water. And, even if satellite towns and transport systems destroy landscapes, there are protected recreation areas near the cities or farther away. Losses of this kind, even if people are conscious of them at all, are put up with as falling under the decisive question of man's utilization of the living world: land use is obviously necessary in view of the economy, industry, the gross national product, jobs, the securing and raising of our accustomed standard of living.

There is no doubt at all that for the average person the natural conditions of life and their use by men and women in our parts of the world are anything but a vital question, even when deficiencies are felt here and there. Natural conditions at our disposal are so much a matter of course that to reflect about the connection between life and the natural conditions of life, as this has a bearing on men and women, seems in our area entirely theoretical and artificial; while in its bearing on the threat to other forms of life, which are of no direct human use, it appears to be of secondary importance. For our average consciousness, the vital questions are to be found on a different plane: not in the field of the natural elements of life, but in the sector of political, economic, social conditions and decisions, and in the scientific and technological developments of every kind that are decisive for the specific world of the individual and its quality. It is not without reason that Dieter Lührmann writes: "For us seedtime and harvest are no longer the cycles with which hopes and fears are bound up; now it is the cycles of inflation and the economic situation."[16] The prospects and fulfillments of the individual's life are primarily decided in the sectors where man builds his own life, not in the elemental sphere of natural life, which is completely a matter of course. And it is from there that the shadows, fears, and burdens of the individual's own world are also derived. The precipitously growing complication of technical, economic, and political processes is rapidly turning our modern, enlightened world into a riddle. In addition, widespread strain and exhaustion is often the outcome of a relationship to the world that, on the emotional level, is highly sentimental and yet offers diminishing opportunities for entering into and preserving relationships. Many find it increasingly difficult to accept and endure their own lives, and the world around them, with imagination and a love capable of suffering. There is an urge for maximum freedom, but detached from equivalent responsibility as an essential part of liberty, because with responsibility, liberty is forced back into those compulsions in life from which it wants to escape.

On the other hand, in recent years the media have confronted us with a multiplicity of environmental institutions, measures, and spontaneous initiatives, which have brought the realm of elemental, natural conditions for life and survival into the limelight. Explosive though they are, however, they have found it hard to gain a hearing from our general consciousness beyond a circle of locally affected people, simply because such data does not fit into the framework of our present experience. So global predictions are bound to slide off public awareness even more, when they point to the threat to our survival posed by an endangering of the ecosystem in its elemental, fundamental significance for all living things, including man. Even such challenging titles as the following, collected at random recently, indicate a detached viewpoint: "Grow Up in Freedom—for Death" (report in the *Süddeutsche Zeitung* on a conference of the Catholic Academy in Bavaria), "Planetary Nightmare" (headline in the same newspaper), "Man at the Time-barrier of Survival" (K. Müller), "Agriculture and the Survival Crisis" (K. Egger), "From Exploitation to Cooperation" (G. Liedke), "Creation in Front of the Abyss" (G. Altner), "A Planet Is Plundered" (H. Gruhl). These are visions of an elemental threat of comprehensive and unimaginable scope, which cannot be permanently endured by the general consciousness and simply ask to be repressed. And this is the case all the more because the individual seems to himself to be utterly powerless in the face of these threatening developments in a world he can no longer see through. If he accepted the truth of these predictions, they would be contrary to what his actual experience of the world tells him.

And it would be contrary to his long-cherished expectation that specific, individual measures to protect the environment (measures to protect the landscape, water, and air; measures to reduce noise; measures to protect threatened animals and plants), together with new technologies and long-term crisis management by the people responsible, will knock the bottom out of fears of this kind.

In this conflict, a desire for soothing reassurance is all too understandable. But is it realistic? In recent years scientific discussion about the world and the environment has arrived at essentially different opinions. It has ushered in a radical change which teaches us to view the present situation with different eyes.

b. The radical change of opinion and the support to be found for it in the present situation

Only a few years ago our general awareness was entirely concentrated on human society, in line with our general view of the world. Mental, political, and economic activities were concentrated on the social relationships among people and on the capacity of social systems for realizing a high quality of life on a wide scale. Peace, liberty, equal rights, and social justice for all were the target concepts in discussion, and still are. Apart from isolated protective measures, the natural world and environment as given *datum*, together with the use and shaping of it so as to secure shelter, sources of food, and raw materals, was only viewed in the perspective of the society of men and women living here and now. It was only a problem insofar as it did not as yet display an equal, just supply when measured against prevailing human standards of living. People had to bring this about by means of technical operations and social and economic policies, so that injustices and inequalities could be adjusted in such a way as to make utilization and exploitation of the world's resources as just as possible. The given datum in this view of what had to be done was the natural world and environment as an object of exploitation, as raw material, and as the substance for shaping and organizing human life. It was viewed as something quite other than man. The impulse behind this view of what had to be done was man, absolutely and exclusively orientated toward his claims to a high standard of living. The goal, finally, in the familiar descent from north to south, was to increase or preserve the same standard of living, or at least to reach it in the forseeable future, in the southern regions.

Certainly, besides this exploitation of the world and the environment in order to produce what is necessary for the dictated standard of living, there stood, and still stands, the more harmonious experience of world and environment in leisure and tourism, as a factor of physical and psychological relaxation—though this too is anything but free of human marketing, and man's need for relaxation must be content with the reservations that have been laid out or with the surrogates provided by the media. This need is optional, private, and without obligation, compared with the dominating, grabbing exploitation whose purpose is to raise the standard of living.

But this interpretation of the world which is totally oriented toward man has been undergoing a radical change in recent years. The trend of this change is as follows. The problem of our time is no longer solely man in his social aspects, seeking the widespread realization of a high quality of life, because existing resources in the world are no longer unquestionably at our disposal. On the contrary, the whole problem of our understanding of the world is now broadening out, in a significant development of the critical consciousness, to cover the sphere of the world's natural resources and conditions. The change is directed toward the subject world and environment as we propose to interpret it: namely, the effects of human actions on the whole context of the world and living things in general.

The oil crisis acted as a warning signal, and for a time it even stirred up general awareness. It made clear to people, in a form they could actually experience, something that experts had long known through scientifically calculated forecasts (by the Club of Rome especially, at that time): the fact that the earth's resources of the highly important raw material crude oil are limited. We can forecast the time when they will be exhausted, if we continue our present exploitation, let alone increase it. The calculation of the time limit has meanwhile been brought to the notice of every user of the mass media. Similar time limits apply not only to oil but to all sources of energy that are relevant at the present time. Time limits have been worked out also for sources of other raw materials and foodstuffs. "We can take this," writes the physicist Klaus Müller, "as an indication of the fundamental change of aspect introduced simply by the fact that all undertakings are faced with the pressure of a calculable date, a date that is irrevocable. But it is this very fact—the fact that we have everywhere to reckon with ultimate time limits—which is the new situation that we . . . find in every sector."[17] This makes the most important factor in the upheaval clear: it is the time factor. Hitherto the experience that molded the outlook of the average person was a static one, the ecosystem was an inexhaustible reservoir of vitally necessary supplies with unproblematic possibilities for exploitation. Today people can no longer look on the ecosystem in this way. Even if we continue our exploitation as before (and even more, if we increase it, which is probable because of the increasing population), the elemental world of man's life is now already presenting itself—in terms of foodstuffs, raw materials, and energy—as a finite, limited foundation for existence whose time limit can be calculated.

Time is the revolutionary factor that is changing everything today. But subordinate to this, the natural world and environment has a further sector of given data and circumstances: the habitat or living space. Expanding industrialization, increasing population, and the resulting social problem of providing work, and also a measure of satisfaction of demands for a high quality of life, have had certain results. The exploitation of the vegetable and animal world, the introduction of harmful substances, and the intervention of technology, have led to an increasing strain on the biosphere, and to growing modification of and damage to the water, air, soil, and climate of the space in which life exists. These things, in their turn, mean a continually spreading disturbance of the controlling and regulative processes of the ecological cycles. And again the time limits are foreseeable. In accordance with this revelation, the subject of the world and the environment is

today going beyond individual problems. Under the pressure of
the time factor it is presenting itself as an environmental crisis
with the character of an elemental crisis of survival.[18]

This perspective of a threatening survival limit for all living
things on earth is not intended to point toward a rarified
counter-picture of virgin nature or a purely agrarian utilization
of nature, free from technology and industry. It rather realizes
that an upheaval, reaching to the very roots, is going on with
regard to the connection between the elemental, given world
and man's use and shaping of it to secure his own life. It
perceives the upheaval that has taken place because the degree
of human utilization has now reached a point that makes the
deadline facing the world and its life (including man)—the
world's coming annihilation—a fact that can be forecast. This
upheaval acquires harshness and inescapability because its
development cannot simply be brought to a halt, let alone
reversed, through the further perfecting of scientific and
technical measures; the complex reciprocal effects of the crisis
phenomena, to which Klaus Müller especially has pointed,
would alone make this impossible.[19] In this situation, progress
in science and technology does not bring sufficient power to
master the survival crisis.[20] C. F. von Weizsäcker is breaking
new ground when he says, in the final section of his book, *Wege
in der Gefahr:*

> We have not added our voice to . . . the criticism of
> technology in principle; nor have we assented to the
> fundamental optimism about technology. The main charac-
> teristic of our attitude was the thesis that . . . there are
> technical methods to counteract technically caused dangers.
> The real dangers are the ones that are brought about by
> human beings. In the language of today we might put it as
> follows: technology is an instrument of the reasonable will.
> Technology can be controlled as far as our reason extends.
> But technology cannot compensate for the failure of reason.[21]

The consequences of his upheaval are of elemental clarity. In the
past what dominated man and the relations between individuals,

groups, and nations in daily events and experiences were the levels of life to which political, economic, and social activities applied. Now, beyond his threatening wars of annihilation, man is having a new dimension forced on him: the perspective of the elemental world of life and its elemental potentialities of existence. This is being laid on him as a problem for worldwide mental and political activity, with the shadow of the threat to his survival presented by the deadline set for the world's existence. If we follow up this perspective, the differentiations and differences in human society are reduced to the subject man, which includes all and everyone—man in relation to the world and the environment, as the fundamental, spatial and temporal ecological system. This system asserts its claim, not as the environment of the specific individual, but as all-embracing totality, because the damage and destruction which are showing themselves affect it as a whole. At the limits of man's unquestioning disposal of things, it simply shows him that he himself is a highly dependent element within this natural world, that he has elemental needs, and that the natural world's end also means his own. It shows man that world/environment and man have a common future, and that it is now being decided how and whether people can live after us. It shows man that with the annihilation of nonhuman life, we are determining the fate of human life as well. In the face of the inescapable time factor, the crisis in the use and molding of the elemental life of all living things throws back at him the simple but decisive question: What will be the future of human and nonhuman life that wants to follow us and live?

c. The reasons for our present situation

We may use the catchwords "environmental crisis" or "survival crisis" to describe our present situation. But if we ask about the reasons for it and its background, the literature on the subject will bring us up against extremely complicated connections and interdependencies between many sectors and phenomena. This being so, we cannot even approximately describe them within the limits of our present framework. The interested reader may turn to C. F. von Weizsäcker's latest book,[22] or to the work of Klaus Müller[23] or Günter Altner.[24] I should like also to draw special attention to the extensive compilation on environmental strategy published in 1975 by the Sociological Institute of the Evangelical-Lutheran churches in Germany.[25] In our context we must select and concentrate primarily on the reasons and aspects that are of essential importance in a confrontation between this subject and the biblical texts.

Plants, animals, and groups of people have always suffered from limited stresses and strains and damage to their ecosystems, and the radius of this damage has ranged from the very small to the relatively extensive. The fact that today, in contrast, the ecosystem as a whole is drifting toward the limits of survival (according to well-founded forecasts) is due mainly—if we take a superficial view—to the ever-widening encroachments of man's modern world, with its industrialization and mechanization. But this is to name only a secondary cause, not a primary one. In considering this secondary cause, the crisis-conscious critic should remember, before making any hasty and illusory condemnation, what positive effects industrialization and mechanization have in controlling danger to human life from the natural world and in the human development of life—effects which we cannot now imagine ever doing without.[26] Even the pressing problem of unemployment makes the facts clear today. The results of the present situation in the industrial and technological sectors are inescapable. But when we are inquiring as to reasons, we cannot be content with an illusory and simpleminded condemnation of industry and technology. On the other hand, even though the intensification of technical research is and will remain essential and unrelinquishable for the control of individual elements of danger, yet there is general agreement that this will bring no essential turn of events in itself. The basic reason for our situation is not simply that, at the present time, we are lacking in the technologies to eliminate the approaching survival crisis. Optimistic and superficial views of this kind start from a complex in which the reasons for strains on the environment and environmental damage are of a purely technical kind. The environmental crisis is therefore seen as the problem of an inadequate but adaptable technology. It is consequently also seen as the sum of part-problems, which can be isolated, and whose solution is striven for and expected by means of a technology of production and waste-disposal which must be continually pushed forward.[27]

In building up the economic systems in the developed countries through their industrialization and mechanization, people did not yet comprehend the heart of the problem, even though subjects central to our present discussion were frequently touched on. Evidence has been offered to show that it is not the systems but their presuppositions which, if they are laid down in a certain way, produce corresponding crisis phenomena.[28] In spite of all the differences in their structure, economic and social systems are the executive media in the industrial countries and are oriented toward quantitative growth. However, the actual impetuses and impulses that direct them still lie behind the systems themselves. In the introduction to the compilation on "Environmental Strategy," the essential reasons for our present situation are precisely located and tersely formulated.

This way of looking at things [i.e., the explanation of the environmental crisis as a merely technical problem] . . . does not lead to an adequate analysis of the reasons for our environmental problems. For it does not take into account the motives, values, and goals which stamp economic behavior, conditions of production, consumer-wants, and our whole economic and social system in such a way that material progress leads simultaneously to wrong social development and an endangering of the ecology. It therefore disrupts the cohesion of cause and effect whereby strains on the environment are the consequences of behavior which is directed toward a certain goal in a certain way. If we follow up this connection, the environmental crisis proves to be the crisis of our individual and social models and ways of living.

The question about the operative values and norms then
becomes the key problem for the continuance and progress
of industrial society.[28a]

It is stressed that "the goals that dominate a society and the
attitudes toward nature expressed in them have essential
importance for the environmental crisis."[29] To sum up, "The
environmental crisis is therefore only properly understood
when the models and patterns of behavior of the given society,
which are the cause of that crisis, are brought to the surface."[30]
The goals, attitudes, models, ways of behavior, values, and
norms of a society, in individuals and collectively, are
accordingly the domain where the determining causes are to be
found. And this exposes man, in his social character and
because he is stamped by the history of his civilization, as being
the true originator of the situation.

What is it about man's goals, attitudes, models, ways of
behavior, values, and norms in modern industrial society that
cause such serious effects—effects which are so far-reaching
that the limits of survival can be prophesied—in the realm of
the natural world and environment even though these attitudes
are paradoxically bound up with the quality of human life?

Following the pioneer insights of C. F. von Weizsäcker,
representatives of both science and the humanities have put
forward analyses that touch on the roots of the survival crisis.
These analyses put foremost the far-reaching effects of modern
science insofar as these have molded the minds of people as a
whole and the attitudes, aims, and expectations behind human
activity. Klaus Müller actually coins the term "the scientific
catastrophe"[31] and feels able to say about it: "It is the
quintessence of all the hazards caused by an outmoded attitude
to science."[32] After an analysis of physics, Müller goes on to
show the far-reaching effects in this field also.[33] Günter Altner
shows similar trains of thought in the sphere of biology.[34]
Christian Link concentrates on the epistemological field and
the realm of scientific methodology.[35]

What insights have emerged? Of course, we shall be forced

to concentrate on highly simplified, basic aspects. The starting point of these analyses is the view of cognition (or the act of knowing) and reality that rests on the essential separation between the perceiving human subject and the object of his cognition. This notion is somewhat vaguely associated with Descartes. Reality—i.e., what can be explained scientifically—is accordingly whatever can be established as being the generally applicable answer to the mathematical and logical questions of the perceiving person. The answer is generally applicable under the same conditions because its structure follows certain laws. Included in this definition of knowledge is the basic notion that man as the perceiving subject is in principle detached from the object of his cognition. What he establishes as being real in the external world he is investigating is whatever emerges as the logical explanation according to the laws about which he is inquiring. It cannot be doubted that reality does emerge from this attitude toward knowledge; the possibilities of controlling nature technically and economically, and our insights into the correlation of controls and laws in organisms which characterize modern science would otherwise be inconceivable.

At the same time, this attitude toward knowledge, which dominates our scientific and technical world, is seen as a central problem of our situation. For it is no longer possible to suppress the question of whether this overemphasis on rationality does not perceive too little—dangerously little—from the point of view of our survival and whether it does not lead to serious deformations with regard to the object of our knowledge—i.e., the natural world and environment—and with regard to the perceiving subject, man. Does it not abbreviate and do injury to reality on a scale that is today gradually becoming heavy with impending catastrophe?[36] The analyses we have mentioned show that this dominating attitude toward cognition, and its ideal of an objective knowledge which is, in principle, equally accessible to every observer, leads to three serious and narrowing restrictions.

First: The objects of investigation lose their wholeness and their direct unity, because the methods of experimental questioning lead to a way of thinking "which divides, isolates, classifies, and catalogues in order to be able to handle the 'problems' that arise one by one, and one after another: it is the beginning, that is to say, of a particularist way of thinking."[37] Particularist cognition of this kind cannot preserve the given, direct unity of the thing known, because the whole is more than the sum of the part-structures—because it is greater, even if the relativity of the cognitive processes is reflected in time, as is the case in quantum physics.[38] Corresponding epistemological discoveries about the loss of reality are met with in the field of biology, for example, [39] not to mention the pioneer insights of the psychosomatic medicine of Viktor von Weizsäcker,[40] which are taken up again in this context.

Second: Not only the wholeness, but also the temporality and future of the object is also excluded in the wake of this approach to knowledge—that is to say, the temporal and qualitative character of process in the thing investigated. Objects are reduced to descriptions that are timeless and structural. Their temporality is merely the "prepared time," in Klaus Müller's phrase, of the experimental situation.[41] According to Müller, "physical time is itself . . . a preparation for the fullness of time," "preparation" meaning the preparation, or reduction, of facts necessary in the setting up of an experiment (p. 240).[41]

Third: This reduction of wholeness and temporality not only affects the object of cognition, it implicates the perceiving subject, man, no less. For any education in knowledge of the external world results from the separation of the subject from the external world as a matter of principle. But by that very fact the essential role of perception in gaining knowledge is excluded, by and through the reduction process, and its significance in the discovery of truth is in principle denied. For perception does not take place in the separation of the subject from its object, perception comes into being in the subject's link with the object of knowledge, in mutual dealings with it, and in receptive encounter with it. This is the way in which it comprehends that whole and temporal *more,* which is lost in the scientific reduction of perception, to timeless, repeatable, and logical structures, and in the preparation of objects through the experimental situation.

Klaus Müller[42] and Christian Link[43] have described this separation impressively, showing that it excludes and indeed destroys the original, given link between subject and object which binds the two together in a total event of encounter and living association comprehending both. Under the dominating dictatorship of scientific premises about knowledge, the loss of the perceiving subject's wholeness of perception, in living and encountering the thing that is to be known, goes hand in hand with the loss of the whole sector in which total, temporal perception takes place: the field of experience. For under these premises and in the sense of reality open to scientific substantiation, experience that is more than subjectively arbitrary—and therefore nonbinding—can only exist as insight into laws and structures as these appear from the angle of the detached observer. But what is left out of the question is Christian Link's formulation, following Viktor von Weizsäcker. "At all events, an experience which one has *with* (as our languages expresses it) people, things, or events seems only to be possible under the condition that the experiencing person does not place himself in the magisterial role of the Kantian judge, but, on the contrary, enters into a relationship of positive dependency on the 'object' of his experience—that is to say, is prepared to learn from it."[44] The unanswered question is why some things do not take place in line with general laws and structures, and yet really happen to someone. Why a person meets with such events and why they become confronting events for him is excluded from this perspective, as is perception and experience. Correspondingly, events in the world are reduced to the happenings achievable by man. We are facing the same problem when, as a result of this definition, people notice the inevitable "loss of love, sensuous experience, and beauty."[45]

K. M. Meyer-Abich has recently written as follows about the origin of the "deformation of the human capacity for perception":

The crucial point is Descartes' statement that man is most certain of himself as *res cogitans*. Consequently, one only sees what one knows, and the *res cogitans* only sees what can be grasped *clare et distincte*. . . . This is the origin of the degeneration of our senses in the environment, because the result is that the sensory world fades into the mere *res extensa*. For extension in space was the only characteristic of sensory things by which they could be grasped as the objects of mathematics (the mathematics of that day, that is). No other characteristics of the sensory world can be perceived by the *res cogitans*. In particular, it cannot grasp beauty and ugliness, the appearance of good and evil in the sensory world, because its aesthetic feeling is limited to geometrical structures, and even in these excludes the coperception of the Good.[46]

And Christian Link writes similarly.

Modern thinking has detached man's rational capacity from his sensuousness, i.e., has destroyed receptivity and spontaneity, which are the bridge joining sensuousness and reason. The senses merely provide material for the logical functions of the judgment. Reason has admittedly paid a high price for the triumph of thought over the assertions of the senses, which has thus been achieved. Like Minerva's owl, it is always too late. Reason can reflect on what has been perceived, but cannot grasp the real itself. Modern science only glimpses reality in reflected form. . . . The possibility of knowing truth rests on a mere reflection of nature in the inner space of consciousness, not upon the original link between nature and the subject.[47]

Now all these views are by no means insights that would have relevance only for the intellectual field or would be of importance only in the sheltered regions of epistemological and methodological discussions about the process of acquiring knowledge. As the German word shows, the process of perception—*Wahr-nehmung* ("The *taking* as true") includes an active, positive reaching out to what is perceived.[48] That attitude toward knowledge has a direct influence on aims, .

attitudes, models, values, norms, and behavior in industrial society, and is therefore of essential importance for grasping the reasons behind the signs of crisis in the natural world and environment today.

The division between subject and object in the process of cognition, between *res cogitans* (man) and *res extensa* (the external world) means that in the economic and social sphere, the whole theme world and environment cannot be perceived at all, if it means a view of the whole elemental world in which everything, including man, lives in its total context. Nature and man do not only diverge to the extent in which man also acts in nature—as he has done from time immemorial, cultivating it and modifying it through his labor—here nature and man enter into opposition in principle, and *nature* disintegrates, not merely for the processes of cognition, but even highly practically, in the processes of action, as the object in a multiplicity of individual human fields of activity. What is essential and real about nature, as the nonhuman external world, is what man wants to extract from it. Nature is reduced to an object for man's exploitation, to a material world for human purposes, experiments, economic projects and utilization. In the wake of this approach, nature is truncated and becomes the timeless, inexhaustible, and indefinitely exploitable revenue-potential for man. The totality of a life-complex that includes man, with its own significance and its own value, is faded out, dissolved into a readily available sum of logically, scientifically, and economically applicable part-aspects of man. And these only seemingly find their way back to the original totality of the world-environment event, by way of such systematic designations as biology evolves. Man's special position in, and in relation to, the natural world and environment turns into a dominating outsider's position. And this forms the foundation for man's essential, leading ideas about his outward world, ideas that are the basis of his actions in industrial societies.

If, in the basic approach we have described, this view of nature as an object of economic and social action is the logical continuation of its truncation as the object of knowledge, then something corresponding applies on *man's* side as well. The

position he has chosen for himself as dominating subject in the
cognitive process corresponds to his self-understanding as
regards his activity in society and the economy, where this is
focused on nature. We have seen that in the cognitive process
man blots out the temporal and total event of world and
environment, as the elemental, fundamental life-complex,
which includes man himself. Instead he enters the stage as
authoritative interrogator and judge,[49] holding only that to be
real which nature indicates as laws. But the dominating
character of man's interrogation always means that he already
influences, breaks down, and destroys what is given, in order to
extort from nature answers that are in accordance with the
nature of these questions of his—questions which in fact can
only be part-aspects of reality under predetermined conditions.
In his active dealings with nature man acts in accordance with
the same principle. It is human society, man, that determines,
quite independently, the use to be made of nature. It is he who
sets up the claims which he exacts from nature. It is his
continually growing demand for humane quality of life which
direct his activities. The values of his self-created human world
are the only things that matter. Nature degenerates into the
mere means of putting all this into effect.

Of course this attitude on the plane of human society and
its constellations of power has long since acquired a highly
complicated autonomy of its own, in the form of current
political requirements in the economic, social, cultural, and
defense sectors. But for an explanation of the prophesied
survival crisis in the elemental sphere of the natural world and
environment, the essential thing is to trace back the thorny
political phenomena, which are plain to be seen, to the ruling,
fundamental convictions, to the leading ideas and values that
underlie them. In short, we must follow these secondary
phenomena to their source, in the basic attitude toward nature
prevailing in all industrial countries, an attitude which sees
man, and man alone, as the subject who determines the
purpose, use, and goal of activity with regard to nature; and
which sees nature, again unquestionably, as an exploitable
instrument for realizing the world of human life determined by

human demands. It is obvious that in the face of the grandiose scientific and technical successes of modern times, this basic attitude is linked with the fundamental conviction that the human world demanded is in principle achievable by political and technical means—in the sphere of the natural world and environment, as well as in the fields of man's physical, psychological, and educational world. And it is no less deeply associated with the continual nourishment of this fundamental attitude through a worldwide belief in progress, which expects an inevitable higher development of scientific, technical, and economic possibilities to produce, just as inevitably, the realization of the world of man to which people aspire.

Even if, taking the awareness of a wide public as a whole, our eyes are kept from seeing the havoc which this fundamental attitude produces, for example, in its application to the spheres of psychology or education, [50] in the realm of the natural world and environment the ravages are obvious. Nature, even human nature, is everywhere rebelling against the universal domination of this mental and practical approach. The devastation does not only show itself in the destruction of the ecological quality of the natural world and environment, for all our insight into the time-limit set for it, in the foreseeable exhaustion of its resources and the threat to the life-expectation of living things on earth. It appears no less in man himself, in the sharp increase of mental illness; for, as Klaus Müller shows, "An environment of this kind, which is 'purged' and controlled by the logic of practical technical compulsions, makes people *ill*."[51] But the ravages are shown too in the reduction of reality which prevails today—the reduction of actual, lived life to precise, timeless concepts free of association, [52] and to formal and quantitative processes of planning, opinion-forming, and decision; in the reduction of education to what is technocratically obviously "useful"; in the reduction of language to "objective" structure-analysis; and much more of the same kind of thing.

Under the dominating dictatorship of this fundamental attitude (which takes its bearings from science and technology) and its definition of reality, one thing in the general web of the results forfeits its general importance more than any other:

experience. Yet it is experience that ought to be of preeminent importance for the broad reception of reality, for the total and living movement of man in the world and the environment, and for the orientation of meaning and values which follows from it. Experience, experience based on life, experience of the whole, ought to precede theories and concepts, and retain its efficacy as a critical, broadening corrective. But today—apart from the private, and hence optional, sphere—it is reduced to its "scientifically proven" facts, which can be grasped in terms of concepts and laws; and it is manipulated in favor of an all-prevailing, second-hand perception. It is replaced by *ersatz* or surrogate experience, through the dominance of demands, consumer-wants, and compulsions created by man himself. So Klaus Mülluer can provocatively put it as follows:

> A few scientists (only a few, initially) are beginning to realize that science is in essence murderous; and it does not only become murderous because it is wrongly applied. But because we are already murderers even when we merely follow the laws of nature and pursue logical perception, the crisis is of an undreamed-of depth; and there is apparently no way out. Science has taken over the world, and in the wake of its progress the crisis has been able to escalate into the unparalleled crisis of survival whose warning signals are today clustering together more and more thickly before our very eyes.[53] . . . The crisis of survival is world history's requital for a long-practiced exclusion of temporal truths in favor of timeless, "eternal" ones.[54]

Today the natural world and environment itself is forcing us toward the life-threatening frontiers of this fundamental attitude. But are people in general coming to realize how problematical, destructive, and detached from reality this fundamental attitude is in itself?

d. *Some questions and the tasks before us*

In the previous section we tried to deduce from the current discussion basic lines of approach, a standpoint on which to base the subject of the world and the environment, as this presents itself today. If we follow up these lines of approach, it is clear on what level the essential tasks and questions for a comprehensive and long-term change are to be found. We have to arrive at the fundamental level of man's relationship to his natural world and environment. This level lies beyond the necessary technological counter-measures which, though working for short-term, partial help, remain within the framework of a longer-term basic attitude that is highly problematical. It is beyond the conflict between interest groups in society and beyond the political discussion about the utility of economic systems—discussions which would like to exclude from critical reflection man as the cause of the environmental crisis. But, equally, it is beyond the wholesale, illusory condemnation of scientific activities. It is here, on this fundamental level, if at all, that the perspectives of a transformation must be found. It is here that we have to discover the conditions and marks of a fundamentally altered attitude on man's part, whatever political, social, economic systems he may actually find himself in today. It is only with such altered viewpoints (which can work toward changing aims, attitudes, and models, and the definition of values and norms in man's everyday consciousness) that there will be any prospect of human behavior and actions in man's natural world and environment which are capable of penetrating the mere illusion that the survival crisis can be prevented by technical means, and which can break through the reduction of responsibility to the point where it means only the security of one's own life. It is only this that could allow us to expect practically directed, effective retroactive influence on the complicated processes of the political and social organization of human activity with regard to nature.

Seen from this angle, the tasks open to us are concentrated first of all on highly elemental, basic questions. All these basic questions do not aim at eliminating scientific and technological ways of thinking, experiencing, and acting; but in view of the appalling results, they do aim at limiting them as the prevailing fundamental attitude on the part of man in his relationship to the world and the environment, and at limiting them by means of overriding aspects which will contribute to a new orientation.

The first of these basic questions is directed toward a comprehensive view of the relationship between man and nature that will be in accordance with reality. Even if the division between man and nature (which dominates the form of human existence everywhere in the modern world) cannot be reversed, can we not restrict it effectively by means of an overriding viewpoint? A viewpoint in which man no longer sees himself merely as outside nature, but as within it, together with other living things? Sees himself as a being also affected by the process of the worldwide event of elemental living conditions for all life, where he, like other living things, is met by the event of an environment of constitutive, natural conditions of existence? What we are asking, therefore, is whether the ecological perspectives of biology, instead of being one, analytical, scientific part-question among others, can be the impulse for regaining an elemental total perspective, a perspective that can grasp from the very beginning the given, essential connection between living things and the natural world, man included, and can grasp it in such a way that this connection is seen as a fore-ordered and permanent totality essential for life.

This does not mean the surrender of man's special position; nor does it mean his illusory return to a pure state of nature, like the state of other living things.[55] But it does mean the task of so determining this special position that it will be, not parallel to, but *within*, the overriding, total framework of the natural world and environment as an overriding complex of life. Selective scientific questions and acts touching on the technical use of nature and its modifications are not excluded either. But they are part of a wider context, limited in their dominance and given a new position as merely partial aspects. It is in line with this basic question that in the latest discussion stress is laid on the necessity of a new concept of nature (by Christian Link, for example);[56] or on the "task of expanding the concept of knowledge as this has come down to us."[57] On the other hand, people are seeking the inclusion and participation of man in nature, in a changed definition of his position; and this is finding expression at present in terms like "co-creatureliness";[58] while the old view of a dominating subject-object relationship is being overcome by a new one, defined as cooperation[59] or partnership,[60] which actually proposes to concede to nature its own subjectivity.

Our first basic question had to do with the possibility of confronting a many-sided and dangerously limiting division between man and nature, with the world and the environment as the event of an elemental, total cohesion of fore-ordered living conditions and a life-securing organization and use of them which will be to the advantage of all living things, including man. A *second basic question* takes the first one farther in the sphere of the epistemological perception of these elemental perspectives. What is at issue here, therefore, is a banning of that approach to knowledge which divides man and nature as a matter of principle, because of man's all-dominating position. This approach is to be overridden and limited by a perception that glimpses the world and the environment, including man, in a total and elemental sense. It is a view that is reconstructible by the different subjects concerned, scientifically demonstrable, and without the blemish of being subjectively optional and arbitrary. Klaus Müller[61] and, especially, Christian Link[62] have pointed to the need for such a new perception. They have investigated its relationship to scientific findings, natural laws, world views, and world designs, and have tried to define it epistemologically as a scientific process.

A *third basic question* proceeds from the problem of knowledge about the world and the environment to the presupposition of knowledge, that is, to the experience which opens up, and continually keeps open, direct access to the world and the environment as an elemental, total event. Christian Link can put the critical question to science.

Does science perhaps experience too little? Is the assurance of science perhaps merely a bad con-science? In other words:

Has modern science—ever since it began to permit man to play the part of the God who had been lost, clothing him in the dignity of the Creator—perhaps pushed aside and repressed an experience which is now going over to the attack in a merely negative way, stabbing science in the back as it were?[63]

But what kind of experience must it be, of nature, and of man himself, if man is to be conscious of his vital link with nature and of his inside position in the world and environment, and is to remain conscious of it, without any repression? What elemental content of experience is essential and important here? What content of experience has to be laid bare, if a breakthrough of effective dimensions is to succeed, and if the opposition between man and nature as subject to object is to be successfully restricted?

While the first three basic questions are related to the perspective, knowledge, and experience of the connection between man and nature, as this is contained in the theme world and environment, the *fourth basic question* turns to the quality of meaning of this whole complex. If it can no longer be simply man who, as autonomous subject, lends meaning to this complex through his questions to nature and his demands on it; and if it cannot be merely a neutrally described cohesion of given ecological facts, and the relations and laws they display, then questions arise. Do total experience and knowledge of the natural world and environment come upon meaning within this complex itself? Do they arrive at any overriding authorities, fundamentals, meanings, values, and norms, which link nature and man, and which of themseves also include nonhuman life and its world, and which concede to this more quality than merely that of providing material for exploitation by human demands, while also pointing out the limits of those demands?

The *fifth and final basic question* is concerned with conclusions arising from what we have already said about man's special position, and the conditions of his actions in world and environment. Here, that is to say, we are inquiring about man's legitimation, and his responsibility for the shaping and use of world and environment, which must preserve what we have shown to be the total context in which he stands, together with all living things, and which serves the life of the whole. The question about man's basic attitudes, models, modes of behavior, and orientations of value belongs within this framework; for it is these that provide the foundation for specific decisions, for considerations of changes, and for pros and cons in economic, social, and socio-political processes. Other questions belong within the same framework too. There is the problem of whether man would not simply lose his liberty and his self-consciousness if he were to step back into the interlocking system of his natural environment. There is the question of what asceticism (a phrase frequently used today) with regard to the environment means.[64] There is the question of the extent of human responsibility, which may possibly include nature for its own sake, not merely for the sake of man's continuing existence. And last but not least, there is the question of how standards of quality in the environment and man's life can be evaluated, out of responsibility for the whole and not merely out of the drive of human demands.[65] All this may be exemplified by aspects that are touched on in this final basic question, not to speak of educational measures designed to implant the necessary attitudes in the general awareness,[66] as well as effective political measures on a worldwide scale—though we must avoid implementing these measures by dictatorial means.[67] This final question aims, as J. B. Cobb says, at the decision for ecological awareness which has to consider that the price of technological and economic progress can be too high, that there are limits so narrowly drawn, that man cannot go beyond them. We must attune ourselves to these limits if we do not want to perish.[68]

e. *Questions we must put to theological tradition*

This thrusting of the discussion through actual individual phenomena to the elemental basic questions raised by the subject world and environment makes it appropriate to include the theological tradition, when it is a question of illuminating the present situation and finding out what the basis of its transformation must be. The discussions that have gone on between scientists and theologians in the last twenty years show how theology has come to be drawn in. Recent working groups, conferences, institutions, and publications on the subject of the world and the environment demonstrate this also. On the scientific side the names of C. F. von Weizsäcker, Günter Howe, and Klaus Müller may serve as examples of people involved in the discussion, while for Protestant theology we may mention Wolfhart Pannenberg especially. The physicist Müller reaches out to theological tradition for perspectives of a transformation,[69] as does the zoologist Gerd von Wahlert,[70] and Günter Altner in his biological comments.[71] The philosopher K. M. Meyer-Abich has published reflections on the concept of a practical theology of nature.[72] There are, meanwhile, many theological publications which pick up the challenge of the current world and environment theme. Names such as J. B. Cobb,[73] K. Scholder,[74] Altern,[75] Liedke,[76] Link,[77] or Ole Jensen[78] may stand as examples here, out of many that might be named.[79] In addition, the Sociological Institute of the Evangelical-Lutheran churches in Germany has published an interfaculty compilation on the theme of environmental strategy, while the periodical *Evangelische Theologie* has devoted two special numbers to contributions on this subject: *Anthropology and the Relation to Nature (Anthropologie und Naturverhältnis)*, 1974, and *On the Theology of Nature (Zur Theologie der Natur)*, 1977.

It is a fact that inquiries in line with the basic questions we have raised, and directed toward a critical surmounting of the prevailing and serious division between man and nature, meet with a long and continuously cultivated doctrinal tradition on the subject in theology. According to this tradition, man and nature stand in the context of the creation process, which overrides and comprehends both; while in God the creator they have a fore-ordered relation of meaning and value. At the same time, the challenge of the current world and environment theme also brings doctrinal development face to face with new questions and new groups of problems, in contrast to the ones that were dominant in theological discussion under the dictatorship of a despotic scientific knowledge and the technical organization of the world. J. Track has pointed this out in an impressively informative essay.[80] For the suppression of God in a world that has become theologically neutral allows Christian doctrinal statements all too quickly to become statements of faith without any foothold in modern experience of the world—statements which are defended more laboriously than effectively. In the face of this, theology still sees itself with its back to the wall when asked for its contribution to the subject of world and environment. The situation has been recently described by G. Noller,[81] K. M. Meyer-Abich,[82] H. Dembowski,[83] and J. Hübner,[84] and has been discussed in some detail by Link.[85] And even within the confines of theology itself, the question arises: From which aspect should theology attack the subject of the world and the environment? In the context of the doctrine of creation, in the light of christology or pneumatology, or from the standpoint of a new interpretation of nature?[86]

So the obvious approach for a theological participation in the world and environment discussion would seem to be to return first of all to the fundamental biblical statements that lie behind the formation of theological doctrine. For this return, it is an important fact that the current discussion about the world and the environment has, for its part, pressed forward into fundamental questions, because these fundamental questions show links with the biblical understanding of the world. For, as we shall be showing in detail, according to the Bible's interpretation, the natural world, including man, is a total, elemental process of historical movement and future which is closely bound up with experience. It includes determinations of meaning, value, and norms for the experience, spiritual grasp, and shaping of the natural world. That is to say, it includes just that decisive *more* which is excluded, with such momentous consequences, when nature as object is divided from man as autonomous subject. The Old and New Testament statements about the world as creation, our perception and experience of it, and its unity and quality of meaning as the act of God the creator, must be considered especially, along with statements about the human shaping of the world. It is not surprising that it is texts of this particular kind that are drawn expectantly into the current new way of looking at things by nontheologians such as Weizsäcker,[87] Klaus Müller,[88] and K. M. Meyer-Abich,[89] as well as by theologians such as Altner,[90] Liedke,[91] or Link.[92]

Yet here too difficulties arise. The first of them is connected with the reproach (which has been vehemently put forward more than once) that the biblical statements about creation, with their command to man to subdue the earth and have dominion over it, have themselves contributed essentially to our contemporary environmental crisis. So, if it is the origin of the crisis, how can this tradition contribute to its solution? We must consider this reproach levied at the biblical texts in the appropriate place in our confrontation. And we must do the same with the other reproach, which constitutes the second difficulty: the reproach that the biblical tradition is unsuitable for a fruitful contribution to the discussion about the world and the environment because contempt for the existing world and the negative assessment of human potentialities led to a flight from the world in the later Old Testament texts, and even more in the New Testament. And, it is asserted, this flight from the world concentrated responsibility and activity, not on this world at all, but on one which is to come some day or other, a world which only God can bring about, not man. A third difficulty is a fundamental one; it touches on the question of whether a fruitful confrontation between the biblical state of affairs and present, topical questions is possible. Even if, on a fundamental level, relationships do exist between biblical statements and topical problems connected with the world and the environment, how can the statements of ancient texts prove fruitful in our situation? For they do not yet envisage the experience and intellectual foundations of a scientifically and technically molded modern world; and further, they live from experiences and intellectual foundations that have long since ceased to be taken for granted, generally speaking. How, then, can the texts be brought to bear on our problems, unless they are robbed of their specific content and unique character through inadmissible modernization? Or unless we think in terms of a no-less illusory return by the modern world to ancient conditions? We must discuss this question in the context of a third fundamental condition for our confrontation.

3. The Importance of Biblical Exegetical Statements in the Context of the Problems Raised by the Natural World and the Environment

We have just referred to the difference in the times, the experiences, the mental presuppositions, and the actual image of the world and the environment, as well as in the technical and industrial possibilities and challenges of the day. All this makes it clear that the biblical texts themselves, as the scholar seeks to interpret them, in their original historical sense, cannot yield any direct solutions and specific directions for the questions and challenges of the present day. These can only be extracted at the price of inadmissible, and consequently ineffective and dangerous, curtailments on both sides. In order to bridge this difference, we have rather the task of bringing about a reconciliation, based on evidence, between the Bible and the present. But this task, necessary and inescapable though it is, goes far beyond what is possible for a biblical scholarship based on exegesis.[93] It aims at the discovery of Christian truth as it appears at the present day in mental, spiritual, and practical contexts. Consequently, it is something that can be implemented in a theological, cross-faculty process in which nontheological and theological disciplines together try to find the current form of Christian truth and life, as regards the world and the environment.[94] Our confrontation can do no more than work toward this far more broadly designed procedure, which can convey theologically the differences in the times and problems of the Bible and the present, and can bridge the two responsibly. This is the only procedure that can aim at working together theologically to discover the truth for the present which is to be found in the fundamental biblical findings; this is the only procedure that can hope to bring about educative and practically effective dissemination in the worldwide political context of our present and future. This common working procedure will present itself differently, as I have shown elsewhere,[95] in its layout and the evidence it offers, according to whether it is confined to theology itself, to the sphere of the Christian churches and the foundations of their faith; or whether it reaches out beyond that, into the discussion about fundamental views of knowledge, values, and action in pluralistic societies, a process deserving of special attention in view of the worldwide political explosiveness of our present subject. But there is no need to go into that again here.

The exegetical and historical findings about the original meaning of biblical statements related to our theme are of essential importance for this cross-faculty theological process, however, and hence also for the forming of attitudes of thought and action in the face of the challenges of our day. They are of essential importance also because these statements, unique in kind as they are, constitute the foundation from which the Christian form of truth (which we have still to work out) takes its bearings in matters of the world and the environment, if it is to be the Christian view of things at all. All Christian thinking, living, and acting take their fundamental direction from these biblical findings. A second point may be added. It is only in a historical exegesis, which preserves the original sense of the biblical texts, that the role for mediation becomes clear. For this makes it evident that the current theological form of truth requires, first, an extension of the biblically formulated background of understanding, in support of the realities peculiar to our own day; and, second, an expansion of our present conditions, for the sake of the substance of what the Bible has to reveal in the way of meaning and values. We have to achieve this expansion by a critical examination of current opinion and conditions.

At the same time, biblical historical exegesis will be able to make an effective contribution on the subject of the world and environment to theology, the church, Christian practice, and the encouragement of responsibility for the world, only if it goes beyond its usual practice in two ways.

In the first place, it must not confine itself to the analysis and explanation of sentences that are in need of it. It must set biblical texts historically in the dynamic context in which they live, with its special conditions and experience. It must see them as the embodiment of life processes and as the linguistic assimilation of lived life. For it is only in this way that they can be related, in their correspondences, differences, and impulses, to the conditions of a world today that is understood as a whole.[96] According to K. Müller,[97] Altner,[98] or Link,[99] a quasi-Cartesian attitude toward knowledge, one which grabs at it despotically in an attitude of cross-examination and experimental analysis, must be superseded by a total perception of life processes, not only in historical scholarship but also in the realm of the world and the environment.

In the second place, it is true that biblical exegesis, as a historical inquiry, cannot of itself also make topical statements touching on the truth of its texts, and the form taken by human life in them; for it is devoted to their original, historical character. Yet it will only work effectively toward a mediation with the present if it tries to bring out this original, historical character of the text's statements with an eye to the changed problems of our time. Indeed, by taking account of present problems, the interpreter can be led to thematically important texts and historical connections, which would not appear at all if the interpretation were directed exclusively toward specialized exegetical discussion. Consequently, in the framework of this encounter a direct entry into the biblical statements about creation seems closed to us, and inquiries about our present problems, as these are reflected in the first and second fundamental conditions we laid down at the beginning, seem unavoidable.

In what follows we shall be trying to describe biblical statements on the subject of the world and the environment in their historical character, as living processes; and we shall then bring out this character of theirs in the light of present

problems. That we can only do this by means of examples goes
without saying, in view of the extent of the subject. Our aim is to
point to fundamental biblical facts which can provide material
that will help us to find relevant theological truth in the present.
But, as I have stressed, the process of finding this kind of truth
and its consequences lies outside the possibilities open to
exegetical work, and hence are beyond the scope of this book
even more. This defines precisely what seems to be open to us
when we are looking at a topical theme in the framework of a
historically exegetical book like this one. But this definition of
the limits does not mean that in what follows the reader is only
to be conducted round a theological and historical vestibule of a
Christian view of the subject world and environment. On the
contrary, he is invited to accompany the exegete on that part of
the way which leads to the biblical foundations, a journey that is
an important one for the Christian faith. He is invited to
perceive the biblical findings in their own historical character,
with the eyes of our own time and in the context of the crisis of
the natural world and elemental life that weighs so heavily on
us; and from this he is asked to take up fundamental insights and
impulses which currently have escaped us, but which are
needed to determine the current Christian content of truth and
life with regard to the natural world and environment, and
which could find their way into the discussions and into the
actions of every responsible person.

These are the aspects that determine the layout of our
book. But before we begin, we must still briefly say something
about the design of our project, in a fourth and final
fundamental condition.

4. The Layout of Our Biblical Encounter on the Subject of the Natural World and the Environment

The perspective that determines our view of things is the
subject of the natural world and environment, in the sense in

which we developed it in the first fundamental condition. That is to say, it is the viewpoint of the vital connection and reciprocal effects between living things and the natural world in which they live, seen as total event. This event offers the given data of life's elemental and natural conditions; on this event depend the utilization and shaping of the natural world by the living thing, in order to achieve security of life; and this event includes man, as being intrinsically a part of it and yet in his special position within the whole.

Taking this viewpoint, we shall first of all, in Part A, go into the Old Testament, inquiring about the view taken there of the natural world and the environment. This Old Testament section is divided up into three parts. First of all, the natural conditions of life in ancient Israel will be described in chapter 1. Then the reader will be invited to make the observations appropriate to our theme on the basis of three exemplary, fundamental Old Testament creation texts, which are under continuous discussion, within theology and outside it (chapter 2). Finally, we shall follow up the Old Testament facts under various thematic aspects, in the light of our own day. These aspects are related to the fundamental questions that we worked out in the second fundamental condition (chapter 3). These aspects can in this way also open up Old Testament impulses and suggestions for the mastery of the subject of the world and the environment in our time. In five of these thematic aspects, the main weight lies on the Old Testament view of the natural world and environment as God's creative event; and this is considered from various angles. We are giving special weight to this because, while it is of particular importance as regards the contemporary problems we are dealing with, it also comes up against great difficulties in being understood in the modern world. However, immediately after this we shall be considering, as final aspect, counter-experiences and problems connected with this view, as these are expressed especially in the later Old Testament, and in post–Old Testament texts dating back to late Israel.

In Part B we shall investigate the guiding viewpoint in the New Testament. This is a much briefer investigation than our inquiry into the Old Testament, if only for reasons of space. But this unequal distribution seems justifiable because the New Testament texts that are related to our subject are fewer, because the fundamental features of the Bible's interpretation of the world can already be described in the Old Testament context, and because, therefore, in the New Testament section we have primarily to bring out the new breakthroughs and additions to Old Testament opinions. In this section too, important features of living conditions in New Testament times will be discussed first of all, and we shall give a survey of the textual findings, developing some examples of texts that are of fundamental importance for our subject (chapter 1). Then again we shall be following up thematic aspects (chapter 2) which develop the coming of Christ, according to the witness of the New Testament, in various ways touching on the view of the natural world and environment, its times, its future, and man within it, emphasizing what we find in the light of Old Testament opinion and the fundamental questions of our time.

A.
THE NATURAL WORLD AND THE ENVIRONMENT IN THE OLD TESTAMENT

I. Natural Living Conditions in Ancient Israel

1. The Geographical Area

Some parts of the Old Testament derive from Israelites who were living in exile in Mesopotamia or in other regions of the eastern dispersion. For the most part, however, the Old Testament is the testimony of an Israel that lived in Palestine, in the area lying between the Mediterranean in the west and the Syrian-Arabian desert in the east, and which stretched from the southern border of Lebanon to the Ante-Lebanon range in the north, and the southern end of the Dead Sea in the south. It is closely linked with the wider region of the narrow strip of cultivated land between the eastern coast of the Mediterranean and the Syrian-Arabian desert. This is the living space with which ancient Israel was faced, and in which it moved.[1]

2. Living Conditions

This area, which is part of the wider belt of land known as the Fertile Crescent, certainly offers acceptable living conditions on the whole, not merely for an extremely varied fauna (which is frequently mentioned in the Old Testament[2]), but for men and women too, both nomads, on the fringe of the area, and people with a settled form of life. The reason for this is the conjunction of favorable climatic or weather conditions and soil constituency, which is characteristic of the Fertile Crescent generally. If we look more closely, however, we can see that natural conditions in Palestine vary considerably, and are as a whole quite different in character from the great river oases of Mesopotamia and Egypt, which offer constant and secure foundations for vegetation, animals, and people because of the regular flooding and the opportunities for artificial irrigation, independent of rainfall. Palestine, on the other hand, is a country that is totally dependent on rain. The early, main, and late rains fall during the six winter months, but in the six months of summer there is no rain at all, and all annual vegetation withers, except for woody plants. The limestone soil of Palestine is very permeable, extensive forestation in our sense hardly existed, even in Old Testament times,[3] and springs, brooks, rivers, or access to the ground water providing an adequate supply of water all year round are only found to a limited extent, and are only significant in certain regions. Consequently the provision of water in the dry summer months is an elemental problem, which can only be solved if the winter rains are sufficient to build up water reserves in cisterns for the summer. The amount of rainfall varies considerably in the different areas of Palestine, however.[4] Adequate rainfall in the plains along the Mediterranean coast, on the western slopes of the West and East Jordan mountains and on the high plateaus behind them are in contrast to unfavorable or insufficient rainfall in the eastern foothills of the mountains, in the areas east of East Jordan, which merge into the desert steppes, and south of the West Jordan Mountains, which, with their scanty watering places and sparse vegetation, only occasionally offer suitable grazing for herds of sheep and goats.

3. The Utilization of the Natural World

The highly varied character of the land in the different parts of Palestine, and the complete dependency on climatic and rainfall cycles, results in wide differences in environmental conditions for plants and animals—and for people as well. Permanent settled life is only possible in areas with a certain amount of precipitation. Apart from these, only a seminomadic, pastoral existence is possible, in which people move from pasture to pasture with their herds of sheep and goats. In the regions of cultivated land, with more extensive rainfall, arable farming is of fundamental importance—though the extent of the yield varies—as is herding (sheep and goats, but also cattle). Grain especially is planted (wheat and barley, also spelt and millet here and there), as well as flax. Trees are planted and cultivated, especially figs, olives, and occasionally palms. Vines and garden crops are grown, especially vegetables such as lentils and beans, along with herbs.[5]

It has often been stressed that these natural conditions make only a modest way of life possible for Palestine's people.[6]

> The inhabitants' livelihood depended on a combination of agriculture and small cattle breeding, varying according to local conditions. Home-baked bread and a variety of milk products, with various seasonal fruits, represented the main foods. Meat eating was always exceptional and limited to certain special occasions and feast days.[7]

And this was the case all the more because there was almost no way of raising the standard of living for wide sections of the population. It was only in certain regions that the food available could be supplemented by hunting[8] or fishing (off the Mediterranean coast, for example, or in the Sea of Gennesaret). Here the nature of the country, in contrast to that of great river civilizations, hardly makes any economically considerable surplus of natural products possible; and any surplus had to be used as barter (or later as payment) for the goods urgently needed by the people settled on the land, whose way of life was aimed at self-subsistence through the cultivation of the soil and the keeping of animals.

It is obvious that this generally modest Palestinian way of life, which involved demanding labor, was bound to come under considerable strain when the areas where Israelite farmers and herdsmen had settled became part of developing states, for these inevitably brought in their wake a society based on the division of labor, with the separation into different classes that accompanied it. To this was added a shift of importance from the country to the town; the requirements of the court, the army, and the administration, and the pressure to import metals and wood into Palestine so poor in raw materials[9] —all this quite apart from upper-class demands for luxuries, as well as the claims of foreign powers, to which Israel was exposed for most of its history. In Old Testament times too, there were periods when economic life flourished, when trade was brisk and commerce profitable.[10] This was so in Solomon's time, for example,[11] or under Jeroboam II.[12] But economic prosperity of this kind, if it profited the people as a whole at all, was the exception or was confined to the towns that were near the coast or that lay on the great trading routes that passed through Palestine.[13]

4. The Hazards

The nature of living conditions in Palestine therefore demands considerable powers of adaptation from plants, animals, and, especially, man, if they are to manage to eke out even a modest existence. These natural conditions meant that the mass of the country people had to rely on a limited economy, in their arable farming and animal husbandry, aimed at self-subsistence and the provision of what was needed for barter or for taxes. This way of life is in any case largely dependent on the natural economy; but there are, in addition, considerable extra hazards springing from the nature of the country, which can have unexpected and incalculable effects. Palestine is threatened by earthquakes, and there were several in Old Testament times (1 Sam. 14:15; Amos 1:1; Zech. 14:5). Much more of a threat—a threat that touches the very life-nerve of the country—is a reduction, or even a complete failure of the necessary rainfall. This could always happen, and was not infrequent in ancient Israel (2 Sam. 21; 1 Kings 17–18; Jer. 14). The Old Testament is full of reflections on this continual danger for man and beast. In the Book of Deuteronomy a drought of this kind is threatened with the words: "And the heavens over your head shall be brass, and the earth under you shall be iron. Yahweh will make the rain of your land powder and dust; from heaven it shall come down upon you until you are destroyed" (28:23-24).[14] Other dangers were grain disease (e.g., Deut. 28:22) and insect pests which attacked the cultivated plants, especially grasshoppers or locusts (Deut. 28:38-39; Joel 1; and frequently elsewhere). In addition, men and herds were threatened by sickness and epidemics, as well as by animals—lions, bears, wild cattle, and snakes.

Altogether, therefore, nothing could be farther from reality than to imagine that there was a harmonious and balanced relationship between man and nature in Palestine. Nature challenged, while man was forced to adapt and had only very limited opportunities for intervention.

5. What Predetermined Israel's Perception of the Natural World?

How did ancient Israel perceive this actual existing world, with its life and its opportunities for living? How did Israel think of it and act toward it? We shall be following this up presently with the help of certain texts, under particular thematic aspects. But we may consider a few predetermined characteristics now, following what we have just said.

First: Israel's own estimate was one of wonderment and delight at having entered "a land flowing with milk and honey." But neither this nor Israel's own interpretation that the world in which it lived was also Yahweh's good creation should blind us to the fact that even in the most elemental sphere Israel had as a whole to make do with living conditions ranging from modest to hard, conditions which were always full of the gravest risk, particularly because of the weather. Israel exposed itself to this instability of its world without any attempt to gloss it over, as the Old Testament everywhere shows. The fact that in spite of this it could arrive at so positive a judgment about its world, must simply be connected with the character of its civilization. We shall have to bear this in mind.

Second: Unlike the waves of immigrants that preceded it, Israel did not enter the country as a conquering class. It did not take over a social position and cultural role as the upper-class of an urban civilization, distinct and inevitably detached from the lower, dependent sections of the population who were compelled to supply their needs directly from nature. Israel as a whole was never in a position for commerce, the skilled trades, or particular processing techniques to provide the foundation for its people's lives. Israel entered the country to cultivate the land and keep cattle. This remained the economic foundation for its people, and they therefore always had close and direct experience of the elemental significance of natural living conditions. This too, no doubt, influenced its perception of the natural world.

Third: The population of later Israel settled down in the cultivated land of Palestine, having formerly led a seminomadic life. This earlier character would not only have contributed to the positive view toward a settled life with one's own share of a cultivated land; it probably influenced Israel's relationship to the natural world in general. It no doubt helped to form the attitude of expectation that was in accordance with a wandering life; the basic knowledge of man's dependency on, and subordination to, natural conditions; the perception, and yet the overcoming, of the risks inherent in the natural environment; and a sensitivity toward the unexpected over which man has no disposal. Even the main risk, the rainfall, was therefore probably also perceived differently from the way it was viewed by people belonging to a Canaanite urban civilization, who often had no direct contact with agriculture and who lived in the more favorable parts of Palestine with a secure rainfall. The former nomadic character of a broadly peasant population, living in an area of considerable risk, was probably of importance for Israel's attitude toward the world.

Fourth: Of course it is impossible to talk about ancient Israel's awareness of ecology, in our sense of the word. But Israel did have certain ways of behaving in its dealings with the land and with animals that did in actual fact have a favorable ecological effect. Man's relationship to the group (including his domestic animals and his herds), which was due to the influence of the nomadic period, probably played a part here, as well as the experience of ecological dependency. This was in contrast to the experience of power through the technical exploitation of nature, which probably emerged from the art of differentiated irrigation refinements in the river oases of Mesopotamia. For there man saw himself in confrontation with a nature which he could control, which he had formed, and which could be made useful.[15] What the Palestinian perceived from his natural world, on the contrary, was rather the bestowing Power on whom he was dependent.

Fifth: The very difference in the nature of Palestine as country, which only yielded isolated areas of settlement and utilization to the Israelites, and even in those areas made varying demands on the adaptation of the people, meant that the world and the environment had at first a very limited radius. It was simply the radius of the people's own world—the territory occupied by the family and the tribe, and later the land of Israel, were the main units, the units that were perceived and in which life was carried on. At the beginning Israel certainly could not talk about the world and the environment in the comprehensive, total sense. For that, particular cultural stimuli and historical developments were needed.

For our initial examination of the world and the environment as it was viewed in ancient Israel, we shall now turn to some texts that display this comprehensive outlook. These texts are selected examples only. We shall be looking at the Yahwist's story of the Creation (part of Gen. 2–11); the great creation psalm, Psalm 104; and the Priestly Writing's creation account (part of Gen. 1–10).

II. Some Observations About the Texts

1. The Yahwist's History of the Primeval Period

a. The text and the area to which it belongs

"The Yahwist's primeval history" is the name given by Old Testament scholars to a series of texts that are part of the first eleven chapters of Genesis. The most important of these texts are the story of the Garden of Eden (Gen. 2–3), the story of Cain and his descendants (Gen. 4), one version of the story of the Flood (included in Gen. 6–8), the story of the cursing of Canaan (Gen. 9:18-27), one version of the tables of the nations (part of Gen. 10), and the story of the Tower of Babel (Gen. 11:1-9). These texts originally formed a self-contained narrative (see Bibliography, 137).

Many scholars think that this whole narrative complex was the beginning of a bigger historical work, the Yahwist Source, which can be reconstructed from the historical books of the Old Testament and which, after the primeval history, went on to tell the early history of Israel, at least as far as the entry into the Promised Land, by way of God's famous address to Abraham (Gen. 12:1-3), which was an important pivot-point in the history. The dating of this historical work has recently become a point of controversy again; but there are still good reasons for placing it, at least in its essentials (including the primeval history), in the period of the empire of David and Solomon,[1] i.e., the tenth century B.C.[2] If it is permissible to take this date, then we have here the earliest Israelite text that can be related to the world and environment theme in the wider sense.

b. The intention of the account

Anyone who reads straight through the primeval history in the framework of the Yahwist's historical account (to which scholars have given the symbol J, from the German spelling *Jahwist*) will certainly not discover its relation to the world and environment theme straight away. He will fail to do so because we inevitably read this series of stories as the account of individual, self-contained events in the remote past. We may admire them esthetically, but we smile over their factual content. For at that time narrator and listener had a quite different viewpoint. The aim was not to satisfy people's curiosity and interest about remote times in a seemingly simple-minded way, trying to explain what things were really like once-upon-a-time. The intention was to clarify the present experience of the world of narrator and listener by showing features that had put their stamp on the experience—the mental and active perception—of the world of the present. For this is predetermined by certain conditions of general applicability, geographically and in time—generally applicable, that is to say, not only to Israel but to man as a whole. That is why in a history of primeval times we are told how these conditions came into being and why; for it is from these beginnings that they retain their efficacy down to the world of the present day. We must therefore look at the Yahwist's history, and especially the primeval history, retrospectively as it were,[3] with the eyes and experience of the people in whose time it was composed and narrated. According to what these texts tell us, how does the narrator see his world? In his account of Israel's early history, from Genesis 12 onward, he expresses the meaning, the chance, and the future of the world as it exists; but in his primeval history he brings out the ambivalent predetermination of this world. We shall consider these two aspects one after another.

c. *The Yahwist's view of the world as it stands*

The narrator sees Israel, the people of the twelve tribes and the country in which he himself lives as belonging to the group of all the nations on earth (Gen. 12:3), from which it itself came (Gen. 10:21, 25-30). With this viewpoint he paces out the whole earth, as the space man has to live in; in accordance with the knowledge of the time, his perspective of the whole world covers the Middle East from Mesopotamia to Crete, and from northern Syria to the Arabian Peninsula and Egypt.[4] This comprehensive, worldwide viewpoint is already opened up in the first sentence of the Yahwist's account: "In the day that Yahweh Elohim made the earth and the heavens" (Gen. 2:4*b*). Even this radius is astonishing. What actually makes the narrator expand Israel's horizon so widely? What makes him go beyond his own area of settlement and his immediate neighbors? On the one hand, it was probably Israel's new consciousness of its international setting, an experience that sprang from the building of the empire under David; though the Yahwist admittedly still depicts these international ramifications in genealogical terms (Gen. 10) as a great association of families (Gen. 12:3), with Israel as nation in the center (Gen. 12:1). Another factor was no doubt the critical integration of Canaanite traditions, which already had an all-embracing perspective of this kind.

But we should be misunderstanding the narrator if we suggested that he is only describing what he knows, though naturally a mass of detailed knowledge and geographical and ethnographical information contributed to this world perspective. The world is for him, not a certain state of affairs, not a static object, which man explains by an analysis of its individual subsections. For him the world is an event, a process. Israel and the peoples of the world, mankind as a whole and the elemental natural world, are all included equally in the movement of this event. In this process "world," a qualitative aspect is now of essential importance for the narrator: the world is for him (to put it in abstract terms) a sphere in which existence is either successful and fulfilled, or not. This is true for Israel and for the other nations, on the level of the world of man. It is true for Israel and the other nations, i.e., for all men, as regards the natural foundation for living. In this historical work the narrator simply wants to show the rise of the conditions that are valid and effective here; but these do not emerge out of deductions about some divine power or other (conclusions which would be accessible to everyone): they spring from the perception of Yahweh, as seen in the early history of Israel, which the Yahwist describes.

This qualitative view of the world as event—a view which takes its bearings from Yahweh—corresponds to a particular basic experience. It is the experience that fulfilled existence, down to the very elements necessary for life, is not possible for Israel and within Israel, or for the nations and their relations to one another, or indeed for mankind as a whole, without the bestowal of success. Success has to be bestowed on all levels: foreign and home policy, social life, and even in the natural conditions necessary for life. Everything depends on this bestowal of success, but it is something over which man has no control; it is not at his disposal; he cannot achieve it by himself. The narrator calls this bestowal of success the blessing of Yahweh. It is in this sense that he makes Israel understand its remarkable existence under the empire of David and Solomon as being the result of Yahweh's blessing. And this blessing began with the speeches of promise and the words of blessing in the early history as he tells it. The people's vigorous, well-populated existence in their own country, their prominent position and power compared with other nations, their victory over their enemies (Gen. 12:1-3; 27:27-29; 28:13-15; Num. 24:3-9, 15-19). But the blessing is to be seen no less in their prosperity and success as regards natural living conditions. Thus Isaac blesses Jacob, the father of the twelve tribes, in the words: "May God give you of the dew of heaven, and of the fatness of the earth, and plenty of grain and wine" (Gen. 27:28);[5] and Balaam is constrained to bless Israel: "How fair are your tents, O Jacob, your encampments, O Israel! Like valleys that stretch afar, like gardens beside a river, like aloes that Yahweh has planted, like cedar trees beside the waters. Water shall flow from his buckets, and his seed shall be in many waters" (Num. 24:5-7; cf. also Gen. 26:12-14).[6] But this is not enough. Against the background of the Yahwist's worldwide perspective, he also envisages blessing for the world of man as a whole, provided that it recognizes the blessing of Israel by Yahweh (Gen. 12:3; 27:29; 28:14; Num. 24:9).

What we see in the Yahwist is therefore a total view of the world, which comprehends the whole earth and all men, their times, their future, and the fulfillment of their existence. It includes specific political and ethnic conditions, and even takes in natural living conditions. This view of the world is admittedly not yet directed toward everything living, and the world of all life for its own sake. It is still entirely concentrated on man, with the risks and dangers of his world. Its substantial unity consists in its understanding that the world is a sphere in which man is absolutely dependent on blessing; and that it is the event of the divine promise and bestowal of blessing for the fulfillment of man's existence. This is preeminently true for Israel, but it applies no less to mankind as a whole, if the peoples expressly

orient themselves toward Israel and its God Yahweh, who is the
conferrer of blessing.

Now, in the light of today we could see this view of the
world, theologically speaking, as over-simplified wishful
thinking, because it excludes contrary experiences. We might
see it as prompted by wishes in which the poverty of the country
and its inherent threats, as well as the guiding concepts of pure
power politics, were the father of the thought, so that the
blessing of Yahweh was simply the symbol for the influx of
necessary, additional power. But this would be a fundamental
misunderstanding of the Yahwist. The fact that there is an
increase of blessing in the world of man, and that there has been
an increase of blessing from the time of Abraham onward, is not
an automatic process for Israel; and for the world of the nations
it is not simply identical with subjection to the Israelite empire.
In the Yahwist's view (and Gen. 12:1-3 indicates the whole
outline)[7] it is bound up with the fact that, for the furthering of
his existence, man is not oriented toward himself and his
self-determined interests, but toward Yahweh and Yahweh's
values, Yahweh's promises and Yahweh's blessing. This is true
for Israel, when it obediently trusts in Yahweh's word, like
Abraham; and it is true for the rest of mankind when they take
their bearings from Abraham/Israel and the blessing Yahweh
has conferred on them. For the Yahwist, the world event—the
sphere where existence is successfully consummated through
blessing—is only possible in man's whole world (with its
political and social relations as well as its basic necessities) if
people turn away from their own self-determination. It can only
be found in man's ties with a third person, who is above him,
Yahweh.

The Yahwist expounds this view of the world as a process
starting from Yahweh's side, with Abraham, and he sees it as
being founded in the early history he relates. Its contours and
depths become recognizable when we notice that here we are
presented with the beginnings that lead to the conquest of a
given, and always acute, state of affairs in the world, a state of
affairs that characterizes mankind's existing condition. This
condition is true of Israel and of all men, and includes the world

of animals and plants. It is this view of the world as it really is,
apart from and before the active tie with Yahweh and the
blessing that man has experienced, which the Yahwist
expounds in the primeval history.

d. *The ambivalent character of the world in its predetermined form*

What the Yahwist shows in the primeval history as the
ambivalent character of the world in its predetermined form is
seen with unparalleled realism and sober penetration. As we
have seen, the series of initial events described here are typical,
comprehensive, and continually valid, not individual and
confined to a particuar incident. What they relate is the genesis
of the world as we see it and the reasons for its being as it is, a
world without blessing and in need of blessing, the world
everyone experiences and suffers from. The world view here is
a total one, even more directly so than the Yahwist's narrative of
the period from Abraham onward, which we have just
considered. The story focuses on the whole living space of the
earth and on mankind as a whole; and here, too, it is the quality
of life that is under consideration. Once more the narrator is
concerned about the success and fulfillment of man's existence
in his world. But what he perceives there, and what he
apprehends in his account of the primeval history is the
faultiness, depreciation, and loss that mark man's life and his
experience of the world.

On the one hand, the narrator sees people as being
endowed with the natural conditions which regulate human
existence and which are not experienced as anything produced,
or producible, by man himself. They are something over which
he has no control, something elemental and positive, and are
simply bestowed on him. These circumstances with which men
and women are endowed are indeed the signs of all that Yahweh
the creator graciously concedes: the fact that man is alive at
all—men, women, children; the fact that people populated the
whole earth (1:19; 10*J*); the fact that the earth where man dwells
is given to him as space in which to live (2:4*b*; 8:22; 9:19), with

all the constant rhythms so necessary for life, "seedtime and harvest, cold and heat, summer and winter, day and night" (8:22); the fact that he has land at his disposal, with soil that can be cultivated and pasture to supply him with food and clothing (2:5; 3:17-19; 4:2); that the land provides animals (2:19-20; 4:2; 6–8J) and plants for his use (2:5; 3:17-19; 4:2, 12), even to the "comforting" vine (5:29; 9:20). It is an elemental outlook, the outlook of the Palestinian peasant. It takes in the whole of the world as man's milieu, with the elemental conditions that constitute his existence, seeing it as a continuous event, fixed in its beginnings and constant from that time on. It always includes man, because of the unfathomable miracle of his life and his natural endowments. It is viewed as a total, always given process, which is permanently oriented toward life as a fundamental value in itself. This process has the quality of endowment, being the gift of Yahweh the creator.[8]

But this is only one side of the matter. This perspective does not filter out the negative features of the human world as we see it. It also includes all the predetermining factors that have a negative effect. The narrator sees the world in which man moves as being no less determined by faultiness, depreciation, and hardship. Man does not see these unpropitious factors as being at his own disposal either, or as being the direct result of his own actions.[9] So in the course of the Yahwist's primeval history in Genesis 2–11, we have the isolation of the snake from the community of beasts and its permanent danger for man (3:14-15); the hardship of birth for the woman and her subjection to man as her lord and master (3:16); the whole toilsome labor of man's work in the fields as he cultivates the soil, which if left to itself only produces weeds (3:17-19); the fact that there are people who have to live as nomads or in towns, without any land of their own, people who have to eke out a living by keeping herds, or by special trades, e.g., musicians or metal-workers (4:17-24).[10] The narrator describes the way people live together all over the earth no less unfavorably. People dominate their fellows on the one hand, and are subjected on the other (9:18-27); their settlements are scattered all over the earth (10J; cf. 11:8, 9); and they are split up by different languages, which hinder understanding and joint action (11:1-9). Here, therefore, is the other aspect of the world, full of unfavorable, predetermined characteristics. This is what it looks like in contrast to the favorable picture of the farmer, who lives in village communities on the basis of family and tribal groups. Accordingly the life of man per se, life as it actually exists, is seen, not as a progressive development toward higher things, but as a limitation and depreciation that burdens and endangers the whole of human existence. This is true even of the natural conditions in which life is passed on, but it is even more the case in the relations between people, in the economic and cultural developments that help to maintain life as it is (food, housing, work, communication between peoples), and in the animal world (3:14); and there is even a glance at threats to the environment. It must be stressed (against contrary interpretations)[11] that even the so-called cultural achievements which the Yahwist's primeval history takes over from tradition—clothing (3:7), the building of towns (4:17), tents (4:20), musical instruments (4:21), the fashioning of metals (4:22), and the construction of towers (11:1 ff)—are not, for the narrator, positive signs of progress. They are simply human efforts to secure survival on the basis of a culpable depreciation or diminution of life (Gen. 3:4); or they may actually be the creations of guilt (Gen. 11).[12]

This ambivalent character of the world in its original form is for the narrator the expression of its striking need of blessing. But it is not a disaster arranged for man, so as to make Yahweh's blessing all the more effective by contrast. It is, in all its ambivalence, a deliberate happening on behalf of man, which has its reasons.

In order to show these reasons for the world process in all its universally experienced faultiness, the narrator's viewpoint penetrates, in the primeval history, to an original portrait of this world without the depreciation, loss, and limitations that are the mark of life in its existing form. At the beginning of his primeval history, in the section on the creation, he shows this world as it was originally ordained for man.

In the day that Yahweh God made the earth and the heavens, when no plant of the field was yet in the earth and no herb of

the field had yet sprung up—for Yahweh God had not [yet]
caused it to rain upon the earth, and there was no man to till
the group; but a mist [spring?] went up from the earth and
watered the whole face of the ground—then Yahweh God
formed man of dust from the ground, and breathed into his
nostrils the breath of life; and man became a living being.
And Yahweh God planted a garden in Eden, in the east; and
there he put the man whom he had formed. And out of the
ground Yahweh God made to grow every tree that is pleasant
to the sight and good for food, the tree of life also in the midst
of the garden, and the tree of the knowledge of good and
evil. . . . Yahweh God took the man and put him in the
garden of Eden to till and keep it. And Yahweh God
commanded the man, saying, "You may freely eat of every
tree of the garden; but of the tree of the knowledge of good
and evil you shall not eat, for in the day that you eat of it you
shall die." Then Yahweh God said, "It is not good that the
man should be alone; I will make a helper fit for him." So out
of the ground Yahweh God formed every beast of the field
and every bird of the air, and brought them to the man to see
what he would call them; and whatever the man called every
living creature, that was its name. The man gave names to all
cattle, and to the birds of the air, and to every beast of the
field; but for the man there was not found a helper fit for him.
So Yahweh God caused a deep sleep to fall upon the man,
and while he slept took one of his ribs and closed up its place
with flesh; and the rib which Yahweh God had taken from the
man he made into a woman and brought her to the man.
Then the man said, "This at last is bone of my bones and flesh
of my flesh; she shall be called Woman, because she was
taken out of Man." Therefore a man leaves his father and his
mother and cleaves to his wife, and they become one flesh.
And the man and his wife were both naked, and were not
ashamed. (Gen. 2:4b-9, 15-25)[13]

Even this primeval world is seen in the light of a comprehensive
viewpoint, inasmuch as the whole milieu of the natural
conditions that constitute existence (at least man's existence) is
brought in, even if this milieu has not as yet the all-embracing
scope of "heaven and earth." Here the narrator picks up the

constitutive, given aspects of human existence, the aspects that are conferred, elemental, not achieved by man, and sees them in their undiminished and undepreciated form as Yahweh's creative event, brought into being on man's behalf. This creative event is man's being alive, a fact over which he has no control (2:7); his endowment with a place to live without any risky, vital dependence on rain, but which always has a secure supply of water (2:5-6); his provision with food which does not require laborious work in the fields but is to be found in an orchard with delicious fruit that only needs to be picked (2:8-9); an activity that does not demand of man the toilsome work necessary if food has to be provided, but is simply the carefree, satisfying activity of tilling and cultivating this garden (2:15) now closed to us forever (3:22-24). This human existence takes its bearings from the directions of the One who is the giver of life and life's necessities (2:16-17), and who confers fellowship with other living things—with animals, which man orders into his world, giving them names (2:18-20), and also with the woman, over whom man rejoices as being completely in accord with himself (2:21-25).

Even if this picture is seen entirely from man's viewpoint, it undoubtedly implies that in the vegetable and animal world everything is excluded that would make life less full and undiminished—certainly as far as human intervention is concerned.[14] What the narrator pictures here is an elemental, perfect world of living things; but we must notice what the impulse behind it is. The intention is not to paint an illusory picture, inspired by the mere play of ideas—peasant dreams of perfection that exclude all unfavorable experience of the world, a picture that has no reality anywhere in the present and that (according to the narrator's view) can never exist again in that form (3:23-24). The impulse behind the narrative is a critical factual judgment about the world of experience as it actually exists, contrasted with the counter-picture of the original world of creation. For a perfect world of this kind, in keeping with man but no less appropriate to the world of flora and fauna, is in line with the fact that there man sees the conditions of life conferred on him, not as the means and materials for his autonomous will, but as a process that happens to him and includes his own activity. The process is a gift, in which consequently Yahweh confers the value and meaning of existence, ahead of anything that man does himself. Consequently, what is good and profitable for man, and what is not, is also determined solely in the light of man's orientation toward Yahweh. The judgment which the narrator pronounces through his introductory account of the creation of man in paradise is that the One who grants the necessities of life is also the One who alone knows what is good for man; and that for the sake of a perfect world, the gift of life and the meaning, values, and aims of human existence must be in one hand, Yahweh's.

In the primeval history, the fact that the existing world is no longer like this but is an overshadowed, diminished, and disturbed version of this original world that came into being solely at God's initiative is put down by the narrator to man's own nature. This is not associated with any notion of doom. But man does not remain close to Yahweh's guiding hand, and to the divine significance and values. Instead he pursues the delusion that he is able to decide himself, quite independently, taking his bearings from himself and his own self-created interests, what is beneficial and what is detrimental for his existence; the delusion, that is, that he is able to know good and evil all by himself.[15] The narrator believes it is the subjection of the world to the interests and values of man as he breaks away from God which leads to the profound damage and depreciation of the created world that is plain to everyone. The character of man as he actually is, the fact that "every imagination of the thoughts of his heart was only evil continually," as the narrator puts it in the introduction to the story of the Flood (6:5; 8:21), finds expression in the rebellion against God, which the narrator describes at the beginning of the primeval history (3:1ff) and at its end (11:1-9). It is equally clear in the corruption of the relations between man and man, which is evident in the accusation of Eve (3:12), in Cain's fratricide (4:1ff) and in Canaan's wickedness (9:18ff). It is man's character and the delusion that he can determine his own goals autonomously in his dealings with the natural world that damage this world in its original form, beginning with the fellowship between man and wife (3:7ff) and between man and beast (3:13), and reaching out to all the losses and depreciation which the narrator perceives as being the unfavorable features that are already imposed on the world. These do not provide the realistic starting point for some Promethean self-striving on man's part to restore paradisal conditions; they are the point of departure for an obedient entry into the movement of blessing which transforms man as he is and his faulty world, and which the narrator sees as being opened up by God from the time of Abraham.[16]

e. The narrator's view of the natural world and environment

Let us sum up a few points at the end of our glance at the great textual complex of the Yahwist's primeval history. We have seen that the perspective of the natural world and environment, as part of the world of life as a whole, is here an essential component of a total view of the world, even if that view is concentrated on human life, influenced by the experiences and judgments of Israelite peasant existence, and related to the field of political experience acquired during the building of the Israelite state. The remarkable thing about this perspective is its relationship to the elemental facts of human experience. Existence, as something that is not at man's disposal, and natural conditions as they are, are absorbed into this viewpoint as being the event of Yahweh's personal bestowal; they are his act and his gift. The activity of man which molds nature is included in this perspective from the beginning, just as much as his shaping of the relationships between people, which are part of human equipment for life. This viewpoint is very soberly applied, and takes into account man's experience of the whole ambivalence and faultiness of his natural world and environment. That is to say, it includes from the very beginning the fact that life lived in the natural world may be either full of delight or heavily burdened.

This in itself is enough to show that the attempt to understand human existence in a world of this kind could not be confined to an explanation and analysis of the world's components, with their separate laws, while leaving the disposal of the world as a whole to the free initiative of human aims. In the Yahwist's narrative, this relation to the world on man's part, its quality and the effect existence has on it, takes account of the character of gift in the natural world and environment, but equally perceives the burdens caused by the · natural world's depreciation. This leads to wider questions about meaning and value, as well as about the place and responsibility of man in the shaping of the world. In this way it penetrates to fundamental conditions and ordinances. The actual form of the natural world is dependent on the activity of Yahweh, since it is not at man's disposal and is embedded in man's behavior toward Yahweh. Accordingly, the event of the natural world and environment is seen by the narrator in the association of two historical movements, one of which overlies the other. On the one hand, man detaches himself from the higher power who is the personal origin of his life and from the necessities of life provided for him; he also detaches himself from the meaning and values of human existence that emerge from an orientation toward God and God's decisions about what is good for man. He determines the form of the world simply according to his own particular interests. That is how the depreciation, faultiness, and ambivalence of the present world came about, right down to the world of nature itself. On the other hand, if man begins to take his bearings from the higher meaning and values of his existence that are revealed to him in the words and promises of Yahweh and in an orientation toward Israel, which Yahweh has blessed, then a counter-movement is set going which not only transforms the political world, but also transforms the elemental, natural world as well, with its animals and plants, and all the phenomena gathered together in the primeval history—transforms it in the power of Yahweh's blessing. This is how the Yahwist expounds the connection between man and the natural world in Yahweh's creative activity and in man's rebellion; and this too is how he explains the division between man and the natural world insofar as it depends on man, and only on him, whether the world bestowed

by Yahweh, before there was any activity on man's part,
remains his world in the shadow of the curse or becomes a world
in the felicity of blessing.[17]

2. Psalm 104

a. Its historical background and theological position

The Israelite background of Psalm 104 differs spiritually
and mentally from the background of the Yahwist's primeval
history. The Yahwist belongs to Israel's traditions about
salvation history as these were cultivated in Judah with its
agricultural character, reaching out from there to the
knowledge derived from Palestine's Canaanite urban civilization, which it integrated—though critically[18]—for since David
this had belonged within Israel's borders. Psalm 104, on the
other hand, stands on highly individual ground, its background
being an Israelite urban theology belonging to the city of
Jerusalem, one in which the ancient oriental character of this
old Canaanite city (conquered by David) was subjected to an
independent, critical Israelite development, which was comprehensive in its thematic scope.[19] This came about in the
context of the temple cult in Jerusalem, as well as through
Israelite cultivation of the ancient oriental traditions of
education, or "Wisdom," in the city, the capital city of both the
Davidic Empire and of the Kingdom of Judah. Psalm 104
belongs to these particular trends in the history of Israel's
theology.[20] We meet them especially in the psalms, many of
which were cultic hymns sung in the temple at Jerusalem, as
well as in Proverbs; but they are also incorporated in the great
·discourse section of the Book of Job. The relationship of Psalm
104 to the theological view of creation taken in the Jerusalem
cultic hymns and in Jerusalem Wisdom is evident, as I have
shown in more detail elsewhere.[21] (In what follows I am
drawing on the conclusions arrived at in my earlier essay.) It is
not certain whether Psalm 104 itself was composed for use as a

cultic hymn. Nor do we know its exact date. It was probably composed in the period before the Exile, however, in connection with the first temple.

Like Psalm 8, Psalm 19, and a number of other psalms or parts of psalms,[22] Psalm 104 belongs to the group of what we know as creation psalms. The main stress lies on Yahweh's creative activity in the world. This psalm therefore embodies a special aspect within the framework of the wide-ranging themes of Jerusalem cultic theology,[23] which were naturally familiar to the psalmist and were presupposed by him and which also covered the political and social world and the world of individual experience.

The special aspect considered here is Yahweh's activity as creator of the natural world. For the cultic theology of Jerusalem, influenced as it was by ancient oriental, Canaanite elements, this was in general the fundamental sphere of Yahweh's activity, and it also determines the theological viewpoint in other respects.[24] This means that here the perspective of natural world and environment is completely congruent with the thematic aspect which Psalm 104 handles—far more clearly so than in the Yahwist's primeval history, which also takes ethnic, social, and cultural features in the world of man into account. As we shall see in detail under the theme of Yahweh's creation, the psalmist concentrates on the elemental connection between natural, constitutive living conditions and living things, as the fundamental, given datum and as the sphere that is to be used for the securing of life.

b. The first differences compared with the Yahwist's primeval history

If we look at Psalm 104 and then look back at the Yahwist's primeval history, it is noticeable that in Psalm 104 creation is not a quality of life that has been diminished in many ways or overlaid or withdrawn again; it is something that can be directly attributed to the natural world and environment. Here the visible natural world is described directly as the world of creation,[25] and not simply in an etiological way as an explanation of origin expressed in a story of a primal era. It is viewed as creation quite directly. Indeed the perception of the natural world and environment is so overwhelmed by the divine dispensation of this world that in this psalm the contemplation and experience of the world are simply expressed as praise of Yahweh's kingly rule. It is a hymn that has its characteristic introduction in verse 1a, has its close in verses 33-35, and in the body of the hymn (1b-32) names the features of the natural world that constrain the singer to praise Yahweh and justify his praise.

Also different, however, is what we might call the depth of perspective in which the natural world as a whole is viewed. Whereas the viewpoint in the Yahwist's primeval history was concentrated on the small farmer's world, the world of the dweller on cultivated land, and everything that is bound up with it, in Psalm 104 the eye is also directed to other regions as well—the air, the sea, the mountains, the woods—and the different features that characterize them. The psalmist is unmistakably interested in pacing out the whole of the natural world against the background of his knowledge of natural history in all its sectors.

c. The world as it is perceived

But now let us look at the text itself. What does the psalmist see as the natural world? In accordance with the theme of creation, the sector of human relations—political or social life—is not the subject here; it is merely touched on at the end, in the context of the final petition (v 35). Instead, what dominates the whole foreground is the view of the natural world. For Psalm 104 this natural world is clearly divided into three areas, which the sequence of his statements follows. They are the three great cosmological spheres as they appear to man: the vertical sphere of the air, above the earth (v 2b-4); and then, on the horizontal plane, the land and the sea. Verses 5-9 stress first of all the security of the division between the earth's surface and the sea; verses 10-24 then consider the "dry land"; and verses 25-26, finally, the sea. If we look at the details which Psalm 104 introduces in these different areas, it quickly becomes evident that here the perspective of the world is not simply confined to a tabulated catalogue. Why, for instance, are the birds missing in connection with the air, as well as the stars? What is more, both the birds and the stars are treated in the framework of the dry land (vv 12, 17, 19ff). Here, then, different criteria are quite evidently at work.

We are told about Yahweh's activity in the air, in verses 2b-4: "Who hast stretched out the heavens like a tent, who hast laid the beams of thy chambers on the waters, who makest the clouds thy chariot, who ridest on the wings of the wind, who makest the winds thy messengers, fire and flame thy ministers." Here, then, the psalmist (of course in accordance with the state of knowledge of his time) sees the heavens holding back a reservoir of water above it; he sees clouds and wind, and all the phenomena that are the necessary preconditions for providing water for the earth. In addition he sees lightning, which played its part in giving the earth's surface the stability it has (cf. v 7). He then turns to the permanent stability of the earth's surface and its secure separation from the sea.

> Thou didst set the earth on its foundations
>> so that it should never be shaken.
> Thou didst cover it with the deep as with a garment;
>> the waters stood above the mountains.
> At thy rebuke they fled;
>> at the sound of thy thunder they took to flight.
> The mountains rose, the valleys sank down
>> to the place which thou didst appoint for them.
> Thou didst set a bound which they should not pass,
>> so that they might not again cover the earth. (vv 5-9)

The region of the earth is described in detail in verses 10-24, in the context of the essential living conditions that are conferred on living things, on different groups of animals and on man. It is astonishing what a differentiated knowledge of nature is introduced here, dividing the natural world into different regions with different essential needs for different living things, and perceiving what has been investigated and defined today in terms of our knowledge of different environments and their links with the ecosystems. In verses 10-18 the main idea (How could it be otherwise in the sphere of Palestinian experience?) is first of all the water supply granted to the earth, which quite simply makes the different regions of life possible and provides the means of living.

In line with this, the rivers are surveyed first of all, from their sources in the mountains to the valleys.

> Thou makest springs gush forth in the valleys;
>   they flow between the hills,
> they give drink to every beast of the field;
>   the wild asses quench their thirst.
> By them the birds of the air have their habitation;
>   they sing among the branches. (vv 10-12)

The course of the rivers therefore offers a habitat for the animals of the wild, as well as for birds on their banks. In verses 13-18 the singer then looks at the regions of the earth that are supplied with water, not by rivers, but by rain.

From thy lofty abode thou waterest the mountains;
    the earth is satisfied with the fruit of thy work
        [? out of thy pitchers].

Thou dost cause the grass to grow for the cattle,
    and plants for man to cultivate,
that he may bring forth food from the earth,
    and wine to gladden the heart of man,
oil to make his face shine,
    and bread to strengthen man's heart.
The trees of Yahweh are watered abundantly,
    the cedars of Lebanon which he planted.
In them the birds build their nests;
    the stork has her home in the fir trees.
The high mountains are for the wild goats;
    the rocks are a refuge for the badgers.

The psalmist therefore sees the mountains towering above the clouds, which are watered by the highest waters above the tabernacle of heaven (vv 3, 13a) for the benefit of the mountain animals living there (v 18). He sees the earth with its lofty trees as the sphere for birds like the stork (vv 16-17), and with its pastures and cultivated fields (vv 13b-15), which drink their fill of rain from the clouds and produce vegetation (v 14), so that beast and man can live there, and man can have bread, wine, and oil (vv 14b-15).

Verses 19-23 contribute a second leading idea to the understanding of the earth as a region for living.

> Thou hast made the moon to mark the seasons;
> > the sun knows its time for setting.
> Thou makest darkness, and it is night,
> > when all the beasts of the forest creep forth.
> The young lions roar for their prey,
> > seeking their food from God.
> When the sun rises, they get them away
> > and lie down in their dens.
> Man goes forth to his work
> > and to his labor until the evening.

Here the praise of Yahweh is directed toward his provision of seasons for the supply of food for man and beast: the moon determines the seasons of the agricultural year (v 19a; cf. vv 14b-15, 23), while the sun is seen in the context of the change from day to night, the night being viewed as the time when the wild beasts feed (vv 20-22) and the day as the time when man works in the fields (vv 22-23; cf. vv 14-15).

The third cosmological space, the great and wide sea, is considered more briefly in verses 25-26, again in accordance with Israel's inland perspective.

> Yonder is the sea, great and wide,
> > which teems with things innumerable,
> > living things both small and great.
> There go the ships,
> > and Leviathan which thou didst form to sport in it.

The sea is also seen here as providing living space, on the one hand for individual giants that go their ways there—the tamed being of chaos, Leviathan, which moves in the sea and is now only described as animal—and the ships, which make the sea serve the life of man through fishing and trade.

The world which the author of Psalm 104 sees and brings to expression is therefore an entirely natural world, free from the play of supernatural forces. What he perceives is the milieu of the conditions that make existence possible for all life, man and beast alike, on the level of the basic equipment which determines existence and which is always fore-ordained and given together with life itself. The factors in this equipment are split into quite separate sectors of existence and elemental needs, i.e., into the different environments of living things. They are there to be used, shaped, and even modified, so that animals may live, multiply, and have food, and so that man may settle, cultivate the fields, keep herds, and sail the seas in ships. A wealth of knowledge of natural history—knowledge based on experience—is introduced here. There are even questions about the elemental relationships of being, which are today the subject of research in the model of the ecosystem. Indeed, the facts that are here drawn from experience are in the sequence of the psalm even considered in the light of the connection between presupposition and result. First of all, the psalmist talks about the presuppositions for the provision of water and the stabilization of the earth, and the earth's separation from the sea, making two different habitats (vv 2b-4). Then he goes on to talk successively about this fundamental division itself (vv 5-9) and about the earth's water supply, which guarantees food (vv 10-18); and this provides the starting point for a consideration of the times and seasons when food is supplied. Finally, he talks about the sea. It is a quite logical survey of the elemental presuppositions and conditions under which all life exists.

In the face of this we are tempted for a moment to say that the psalmist sees the natural world as we ourselves do, even though he is obviously working from an earlier level of knowledge, which lags behind our modern information about cosmology, geography, zoology, biology, and ecology. But this impression is deceptive. It is not only the level of knowledge that is different; it is above all the attitude and approach to the whole perception of the natural world and environment that

d. The psalmist's view of the natural world and environment

If we ask how the psalmist sees the natural world and environment, we must first of all look carefully at verses 27-30, the final section of the main body of the hymn. It is given an important place, following immediately after the psalmist's consideration of the cosmological divisions of space.

These all look to thee,
  to give them their food in due season.
When thou givest to them, they gather it up;
  when thou openest thy hand, they are filled with good things.
When thou hidest thy face, they are dismayed;
  when thou takest away their breath, they die
  and return to their dust.
When thou sendest forth thy Spirit [breath], they are created;
  and thou renewest the face of the ground.

Whereas in verses 2b-26 the psalmist looks at the elemental presuppositions that make life possible, here he is considering life itself: life not simply as an empirical datum, but the phenomenon of the specific, actual, contingent granting of life, its existence, its nourishment, and its appointed term. Natural life and the fulfillment of life for everything living, as an elemental value, but as something that is not at the disposal of the living things, life as gift, as an event conferred, upon which everything is dependent. This whole perception of existence per se marks the psalmist's attitude and approach. Accordingly, in what goes before, he has grasped the natural world and environment as being a continual process, as the event in which elemental conditions of living are granted; and the order, selection, and accentuation of what he says is in accordance with this viewpoint. The fact is that man (like everything that

lives) is elementally dependent, in his existence, his equipment
for living, and the term of his natural life. This is the original,
basic experience which corresponds to the event of the natural
world and environment as Yahweh's creation. Consequently
the psalmist has to see the world, in the elemental sense, as
being the event in which life is bestowed, an event which
always precedes all specific living things and is not at their
disposal, since it is the act of God the creator. Here as well,
therefore, the guaranteeing of life is the fundamental category,
based on experience of a sensory grasp of the natural world as
being Yahweh's creation (and in this it corresponds to the view
of Yahweh's activity as seen in the Yahwist's primeval history).
That is to say, that which causes the natural world to be
perceived as creation here, is not the perspective of the world of
empirical experience, which had always been modified by
human civilization. Nor is it the contemplation of the primeval
genesis of all world phenomena. The psalmist's gaze is rather
guided by the fact that the living thing knows that he possesses a
life whose being and end he cannot himself determine, and that
the living thing is dependent on the chances actually granted to
him to eat and to eke out his existence. Consequently, he is
dependent on equipment for living which he never really
creates for himself but always finds ready to hand. That is why
the psalmist can cry in his summing up: "O Yahweh, how
manifold are thy works! In wisdom hast thou made them all; the
earth is full of thy creatures" (v 24); "May Yahweh rejoice in his
works" (v 31). And here "works" are not prototypical individual
objects, but Yahweh's acts in the whole complex in which life is
bestowed. This elemental view, based on actual experience but
related to existence as such, which sees life not merely as
physical survival but as fulfillment in joy for beast (v 12) and man
(v 15), underlies all the statements about the natural world and
environment in Psalm 104. Following this concept, the psalm
(unlike the Yahwist's primeval history, with its perception of
life that is always already in a state of depreciation) concentrates
entirely on the positive, fundamental evidence, understanding
it as the acts of Yahweh and as the results made possible by
those acts. It is then inevitable that he should fashion these

features of the divine bestowal of the world of life as hymn, as praise of Yahweh, the creator God.[26]

Here, then, we can see an essential difference in attitude and approach to the natural world and environment between Psalm 104 and our modern world. In its attitude toward knowledge of the natural world and the shaping of that world, the modern generation begins with man and his interests; the world is something with which he is "confronted"; nature is a potential of material and a reservoir for exploitation by a world which, in the first instance, is to be used and modified in accordance with human purposes. Psalm 104, on the other hand, begins with the actual, known, fundamental fact of personal experience, which tells us that life is something that is not at our disposal, something with its own elemental meaning and values. For modern man the world is the material and potential for human activity, and the result is a "manipulating reduction of all life, including man, to the level of objects."[27] In contrast, for the psalmist, life is first of all an event of the continual inclining of Yahweh the creator, a movement toward the world which comprehends it and man, which is already a given for all existence, and which offers life and life-span, living room and the provision of life's necessities to all living things. Because the psalmist perceives this, the natural world with its different environments is grasped as being an ordained whole; man and nature are together included in the unity of this event, which already has, simply in itself, meaning and value for all life. Here, therefore, the natural world is primarily a highly positive experience of power. It reveals itself on the basis of the experience that it needs the power of God's disposal for the most elemental things to be provided for the living being, things which it cannot give itself. And for Psalm 104 this is the basis for the royal attributes ascribed to Yahweh (vv 1-2a, 31 ff).

But the psalmist talks about God not simply because the author is deducing some divine figure from the known fact that the necessities of life are not at the living thing's disposal; it is because he is connecting the natural world and environment with Israel's familiar One God Yahweh, who transcends the world, and whose power is equally manifested in what threatens life (v 29), in death (v 29), in the provision of food for one living thing at the cost of another (v 21), in earthquakes and volcanic eruptions (v 32). The connection of the natural world and environment with the very uniqueness of Israel's God Yahweh opens up a view of the world that excludes any assessment of world forces as being in themselves divine, as well as any dualistic divine control of their power over life and death. This link between the natural world and Yahweh opens up a world that will be free to have its existing phenomena and their orders investigated and inquired into. The knowledge that has contributed so extensively to Psalm 104 shows this, as does the even broader spectrum in Job 38 and 39, for example. But the acquiring of such knowledge, or science, does not mean the dissolution of the world, as totality, into a multiplicity of definitions of its component parts (phenomena, laws, or cosmogenic and biogenetic explanations based on an under-standing of evolution), with inquiring and exploiting man standing alone at the beginning and at the end of the process. In spite of all the concentration on details, individual connections, and classifications, and in spite of the usefulness of such information, the acquiring of knowledge of this kind is merely a discovery of evidence for a previous fundamental experience, according to Psalm 104, an experience which even "the deformation of the human capacity for perception"[28] has not totally suppressed in science and in the utilization of nature: the experience that even as an inquiring and utilizing human being, man is part of an over-riding significant event that God brings about for the benefit of all life.

When we consider the position of man in this event praised by Psalm 104, we see that no preeminent position is assigned to him. His value is no greater than that of other living things. The fact that life always lives at the cost of other life—not only among animals (v 21) but even among men, where his domestic animals are concerned (v 14)—does not alter the fact that man is completely part of the order of the creative event of the natural world. His life is lived parallel to other life, and his sphere is one among other spheres, intended for other living things, in the framework of a single process of divine activity, which by no means takes place always for man's sake or tends only toward him, but which is intended for the benefit of all living things. It is in line with this that Psalm 104 extends to animals too what is really man's own experience of life, leading him on to the event of divine creation. What man perceives to be true of his life applies to animal life as well, and consequently animals are in principle granted the same right to life as man. Apart from the fact that it is man who is capable of praising God as God is praised in Psalm 104, and that—unlike animals—he supplies his life's needs through work and (vv 14, 23) actively modifies nature for the purposes of living (and the psalm does not, in fact, distinguish these things as being features of man's special position), his special status consists, grotesquely enough, in the fact that it is he and he alone who can act destructively as counter-force in the framework of the creative event. That is why one of the final petitions of the psalm runs: "Let sinners be consumed from the earth, and let the wicked be no more!" because their evil practices in the political and social sphere also infringe the order of life, which is part of the creative event.[29] "He who oppresses a poor man insults his Maker, but he who is kind to the needy honors him" (Prov. 14:31;[30] cf. Job 31:13-15).

3. The Primeval History in the Priestly Writing

We are taking as example a third complex of texts, which leads us into particularly difficult territory. For it is here that we come across the statements that play a particular part in discussions between the Christian faith and the scientific interpretations of nature; and it is these that have recently also been brought up in connection with the origins of the worldwide ecological crisis and the question of who is responsible for it. Just because of this, we shall do well to look first at the texts themselves. What is their unique historical character? And what do they want to say?

a. The texts and their origin

The primeval history in the Priestly Writing is a description which covers a whole series of texts drawn from the first chapters of Genesis. First of all, there is the famous account of the Creation (Gen. 1:1-2, 4a), together with man's genealogy from Adam to Noah (Gen. 5), which documents his fruitfulness and increase. Then comes the story of the Flood in Genesis 6–8, with the blessing of Noah and the covenant made with him (9:1-17), together with the list of peoples, which shows the worldwide dissemination of Noah's descendants throughout the nations of the earth (part of Gen. 10). These texts too were originally a self-contained complex (see Bibliography, 137). According to a widely held opinion among scholars, this textual complex is the beginning of a bigger work, the Priestly Document or Writing (known by scholars under the symbol P), which, like the Yahwist, has been incorporated into the first books of the Bible. The Priestly Writing has been given its name because of the priestly influence it shows. In addition to primeval history, it describes the early history of Israel, at least until the death of Moses. Scholars are generally in agreement about the origin and date of this work. It is the work of Israelite priests coming from the area of the Babylonian exile, and may be assigned to the sixth, or at latest to the fifth, century B.C., when Israel was under the hegemony of the Persian Empire, having lost its independence as separate state, its monarchy, and the integral character of its population in its own country.[31]

b. The aim of the account

As was also the case with the Yahwist's primeval history, we are again faced with the difficulty of deciding how to interpret this understanding and description of the primeval history, especially since this account has a different character. Unlike the Yahwist, the Priestly Writing certainly reports individual points of time in the remote past—even precisely dated events. But these events are not self-contained, individual occurrences over which the river of time has long since flowed. They are completed events which, from the time they took place, have continued to have fundamental, ever-present validity and efficacy. That is to say, these are the decisive beginnings, the foundations of what is and what is to come. With this intention, the Yahwist offered an etiological narrative complex, which explained phenomena that determine even the present world by an apprehension of their origin. P offers a sequence of institutions, decrees, premises, and gifts bestowed in the world's initial situation, with the aim of determining—for his own time and indeed for all time—what has always existed and has always been valid. P's primeval history, therefore, is also no fable about beginnings that no one was there to see. Here, rather, people are looking back from their own time and are perceiving the foundations of their world—what belongs fundamentally to the world as it is and what is valid for all time—as being events with which the world was endowed with from the beginning, events which laid down what was to be valid for all periods to come.[32] P places these fundamental, always valid enactments, given to Israel as guardians of its identity, in the period between Abraham and Moses, which is really also viewed as part of the primeval history.[33] What, on the other hand, applies to the sphere of the world and mankind as a whole in the way of fundamental institutions, decrees, promises, and gifts bestowed is summed up in the primeval history and summed up conclusively. P knows nothing of any universal counter-movement to the situation given in the primeval history, such as the movement that the Yahwist sees as beginning with Abraham. What has to be said once and for all about the world and mankind is laid down in Genesis 1–10P: for the whole world in Genesis 1:1-2, 4a; more particularly for mankind in Genesis 5–10P. These passages sum up the order that is at the bottom of all history and all human activity. Here the possibilities, the framework, and the limits are laid down—and they are valid for all time, not to be superseded or transgressed. But we must guard against a misunderstanding that it is easy to fall into today. This kind of viewpoint and description must on no account be understood as if we were dealing (especially where the sector "world" is concerned) with an ancient form of modern scientific questions about cosmogenic or evolutionary processes in natural history. Although P here wants to take in occurrences at the beginning and in the course of time, its interest is not directed toward scientific processes of development. The narrative is concerned with the all-embracing foundations for life which are seen in the present as being valid for all time and which, as an expression of this, are depicted as an establishing act at the beginning of time which is complete and unique in itself.[34]

c. The world as it is perceived

Before we consider the view taken of the natural world and environment in P's primeval history, let us look at what P sees in its world.

Its viewpoint moves in concentric circles. What P describes last of all is Israel, the holy, cultic community, with its expiatory cult, its sabbath, and its circumcision; yet for the author's approach and the experience behind it, this is of primary importance. As we have said, P describes the institutions, decrees, promises, and gifts that belong to Israel's special vocation in the period between Abraham and Moses. But put before this, in the primeval history, and seen retrospectively, is a vista of the next wider aspect, the world of men (Gen. 5–10P), and finally, widened out completely, the view of the whole world.

If we begin at the end, with the world of man, P looks at the whole population of the earth, with the help of cartographic notions based on family groups, and split up according to languages into various countries and groups of people (Gen. 10:5, 20, 32). It is noticeable that this is the most concrete thing that P wants to say about mankind. A political and historical viewpoint, which would include actual facts about ruling conditions, is evidently deliberately omitted. This is probably a reflection of the situation in the period when the Priestly Writing was composed, in which a meaning and destiny for mankind was sought before the specifically political field came into play, and which presupposed the fact of the Persian

Empire (which was accepted even theologically[35]). *P*'s view of the world of man is total and all-embracing. It stretches farther geographically than the view we find in the Yahwist, as is appropriate in view of the more extensive knowledge of the period. It extends as far as the Caspian and Black seas in the north, to Ethiopia in the south, to the highlands of Iran in the east, and as far as the western Mediterranean region in the west.[36]

What *P* thinks is important in its view of mankind, and what it finds amazing, is the vast number of people (see Gen. 5) and the way they are spread all over the earth, ordered according to languages, countries, and peoples (Gen. 10*P*); this is seen as being an indication of man's vitality. The leading aspect, life itself, emerges here too—the more so, since the astonishing spread of mankind as worldwide population is, for *P*, in a state of tension with another phenomenon that tends in the opposite direction, and that puts a heavy strain on the earth as a region for living. This phenomenon is the existence of violence—brutal, killing attacks on the body and the very life which take place between man and beast (sometimes in the search for food), but more especially between man and man (Gen. 6:11-13; 9:1-17).[37] Here, therefore, *P* perceives that the living together of people with animals and of people with one another presents a serious problem for the world of man, in the sense that this is one of the elemental threats to human life. But *P* also stresses in this connection that the other danger, which is quite separate from the relations between man and beast and man and man, the danger of a premature, violent end to life affecting all living things does not exist. There will never be another flood (Gen. 9:8, 17).

Consequently it is quite consistent that *P* should view the region "world" (which is conceived in Gen. 1:1-4, 4a as being prior to the world of man) as being completely free from chaotic counter-forces that could be a threat to life. This account of the creation at the beginning of the Bible cannot be surpassed in its mental and linguistic precision. We must devote a certain amount of space to it, because, perhaps more than any other biblical text, it determines the understanding of nature and man that takes its stamp from the Bible and that even influences our fundamental ecological discussions.

An earlier investigation of my own into the layout, construction, and original intention of P[38] (together with the work of other scholars[39]) suggests that the view of the world found here is molded by two themes.[40]

One of them is the aspect of time. For P's creation account, it is important that the world was created, not only *in* time, in the six days of creation, but also *with* time as one of its constituents, and with the intention that time should continue. The world event as a whole is a precisely calculable progression in time, which can be determined exactly—in the progression of the seasons as well. In accordance with this, P stresses, as part of its world-picture, that conditions were created to make the determining of time possible. The first of these conditions is the heavens:

> And God said, "Let there be a firmament in the midst of the waters, and let it separate the waters from the waters." And God made the firmament and separated the waters which were under the firmament from the waters which were above the firmament. And it was so. And God called the firmament Heaven. . . . And God saw that it was good. (Gen. 1:6-8)

This sphere of existence, the heavens, was created for the stars belonging to it, one of their functions being to determine time.

> And God said, "Let there be lights in the firmament of the heavens to separate the day from the night; and let them be for signs and for seasons and for days and years, and let them be lights in the firmament of the heavens to give light upon the earth." And it was so. And God made the two great lights, the greater light to rule the day, and the lesser light to rule the night; he made the stars also. And God set them in the firmament of the heavens to give light upon the earth, to rule over the day and over the night, and to separate the light from the darkness. And God saw that it was good. (vv 14-18)

The second aspect is that of life, which is in accordance with the
Yahwist's primeval history. Under this aspect P conceives the
world in its secure existence as natural world and environment.
The writing divides the world up into different areas for living,
with the conditions favorable for life, and into the living things
assigned to each of these areas. These living things are in their
turn observed in their differentiated groupings under the
aspect of their actually being alive at all, as well as in their
continuing and permanent existence throughout all succeeding
time. So, after the dividing off of the upper water through the
heavens prepared for the stars (a division important in Psalm
104 too), in 1:9-12 P views the various regions of life: the sea,
the air, and the earth with its plants, the latter precisely divided
into woody and nonwoody plants:[41]

> And God said, "Let the waters under the heavens be
> gathered together into one place, and let the dry land
> appear." And it was so. God called the dry land Earth, and
> the waters that were gathered together he called Seas. And
> God saw that it was good. And God said, "Let the earth put
> forth vegetation, plants yielding seed, and fruit trees bearing
> fruit in which is their seed, each according to its kind upon
> the earth." And it was so. The earth brought forth
> vegetation, plants yielding seed according to their own
> kinds, and trees bearing fruit in which is their seed, each
> according to its kind. And God saw that it was good.

Relating what he has to say to these divisions—sea, air, and
earth—P names the appropriate animals precisely corresponding to each of them: for the sea, the water animals, ranging from
the large ones to the swarms of tiny ones; and for the air, the
different kinds of winged animals, the birds (1:20-22).

> And God said, "Let the waters bring forth swarms of living
> creatures, and let birds fly above the earth across the
> firmament of the heavens." So God created the great sea
> monsters and every living creature that moves, with which
> the waters swarm, according to their kinds, and every
> winged bird according to its kind. And God saw that it was

good. And God blessed them, saying, "Be fruitful and multiply and fill the waters in the seas, and let birds multiply on the earth."

The terrestrial animals follow, in the context of the earth, and these are divided into domestic animals, creeping things, wild beasts, and people—men and women (1:24-28).

And God said, "Let the earth bring forth living creatures according to their kinds: cattle and creeping things and beasts of the earth according to their kinds." And it was so. And God made the beasts of the earth according to their kinds and the cattle according to their kinds, and everything that creeps upon the ground according to its kind. And God saw that it was good. Then God said, "Let us make man in our image, after our likeness; and let them have dominion over the fish of the sea, and over the birds of the air, and over the cattle, and over all the earth, and over every creeping thing that creeps upon the earth." So God created man in his own image, in the image of God he created him; male and female he created them. And God blessed them, and God said to them, "Be fruitful and multiply, and fill the earth and subdue it; and have dominion over the fish of the sea and over the birds of the air and over every living thing that moves upon the earth."

As a result of this differentiating view with regard to the living space provided for living things, the gift of life conferred on them, and their permanent continuance, we certainly have here a view of the natural world and of the environment (at least in its widest sense) which takes account of the elemental factors of existence, and which certainly brings in the precise natural-history classifications of the time: the different kinds of plants, with their different seed formation (1:11-12); winged beasts that have both air and earth as their environment (1:20, 22); terrestrial animals, differentiated according to their domestication and their way of life (1:24-25).

But from the very beginning P sees a problem in this sphere of the natural world and environment: *the relationship between animals and people.* For the Priestly Writing this is a fundamental difficulty. That is why it is picked up at the point where the position of man is defined (1:26-28). It is a particularly pressing problem in the light of the common life of terrestrial animals and men in their common habitat, the earth. The fact that the terrestrial animals, unlike the water beasts and the birds (1:22), receive no blessing for their increase and spread is a reflection of this problem; on earth the blessing is reserved for man (1:28). The assignment of food in 1:29-30 suggests another aspect of the same difficulty.

> And God said, "Behold, I have given you every plant yielding seed which is upon the face of all the earth, and every tree with seed in its fruit; you shall have them for food. And to every beast of the earth, and to every bird of the air, and to everything that creeps on the earth, everything that has the breath of life, I have given every green plant for food."

This envisages plants as providing food for the animals that are dependent on the earth for their nourishment (such as the wild beasts, creeping things, and the birds). Domestic animals are omitted because they are in any case, by definition, not a danger for man. Moreover, vegetable food is what is assigned to man too. Neither the Yahwist's primeval history nor Psalm 104 touched on this problem, but for *P* it is an essential one and is considered again in the course of the primeval history, in the context of the phenomenon of violence, as we have seen.

d. Theological aims in the perception of the world

Even more important, however, are the observations we can make about the way *P* sees the natural world and the environment, together with the world of man, in the primeval history. We only have to notice what is not mentioned in Genesis 1 (in spite of all the denseness of its reflection about the elemental factors that determine life) in order to see that *P*'s viewpoint is not simply in line with our view of things in the world and the environment. In what detail, and how reflectively, the Yahwist and Psalm 104 consider the earth's vitally important water supply, which P does not mention at all in Genesis 1! The view of the natural world and environment in Genesis 1 is for P not primarily a working-over of empirical experience of the world, and the apprehension of its profound dimensions, seen under the aspect of creation. What is in the forefront of concern here is a demonstration of the basic order that determines the activity of God in the world, in the world of man, and in Israel; and in correspondence to this the actions of the living, including Israel. For this is the way that God's identity can and should be made visible in all spheres of life, for the benefit of Israel's own identity. [42] That is why God's creative activity is gathered together in the period of a single week of seven days (which is made possible by the creation of day and night as God's first work, 1:3-5), for in this way the activity of God himself corresponds to the sabbath order given to Israel. That is why creation is not a continuous divine activity, which is also carried on in the immediate present (as it is in the greater part of Psalm 104), but is strictly confined to seven days of creation. For here, as elsewhere, P sees the world and Israel as subjected to a series of decrees which confer significance and which were effectively set up once and for all, between the Creation and the time of Moses, to be valid forever.

It is an expression of the same intention that the works of creation, in their whole structure, are so formed in every case that the actual existence of this work is laid down by God and given validity for all succeeding time, while the basic prototype made during the week of creation is described afterward. This shows in compressed form that God's own creative activity also has a certain structure, which is characteristic for the enactments and all ordering events in P. [43] This is also the reason for the differentiation of plants and animals, because that is the order in which they correspond to the enactment of the laws about sacrifice and purity, which were promulgated later in Israel. And this, finally, is why the world perspective is focused on the aspects of time and life. For calculable time is essential for the meaning of the chronological system P has elaborated, as well as for the cultic festivals in Israel; while life corresponds to the promise of land (in the context of living space) and to the promise given to the people of Israel (in the context of living things and their increase). Here, therefore, everything is not derived from natural orders. On the contrary, P sees the enactments of salvation history, which were promulgated later, as already shining through the event of creation, viewing this as an expression of God's identity and the identity of Israel.

Of course, P is convinced that the picture conveyed of the creation of the world is also the real course of events, with the creation of prototypical works in a series of seven real days. The writing does not escape into a merely transferred sense. But the observations we have just made about P's intention do show that in its version of the creation of the world P by no means simply intends to give the result of a number of natural-history investigations, which we could comfortably compare with the superiority of modern scientific research into the beginnings and evolutionary processes of the cosmos and life. With the form it gives to scientific questions, P is pursuing more far-reaching problems and perspectives, whose main concern is the continuity of fundamental orders in different spheres, and the evidence for God's identity.

At the same time, the view of the creation of the world found in the Priestly Writing is not merely a means to the end of justifying Israel's own various orders. P's primeval history is a view of the world and mankind that has an order of its own; but for Israel this order is a transparent one. We must now look more closely at this particular emphasis.

e. The view of the natural world and the environment in P

Notwithstanding its own particular emphasis, by seeing the natural world in general as God's creative act, P gives expression to the same fundamental experience as the tradition behind it, which we met in the example of Psalm 104. This fundamental experience is that the living thing perceives the fact of being alive, the elemental, basic equipment necessary for life, and the space in which to live as an endowment that is always preordered and given together with life itself. As we have seen, P draws the gift of time and temporal reckoning into this basic experience as well, and far more fundamentally than Psalm 104:19 ff. P therefore also penetrates the experience of the existing world with everything it displays, down to the very foundation, where a constant, fundamental event emerges. This event is essential for life itself. It is not at man's disposal, nor is it something he can create for himself. It continually confers life on man and the other living things around him, and just as continually equips them with a favorable living space. In this way P's creation account too (in spite of its further theological emphases) includes the perspective of the natural world and environment, the perception of the fundamental connection and indispensible conditions of existence.

Though P also introduces knowledge of the differentiated form of the whole creative complex, the account does not stand still at a description of that complex and its particular structures and individual aspects. The most important thing for the Priestly Writing, as it was for the Yahwist and in Psalm 104, is the miracle of the continual coming-into-being and existence of the living thing—an event over which it has no disposal—and the indispensable equipment for living provided for it. In order to absorb the depth of this present experience of the world in its constancy as long as, and wherever, living things have life, P talks about God's creative activity and sees the natural world that confronts us in our own experience as being founded on will, power, law, and decree which is fore-given to all life and all history.

P does not have available to him that particular sector of reality which is the focus of scientific perception of cosmogenic cycles and biological processes of evolution and selection, stretching over millions of years. Nor is it what he is interested in. What P is looking for in the creation account is, in contrast, the elemental foundation and the ordained character of meaning and value, for the life of the individual and the world of life as a whole. And this is much more comprehensive and total in its quality, and much more closely related to experience, than a merely scientific account. Accordingly P has to talk about the simultaneous creation of all plants and animals at the beginning, in a single creative event—animals and plants as man knows them now and has always known them, without any genetic differentiation. Here again, the difference between Genesis 1 and our scientific knowledge about biogenetics and the cosmos is not simply a difference in our degree of information; it is just as much a difference of approach and perspective in the perception of the natural world and environment.

In accordance with this view of creation, P talks of a thoroughly natural world,[44] with its fundamental phenomena that guarantee time and life. He lays exclusive stress on the sovereign creative power of the divine activity, which does not come up against any forces of chaos, either before (Gen. 1:2)[45] or during the creation (in contrast to Psalm 104:5-9). As in Psalm 104, the initial gift of separate cosmological spheres is named first of all: the heavens that keep back the upper waters and provide a sphere of existence for the stars, the seas, the air, the earth with its vegetation. Each of them provides the appropriate region for the living things assigned to it. The creation of the earth's vegetation is reported in such a way that the miracle of its constant recurrence, with its renewed springing up and its bursting into leaf, is based on the decree of God at the creation—a decree aiming at permanence (1:11-12). This applies even more to the creation of living things. In the case of the aquatic beasts, the birds (1:22), and man himself (1:28), their vital power of constant survival and increase springs from a continual bestowal of power through the divine blessing uttered at their creation. In the case of the terrestrial animals, for the reasons we have already given, it derives from an appropriate decree given to the earth (1:24).

Here P is not aiming to paint an ideal picture of the natural world that would really leave out certain aspects of reality. The narrative does not content itself with demonstrating that the stable regions provided for living, and living things themselves, are in their existence and continuance based on creation, and that everything simply lives amicably side by side. On the contrary, we have already seen that from the very beginning P also considers the problem of the relations of living things to one another, or, to be more precise, the relationship between man and beast. This relationship does not flourish in a matter-of-course way, as it would in some illusory state of nature. Nor is it simply left neutrally to the internal factors of the ecosystem. It is a meaningful relationship which as such has to be shaped and ordered; and P sees this order, which promotes life, as being already inherent in the creative event. In this order man plays an essential part. And in order to perceive what the order is, we must now look in more detail at the much-discussed account of the creation of man (1:26-30).

f. The position of man as "God's image" and ruler of the earth

P describes man's creation as follows:

> Then God said, "Let us make man in our image, after our likeness; and let them have dominion over the fish of the sea, and over the birds of the air, and over the cattle, and over all the earth, and over every creeping thing that creeps upon the earth." So God created man in his own image, in the image of God he created him; male and female he created them. And God blessed them, and God said to them, "Be fruitful and multiply, and fill the earth and subdue it; and have dominion over the fish of the sea and over the birds of the air and over every living thing that moves upon the earth." (1:26-28)

If we compare this passage with the creation of the animals (1:20-25), it is noticeable that P does not confine itself here (as is the case for other living things) to finding the reason for the miracle of human life's existence—for the existence of men and women—and finding it in their creation (1:27). On the contrary, from the very beginning, the text sees God's decision (1:26) and the execution of it (1:27) as a destiny, which is to be man's from that time on, forever (cf. also 5:1, 3; 9:6). People are created to be the image of God. This phrase, as recent discussion has shown,[46] is a titular and functional term, rooted in declarations about kingship. In the face of the fact that for P God's creative activity is completed with the seventh day of creation, this term qualifies man to represent God to whatever lives beside him in the earthly and horizontal region of creation. This defines the central position man enjoys in the whole structure of the created world, and it is a position which is designed to promote the permanent existence of all life. This permanent existence is, as we have seen, laid down for each individual living being at its creation. As regards the dwelling together of all living things, however, the existence of man is to guarantee life's fundamental provisions—in what way, the more detailed instructions that follow make clear. For the task assigned to him (to rule over the whole animal world) is not the content of this definition or a description of man; it is its result, its active expression and fulfillment. Verse 28 underlines this. Man is not merely given the power of increase and the function of "filling" the earth (which is assigned to him alone among all earthly creatures); the blessing of God at the creation also promises him power and success in the subjection of the earth and in lordship over the animals.

The problem of this much-discussed declaration is that in Genesis 1 it is not stated in very specific or graphic form. More—What does "lordship over the animal world" mean when, for example, a reciprocal use of living things for the purposes of food is immediately excluded in the following verses (1:29-30)? Moreover the phenomenon of reciprocal attacks on the life of others is not yet considered by P either. It only crops up later, and then (in Gen. 9:1ff) brings enactments in its train which go beyond Genesis 1 altogether. So what does P mean by saying that, as part of the creative event, man is given lordship over the animals and the task of subduing the earth?

We must notice first of all that at this point P is not as yet laying down any regulations which take account of concrete, existing reality (this happens later, in Gen. 9:1ff). In the framework of the creation account, it is more a matter of a fundamental regulation in principle, which is not tested against the behavior of living things as we experience it in reality but, as is generally the case in Genesis 1, is measured against the sole promulgating initiative of the creating God and the world created and ordered by him—which is previous to, and at the base of, life as it is actually lived in history. The problem which P now sees as being settled is, as we have already said, the future dwelling together of living things in the world of creation that has now been set up. To put it more precisely: the difficulty is the living together of man with other creatures. This problem presents itself in such acute form to P because after the completion of the work of creation the Creator himself no longer intervenes in it, to give it design and form. Consequently the Creator needs a governor on earth, who acts according to his intention, i.e., according to the intention behind the world of creation set up by God. According to P, "acting" here also means, in the context of the dwelling-together of living things, the continual establishment and enforcement of order. But here as elsewhere, order is for P not a rule that implies determination by some outside force—something that diminishes life, or even reduces living things to slavery. It is the framework in which individual life develops, but is also restricted for its own good and continuance, as well as for the good and continuance of the whole. It goes without saying that, in accordance with the ideas of the time, P does not conceive the preservation of this framework as a proceeding for which the whole that has to be ordered is itself responsible. It is a confrontation, a vis-à-vis, in which one, God, sets up the framework of rule for the benefit of the whole; and another, man, implements the rule that God has established for the benefit of the whole. Accordingly, statements about man's task with regard to the created world are made on the basis of ideas of kingship. It is entirely in line with this that the living-together of "the image of God" with the animal world should be termed "dominion" (1:26, 28), in the expression drawn from royal terminology, which includes a massive realization of will.[47] The way the blessing is formulated in 1:28 links this appointment to kingly rule with the express divine bestowal of capability and success.

We hear statements of this kind with different ears, because of our own experience. But, notwithstanding the results displayed in history, we must avoid missing the original meaning of such Old Testament statements because of an unhistorical, modernizing eco-biblicism. People who take a romantic view of ecology today are apt to make a watchword of the phrase "tilling and keeping" nature in Genesis 2:15. The Yahwist is more realistic and knows that the gates of paradise are irrevocably closed.

On the other hand, some people suggest today that the dominating function of man according to Genesis 1 had an ambivalent character and a negative overtone from the very first. But according to P's intention there can be no question but that this ruling function—to dominate the animal world—is understood in a completely positive sense.[48] For P it is a matter of vocation, which is necessary for the successful continuance of the created world. Accordingly, it is entirely included in the divine approval of the world as a whole, which saw it as "very good" (1:31). It is a vocation that certainly does not give man the right of autonomous and autocratic disposal over the animal world for his own self-chosen purposes, detached from God. P still knows nothing of a direct or indirect exploitation or extermination of the animal world, as a result of an increase of economic consumption and the destruction of animal habitats. According to P, man rules in this sovereign office as God's image, i.e., as God's steward in the world, which God created for permanence. Any exercise of rule on the part of man prompted by independent purposes, arrived at apart from God or in deliberate separation from him, and leading to the damage or even destruction of the foundations of the animal world, would be totally contrary to the intentions of what P has to say. On the contrary, man is for P, among other created beings in the one created world, that being who knows the laws God has enacted and who knows his own destiny. We only have to look at God's address to man in 1:28ff, and frequently elsewhere in P. For this very reason, he and he alone can and must be God's steward for the whole created world. The exercise of this sovereign office may certainly include for P, within the framework of the laws of creation, man's permission to draw on the domestic animals that were created for that purpose—as working power in the tilling of the fields, for example (cf.

vv 29-30), or for his clothing; though he must not kill them.[49] But it is no less part of his office to care for the survival and preservation of the world of animals, which is part of creation. The measures which Noah takes, at God's command, according to P's account (Gen. 6:19ff; 7:13ff), to secure the survival of the animal world during the Flood are certainly seen by P as the practical exercise of man's task as ruler. The purpose of preserving the life of the endangered animal world, which is expressly stated in 6:19, 20 is highly significant.[50] Just as man himself belongs to the natural world of creation, in that he lives and carries on his life in the world, so his divine stewardship expresses itself precisely in the fact that he has to preserve the right to live and the contribution to life of the natural world and environment as a whole. That is to say, he has to preserve the right to life of living things apart from himself as well. The steady perspective that is peculiar to P's creation account especially, includes the fact that man and nature have a common history and a common future, and that man's special position does not mean autocratic confrontation, but the active responsibility as God's representative for the natural created world, which is oriented toward life. The function of man's task as ruler is to guarantee the continuance of the created world as a whole, laid down by God in the event of creation, and to guarantee it for the benefit of all created life. In this sense, for P, the whole world of creation takes its bearings from man and is directed toward him as guarantor of the order of the whole, which gives continuance to life. In P's view, there can be no question of the world or of animals being created for man's sake, let alone for the sake of his autonomous exploitation. If we want to find a formula, then P's intention is best represented by saying that the world is created by God for the sake of all life.

The statement about subduing the earth in 1:28 calls for special attention. P thinks of man's relationship to the earth as being a relationship to a component part of creation, and sees it as something that is expressly regulated and ordered. It does not belong within the framework of the sovereign task of God's image, which is directed toward living things, the animals. But here too, as in the case of the animals, man does certainly stand in need of God's bestowal of capability and success in his relationship to the earth. That is why the statement is part of man's blessing.

What did P have in mind with the *dominium terrae*? The activity opened up for man with regard to the earth is heavily qualified; the verb used means "subdue" in the sense of taking possession with unlimited power of disposal (it is also used for possessing the land in Num. 32:22, 29; Josh. 18:1). When applied to people it can also mean reducing to servitude as slaves.[51] But when we are faced with this powerful expression, we must also notice the object of this human activity in P and the concrete form it takes. The object is the earth, i.e., not a living thing, and the concrete form of the activity is shown by the context: the subjection and harnessing of the earth for man's use, for which he is empowered and for which he is given the capacity, points to man's tilling of the soil with the aim of winning food from seed and his growing of useful plants. This is mentioned immediately afterward in verse 29. What man is empowered to do here, therefore, and what he is made capable of doing all over the earth that he is to "fill," is to break up the ground (which puts it at his disposal), to work it, and to use it for growing plants.[52] Here too P (like Ps. 104, vv 14-15, 23 and, in his own way, the Yahwist in Gen. 2:15) talks, within the framework of the promise of blessing, about a certain destiny, and talks about it without any criticism, ambivalence, or apprehension. It is a provision that is necessary and that is judged positively without any reservations.[53] Because it is necessary to provide for human life, the Creator here decides who is to command and who is to serve in the relations between man and the earth. The limitations laid down in Genesis 1 show that for P the possibility of an exploitation of the earth to the point of the exhaustion of its resources, or the contingency that autocratic man might poison and destroy living space on earth, is not remotely considered in this authorization. The subjection of the earth is only so that man may be supplied with useful plants—and in addition the passage presupposes a permanent and completely sufficient supply of wild vegetation for the nourishment of wild animals, birds, and creeping things (1:30).

Consequently the *dominium terrae* is for P embedded in the nature of the world as creation, and is limited by that fact. The world's character as creation also means that killing is excluded as a means of nourishing the living, and that the earth and its vegetation is to be used for the benefit of all.

For P everything depends on the continuance of this character of the world as creation. Because of it there is no unmediated and, as it were, natural and self-sufficient relationship between the different works of creation. The interconnections between living things and their habitats, between animals and their food, between man and beast, and between man and the earth, all take their course by way of God, as processes relevant to life; and they need express regulation and empowerment through the actions and word of the One who created the world as a whole destined for life.

g. The quality and ambivalence of the world of life

As we have seen, in the creation account P perceives that every utilizing or reshaping activity on the part of the individual living thing is preceded by the elemental, nondisposable foundation for life found in the natural world and environment—the world of creation, made by God once and for all, with the aim of permanence; created for living things, man and beast, containing the determinable sequence of time, and with provisions for animal and human activity inherent in its framework. As the formula of approval after every created work in Genesis 1 shows, each one of the works of creation possesses the quality of being good, favorable, in accordance with what was intended. At the end—when the relationship between animals and men, and between the earth and men, has been ordered, and all taking of life for the purposes of nourishment has been excluded through the granting of vegetable food to everything living—we are told about the whole world of creation.[54] "And God saw everything that he had made, and behold, it was very good" (1:31). This is the way in which P expresses that the works of creation as a whole, in their internal structure and their relation to one another, represent a totality that is very good; and "very good" in the context of the thematic perspective of *P* in Genesis 1 means: completely and permanently arranged and ordered for the promotion of all life. For *P* this means that an elemental value is inherent in the created world that underlies all experience of the world—a fundamental quality that embraces everything that lives and its equipment for living.

In Genesis 1, therefore, *P* grasps the permanent foundation of the natural world as being something fore-given, and unreservedly favorable for the promotion of life, and which as such precedes all specific activity on the part of the living. In this it stands beside Genesis 2 and Psalm 104. But, as we have seen, it has to take into consideration a serious difference between the created world and the world as we find it as regards one particular phenomenon. This phenomenon erodes the divine purposes in favor of life at a decisive point, and needs a renewed regulation of its own. God, who saw his created world as very good, looks down at the earth before the Flood "and behold it was corrupt" (Gen: 6:12). For it is full of violence, which has gained ground among animals and people—among "all flesh"—in spite of the edicts of creation. The world is full of killing, arbitary killing, which was expressly excluded at creation as a way of supporting life (1:29-30). That is to say, it is not the evil, self-centered character of man which involves the whole created world, as it is in the Yahwist. It is a particular situation. There is violence among "all flesh," behavior that deprives living things of life, arbitrarily and brutally, and this is corrupting the earth, which had been created to make life possible and to disseminate it (Gen. 1:11-12, 24, 28, 29-30). Violence is debasing the earth as a sphere in which to live. In its version of the decision to send a flood (Gen. 6:13) and the Flood itself, *P* leaves no doubt about how this fact is to be judged and avenged. But the narrative incorporates the experience that the threat to man, through arbitrary and brutal attacks on life by animals, and also by other people, will remain reality even after the Flood (which is indeed a strictly unique event, 9:8ff). For *P* too, therefore, the world of creation in the form in which it proceeded from God's initiative, does not remain unimpaired in the period that follows. The created world is always only experienced together with the threat of violence from other life, which proceeds from animals and people. Yet unlike the Yahwist, *P* does not see a growing overshadowing and depreciation of the created world; nor does he see the new beginning of a counter-movement, which proceeds from God by way of Israel. For *P* the created world, established once and for all, remains in all essentials, in spite of everything, the permanent and ordered consummation of an event that guarantees life to all.

In order to secure this, *P* sees God as enacting new, modifying regulations after the Flood, in the blessing to Noah in Genesis 9. These regulations are designed to restrict violence—indeed they are intended to prevent it altogether. In accordance with the concentration of *P*'s perspective on the world of man, from Genesis 5*P* onwards, these regulations are concerned solely with the protecting of human life against violent attacks by animals and other people. Violent and arbitrary attacks by man on animals are outside this viewpoint. But *P* does not perceive the way thrown open for an unrestricted mastery of man over animal life. This is already shown by the fact that only two basic situations for the killing of animals by man are mentioned in Genesis 9:1ff: the protection of human life which the animal has attacked, and the need to support life by means of food.

As Genesis 9:1 and 7 show, the regulations here are themselves the expression of blessing. That is to say, they are not merely theoretical provisions; they are the divine bestowal of power and success on man in his mastery over violent attacks on his life. It is not only the biblical scholar, therefore—it is *P* itself that makes an express reference to the corresponding statements in Genesis 1:28-30. Indeed Genesis 9:1-7 is nothing other than a modification and expansion of Genesis 1:28-30, which now covers violence toward people: 9:1 picks up 1:28*a* and renews the blessings given to creation after the Flood (the subjection of the earth is missing, because vegetable food, acquired through the working of the soil, is not the question that has to be regulated anew here). The closing verse, "And you, be fruitful and multiply, bring forth abundantly on the

earth and multiply in it" (9:7), again picks up 1:28a and, with its
new stress on the population increase on earth, leads over to
Genesis 10P, to the population of the world, which manifests
the powerful effect of this promissory blessing.

Between these passages come the regulations that are
really modifying ones. Chapter 9:2 picks up the element of
blessing in the lordship of man over the animals in 1:28, but it
now includes experience of the threat to human life through all
beasts except the domestic ones. Accordingly, these animals
are now seen as enemies threatening the life of man and
entering into conflict with him. But where this happens, attacks
on men are restricted by the fact that in this struggle man is
assigned superiority and victory through blessing.[55] Taking into
account the phenomenon that acts of violence also proceed
from animals, the lordship over the beasts given to man is
therefore modified. It is now also the victorious defense of
human life against animals. It is modified further because man
is now empowered (vv 3-4) to eat meat acquired by killing
animals as well as the vegetarian food which belonged to the
edicts given at creation and which 1:29-30 talked about. Both
are new aspects of human rule over animals. This domination
now includes defense against animal attack and the right to kill
them as a legitimate expression of lordship. In both cases, what
we have is a regulation of arbitrary force.

Like 9:2, 9:5-6 finally shows that P sees the use of force in
attacks on man's life, by both animals and men, as a basic fact of
existence—not, indeed, belonging to the world of creation, but
certainly to the world as we find it; and it is a fact that cannot be
surmounted. These verses show how people are to act in order
to restrict violence in each specific case. The elemental value of
human life, and of human life alone (which does not consist of its
spirituality or anything of that kind, but in its function as "image
of God" for the whole of creation and its continuance), is
expressed in the fact that God himself avenges every act of
violence against man which leads to death—and avenges it with
the death of the attacker, whether it be beast or man. In the
long run, this vengeance through God himself is carried out in
practical terms by man, who in this respect also has the function

of acting as God's steward in the world of creation. "Whoever shed the blood of man, by man shall his blood be shed; for God made man in his own image" (9:6).

Here as well, therefore, man is for P the guardian of the "good," that is to say, the elemental quality of creation in the world that promotes the life of all; and he is its guardian, not only for himself, but for all living things. His task of restricting and avenging "corruption" in the world (Gen. 6:12), given him at God's command and with his authority, also takes its bearings from this given, all-embracing relation of value.

This blessing to Noah, the covenant with Noah that follows (which guarantees the permanent stability and preservation of the elemental world of life) and the manifestation of blessing shown in the tables of the nations means that the given and basic endowments and fundamental provisions for the natural world, and for the world of man, have been established from this time on, permanently, once and for all. God will give no new edicts and regulations in this sector; and he does not need to do so. There will be no higher development of the natural world of creation or the world of men to supersede these basic provisions, and there will be no complete conquest of violence exerted against life. Historical developments, political changes, and social transformations will come and go; P does not include them. What is essential here is that God has permanently endowed and ordered even the natural world and environment in their elemental, essential foundations. He conferred and realized these conditions for man, and for all other living things, before man could do anything himself; and they are not at man's own disposal. God points man to this order and endowment again and again in the vocation assigned to him. It is from these that he must take his bearings; it is to these that he must always turn again. He must continually test his actions against the gifts that God gave him with his creation, so that the world of creation and the world of man can continue to live.

This static quality in the elemental understanding of the world[56] points toward the elemental value of life, which belongs to all the living, and comprehends man, giving him his bearings.

For *P*, being alive never means unlimited life without death, any more than it did for the Yahwist or in Psalm 104. It means having the space to live and the necessary presuppositions for making a living. For *P* too, this is the fundamental value with which the world of creation is endowed, the value that is built into it. And man has to preserve this value absolutely, toward nonhuman life as well, apart from the necessities of defense and providing food for himself. This fundamental value makes man's own life absolutely sacrosanct. The violent destruction of human life is intervention in the fundamental order of the world, which must be avenged by men and women through the killing of whoever is responsible. For *P*, therefore, the wholesome promotion of all life in the natural world, and the living together of men and women, is only guaranteed when the ordained quality of endowment, which belongs to creation, also includes the fundamental values and orders that determine the freedom, the bearings, the obligations, and the limits of human activity. As the "image of God," whose activity shapes the world, man also contributes to the character of the natural world of experience, which points to God. The fact that for *P* God is no longer continually active in the world of the present as creator, is no contradiction. The experience that the undisposable foundations of life found in the natural world are not at man's disposal is made clear through the permanently valid enactments of time and life to which *P* testifies and which were given by God the creator in the beginning.

III. Thematic Aspects

The previous section offered some observations about the world and the environment drawn from exemplary and much-discussed Old Testament texts on the subject of creation. The purpose of this third section is now to follow up the Old Testament facts, summing up what they have to say to us in the light of our own present-day world. We must do this under various thematic headings, which are related to the fundamental questions of the present discussion and which we worked out in the introduction, in the second essential condition. In the first aspect of our inquiry we shall consider the finding that the scope of what Israel understood by the natural world and environment varied considerably. The radius of the world and environment in the Old Testament differs to no small degree.

1. The Growing Scope of the Natural World and Environment

a. The textual findings

When we were discussing natural living conditions in ancient Israel in the context of Israelite settlement, we pointed out that the perspective of the natural world and environment was not always a comprehensive and total one. It did not always envisage the whole earthly milieu of the essential conditions of existence for all living things and all people. It first of all moved in the much more limited radius of its own, specifically experienced world of life. It only grew to total range in the course of time and under the influence of special cultural conditions, and even then it was only at home in this total outlook in certain fields of Israelite interpretation of the world. The textual findings—each viewed in its historical context in ancient Israel—show this quite plainly.

According to the traditions preserved in the Old Testament, a total perspective is only to be found from the time of the building of the empire under David and Solomon. It remains characteristic of the urban culture of Jerusalem (which also influenced the land of Judah in the pre- and post-exilic periods) as well as the area occupied by Israelite deportees in Babylonian Exile. This explains why the most important evidence is to be found in the traditions that have come down to us from the temple cult and the Wisdom cultivated in Jerusalem. Under this influence we find the viewpoint we are considering in Deutero-Isaiah and in the primeval history of the Priestly Writing (both of which date from the Exile), and finally, under the same influence, in the traditions, stemming from post-exilic quarters, that took their bearings from Jerusalem (prophecy, theological Wisdom, and apocalyptic). We have seen that the Yahwist's primeval history shows a significant link between the total perspective and traditions deriving from the country of Judah. And this is not by chance. The total scope of the perspective is not an intrinsic feature of Israelite faith. It derives from the sphere of oriental civilization,[1] which exerted an important influence, in Jerusalem especially, and then in Israel too, by way of the civilization of the Canaanite cities.[2]

Israelite traditions dating from the centuries before the Davidic Empire, on the other hand, show a much narrower view of the natural world and environment, and the same may be said of traditions deriving from the succeeding period, in which the prenational character remained, even in changed circumstances. We must turn to this viewpoint first of all, because we can perceive features in it which also determined Israel's critical adoption of ancient oriental perspectives with their wider outlook.

b. The world as the milieu of group and people

As we have stressed in connection with its natural living conditions, Israel emerged from population groups who had migrated into the Palestinian area. These nomadic groups, with their herds of sheep and goats, did not enter the region as superior classes, ruling over Canaanite urban civilizations. They settled in less-populated areas, where the soil could be cultivated, where they tilled the fields and herded animals. If we adhere to the picture of Israel's religious history and character drawn by Alt[3] and his followers (a view which has admittedly been considerably altered by H. H. Schmid, for example, in an impressive counter-picture[4]), we may say that in the first centuries of their settlement these proto-Israelite groups were able to preserve the unique character they had inherited and to develop it relatively homogeneously in line with their new circumstances. This was especially true of their henotheistic worship of *one* God (their worship of Yahweh alone was not an assertion of the actual nonexistence of any other gods).[5] Even attempts to fuse these groups (in contrast to the country's other inhabitants) into the unit "Israel" and to amalgamate individual settlements into "the land of Israel" on the basis of their common religious and ethnic foundation did nothing to alter this. Indeed, even under the new conditions of the Israelite monarchy, these characteristics remained dominant to a certain degree, and were critically applied in the farming area of Judah, and above all among the people who carried on the traditions of the Northern Kingdom, which are preserved for us in the Old Testament. These early religious, social, and cultural conditions exerted an influence on the prevailing attitude toward the world and the environment.

For in this framework the attitude toward the world is determined, not by the spreading integration of ancient oriental education and knowledge, but by people's direct dealings with what were the obvious and essential conditions of existence. The viewpoint is, accordingly, certainly limited and directed toward pasture, tilled fields, and settled land; to springs, herds, clans, people, and territory; to the increase of the group, the people, and the herds; to the fruitfulness of one's own land; and to unthreatened security and protection from enemy groups and neighboring peoples beyond the group's own world. Here, therefore, the natural world and environment is no longer the specific field of living of the proto- and early-Israelite groups. Of course, here too the life-promoting natural endowments of the milieu are not accepted as a matter of course, but are seen as God's gift, under the guidance and conditioning of earlier religious attitudes. Nonetheless, they were not viewed in a breadth that would correspond to the divine creation of heaven and earth, but—as traditions passed down to us in the books of Genesis to Joshua show—as a divine "allocation," grant, and

promise, an authorization conceding the possession of the
settled territory of the group—the land of Israel. It is not the
provision of water for the earth in general that is of interest
here, but the springs, brooks, and wells in the people's own
immediate vicinity, and the rain that falls at God's command
(1 Kings 17–18). It is not the vegetation of the earth or the
animal world as a whole that is envisaged, but the conditions,
exigencies, and dangers of the immediate environment. The
specific features of this limited perspective are quite evident
in the blessings and curses in Leviticus 26 and Deuteronomy
28.

Even if this immediate environment of Israel's is divided
according to grazing areas or can be split up and differentiated
according to the geography of the tribes, the outlook on the
natural world and environment is not a descriptive or static
one, in spite of this limiting perspective. As the way it is
treated in the blessings or curses makes clear, it is the
perception of an *event* that bestows on Israel, or denies to it,
the necessities of life that are not at its own disposal.

This event of the natural world and environment is not
seen in isolation, however; on the contrary, it is viewed for its
part as one component in the single, fundamental event to
which Israel owes the fact that it succeeded in moving away
from its early nomadic state to settlement in cultivated
country, and was able to become a people. It is the event of
the constant leading of its God, as Israel visibly experienced
it. This story was told again and again in different strata of
tradition and at different periods, as a great complex of
salvation history, stretching from the period of the patriarchs
down to God's guidance of the people into the cultivated land
of east and west Jordan. This means that the natural world of
life in the country in which the people are living is, from the
very beginning, seen together with the life of the group and
its continuing existence. Israel is no more a matter of course
than the natural world in which it lives; both are the event of
God's guidance, which is not at the people's disposal, and
which is directed toward Israel's favored and blessed
existence, which endures and lacks nothing. This link is very

important for the character of Israel's view of the world and
the environment, even within this restricted radius. For the
experiences of guidance which the Israelites had with their
God from the nomadic period onward also put their stamp on
Israel's perception of the natural world and its endowments in
the country of Palestine. As part of the event of salvation
history, to which Israel owes its own existence, the natural
world and the equipment provided for life itself is seen
historically. That is to say, it is included completely in the
movements and conditions of Israel's history with its God. Of
course, this is not a vista of a "history of nature," such as grows
up on the soil of modern science; but it is a perception of the
elemental foundations of life, arrived at by a group, a people,
which understands the "nondisposable" nature of its existence, and the fact that it exists at all, as being the event of
God's continual leading and bestowal—or, it may be, God's
avenging denial of his guidance and gifts.

To the extent that Israel took its bearings from God's
guidance (and in actual fact it was certainly not equally
conscious of this at all times, or with equal certainty in all
sections of the population), any attribution of divinity to the
forces and rhythms of nature itself was excluded. Israel had to
enforce this limitation and see it through, especially with
regard to the god Baal, who was worshiped in Palestine and
whose activities were seen in the nondisposable, elemental
foundations of the natural world.[6] In this connection, H. H.
Schmid has rightly pointed to the fact that the rejection of all
such Canaanite fertility religions goes together with the
Israelite incorporation of the natural foundations of life into
Yahweh's historical activity on Israel's behalf.[7] He sees
Israel's consciousness of this exclusiveness as only growing up
later, however, as a result of the scriptural prophets; he does
not think that it was an early phenomenon. But Israel's
orientation toward the leadings of God in its own historical
existence equally excludes a natural relationship to nature,
which makes human aims and purposes the sole yardstick by
which to judge the way man molds his natural surroundings.

The reason for this particular character of Israel's view of the world and the environment, however, is its henotheism: the sole worship of Yahweh in Israel's world. From very early, this was expressly and emphatically enforced, at least in those circles in Israel that determined the traditions passed down to us. This sole worship of Yahweh is the reason why the experience of the natural world is fused theologically with the whole activity of God for the group, the path it treads and its history. This is the reason why the experience of God is freed from its ties with the notion that natural events point to the power of some inherent deity, and why a polytheistic or dualistic view of the natural world was made factually impossible (though we must not, admittedly, be under any illusions about the practical consequences in preexilic Israel). God is accordingly essentially transcendent, as regards the world of the people.

The characteristics which Israel attributes to its world are in line with this. The world is not God, even in those phenomena that are constitutive for life. On the other hand, the world is not at Israel's entire disposal either, as if it were something quite neutral. The land belongs to God; it is his property; and it is because of this that he has given it to Israel.[8] It is a good country (Exod. 3:8; Num. 14:7; Deut. 1:25), well-watered, fruitful, with more than sufficient food (Deut. 8:7-10; 11:10-12), a land flowing with milk and honey (Num. 13:27; Deut. 6:3; etc.). This view—that Israel has been given its elemental world of life by God, who himself remains the country's owner—also finds concrete expression in legal regulations about land, according to which the different shares in the country cannot be freely sold.[9] We also find it, similarly, in regulations that envisage a regular fallow period for the land every seventh (sabbatical) year according to Exodus 23:10-11; Leviticus 25:1ff, 8ff, or every fiftieth year (Year of Jubilee), although this fallow period for the land was not, of course, based on ecological insights, and its regular observance, in any case, remained theoretical. But more remarkable are the social reasons given for the sabbatical and jubilee years. They show that Yahweh's gift of the land was seen, not only as being made for the benefit of the Israelite citizen with his own portion of ground, but as being an elemental condition of life, which as such had to be preserved, and which applied to people who were in a socially dependent position, and to domestic animals and wild beasts as well—that is to say, to everything living in the land of Israel. This land given by Yahweh to Israel is therefore conceded even to the wild beasts as sphere in which to live. But, above all, it is the domestic animals used by man whose independent right to life is expressly established (see, e.g., Exod. 23:4-5; Deut. 22:1-4, 6-7, 10; 25:4; Prov. 12:10, and, in the sabbath ordinances, Exod. 23:12; Deut. 5:14). Indeed these animals are actually seen as having a living tie with man that makes them part of the social group;[10] and appropriately they are included in the criminal law as well.[11]

Thus the elemental world in Palestine, with cultivated land, animals, and people belonging to their own group and their own nation, meant that for Israelites the life surrounding them certainly had the emotional quality of what we call homeland—the ancestral, familiar sphere of life that can be conceived and visualized as a whole, and which is accepted as ordained and conferred. It is the sphere of experience that shapes the people in it; the sphere of fulfillment granted to them, the sphere worth preserving. It is not just the world at people's disposal, there for the autonomous construction of surrogates for a true homeland. It is the sphere formed by the experience of affirmed and obligatory definitions of the meaning and order of society, as Israel found them when it viewed this world in the framework of the path trodden and the history experienced with its God.

For Israel, consequently, this view of the natural world is by no means concentrated on the God-givenness of merely the minimum conditions necessary for survival. On the contrary, this whole world is the sphere of a happy flowering of life full of blessing, where every man may dwell in safety "under his vine and under his fig tree" (1 Kings 4:25; cf. the evaluation of this Israelite world in Deut. 11:8-15). At the same time, this view of Israel's own world in its own country is not a selective one, only taking into account, theologically,

the positive elements that benefit life, and excluding the
negative ones. Israel is undoubtedly aware of the threat from
enemies, which also destroy the conditions for living and
which involve the animal world in ruin as well; it sees the
dangers from wild beasts, epidemics, sickness, insect pests,
and interruptions to the vitally important rainfall. Yet even
these threats to the elemental world of life do not by any
means lead to polytheistic or dualistic utterances in Israel.
The emphatically exclusive worship of the God Yahweh and,
resulting from this, Yahweh's transcendence with regard to
Israel's world mean that even phenomena involving a threat
to life are viewed as being the actions of the same God; the
curses in Deuteronomy 28 and Leviticus 26 show this
unmistakably, for example. Wherever Israel experiences its
elemental world in its own country, it encounters Yahweh and
Yahweh alone—no other divinely present power. The first
commandment, and the exclusive bond with Yahweh
enjoined there, is the root of Israel's outstanding freedom
toward its elemental world, in which the important thing is
not to bow down to the antagonism of any supernatural forces.
The world given by Yahweh is instead exclusively bound up
with Israel's responsibility toward Yahweh's ordinances.
Israel's way of life decides whether this world, with all the
living things in it, develops in blessing or depreciates under
Yahweh's curse.

c. The widening out to a total perspective

This limited view of the natural world and environment,
as we have just indicated it, is confined to the elemental
foundations of the life of the group, the people; and it is this
that determines the radius of perception. What is dominant is
the pragmatic, limited world of what is to be seen and
experienced every day and which affects the private and
communal sphere of the individual down to the present day.

But things were different among the closest neighbors of
the Israelite settlements, the Canaanite towns, each of which
had its own individual version of a mixed, ancient oriental

civilization and its own direct influence. There, instead of the limited view, closely related to a particular group, there was a comprehensive perception of the natural world as a whole (within the framework of the particular field of knowledge). This included the earthly world in its whole extent and also the concept of divine creation and preservation of the earth, the heavens, plants, animals, and man per se.[12] Here the horizon of the natural world is, in principle, the scope that is essential if we are to relate this early outlook to the present world and environment theme under a common perspective.

How did this total perspective grow up? How did it develop? What were its specific characteristics at the time when it found an entry into Israel's thinking? We still know very little about all this. An expansion of the horizon beyond the narrow individual sphere of living was certainly one element. This evolved between 2,000 and 1,000 B.C. in Mesopotamia, but also in Syria-Palestine (as a coastal region and a sphere of interest for the imperial powers). It developed from the proximity of the city states to one another, out of political and economic relations, and through an extension of individual spheres of interest. Here viewpoint and experience as well as cultural exchanges offered a starting point for a worldwide orientation, and encouraged a reaching out to global conditions and relations. The use of technical, architectonic metaphors[13] for the creation of the world, and for the functional nature and relations of individual natural phenomena as these were perceived, shows one presupposition for this total perspective. The division of labor and the differentiation of the social order in the urban states set the mind free to perceive a total cohesion, to collect and classify world phenomena, and to answer the question about the process of the natural world's creation. To this was apparently added a focusing of perception which differed in character from Israel's more limited one. There, as we have seen, utterances about God were related to the constitutive experiences of the group's progress and history, which included the gift of being allowed to live in a world of cultivated land. Here statements about the divinity are apparently related primarily to certain territory with universal significance, which lends a worldwide dimension to the activity of the god who is manifested at this place and is worshiped in its temple. Anyone who lives in this place and rules it, shares in the worldwide power of this god. The essential link between statements about the divinity (in relation to the creation of the world too) with ideas about the mountain of God and its universal dimension must, above all, be mentioned here. [14]

Much about the pre-Israelite character of the total perspective of the natural world and environment is still inevitably unexplained; but in the context of our whole question about the biblical findings, the essential thing is primarily that Israel absorbed this total perspective from its neighboring civilizations from the time of the building of the empire under David, especially in Jerusalem; and that it thereby came to see the activities of its God Yahweh as having universal scope. For the development of knowledge of God as we find it in the Bible, the important fact is that Jerusalem's pre-Israelite–Canaanite tradition[15] was taken over on Yahweh's behalf in the wake of the city's capture by David, with the transfer of the Ark and the building of Solomon's temple. The essential result was that Yahweh was no longer only the God of a group of tribes, an ethnically and historically coherent alliance of peoples. As the God of the Israelites, who had taken possession of the city of Jerusalem, he now proved himself the "highest" God, who was enthroned on Zion, the Mount of God, and who, as creator and controller of the whole world, and by virtue of that very fact, had a relationship to the whole of the world and to the whole of mankind.

This expansion of Israel's mental horizon to take in the universal conception of the natural world—an expansion deriving from the Canaanite sphere of ancient oriental civilization—certainly did not take place at any one particular point in time. It was a long-term mental process. It went hand in hand with the wider integration of the content of ancient oriental culture in the sphere of the natural world as a whole, as this was known at the period: ideas about the stability of the

earth, about the division between land and sea, about the
origin of meteorological phenomena, the course of the sun,
the behavior of animals, and the like. But this process was,
ultimately speaking, a process of critical and selective
adoption (even if it required a considerable period of conflict,
clarification, and definition of what was in accord with
Yahweh and Israel, in the spiritual and the practical sense[16]).
And in this process Israel finally and emphatically called into
play the earlier features of its unique character, as we have
already come to know them in their limited reference,
according to the picture given us by the traditions that have
been preserved.

This happened mainly because Israel's sole worship of
Yahweh in his transcendence of the world[17] was firmly
preserved and expanded beyond the limited field of Israel
itself and its world. The one God Yahweh is now, as creator,
related to the whole of the natural world in general and to
everything that lives in it. We have already stressed Israel's
own, historical view of its restricted natural world as the
sphere in which Yahweh was to be preceived. This now
acquires an all-embracing dimension. The view of events
which are essential for the elemental living conditions of
group and people now widens out to a view directed toward
the whole natural world and environment, an event to be
narrated and praised as the activity of Yahweh the creator.
Israel perceived the totality of the natural world as possessing
the same character of event as the history of guidance leading
to its own existence. So it is quite consistent that mythical
conceptions of a dualistic or polytheistic kind should now be
excluded—in the wake of this conception of the whole of the
natural world as being Yahweh's creative event—so that it is
no longer merely Israel, in its individual world, but man, in
the natural world in general, who comes face to face with
Yahweh alone as divinity. This in its turn conferred
naturalness to the whole elemental world, in which the
human being, with his shaping powers, could move freely,
without reckoning with the play of power of any divinely
imminent forces in nature itself. Certainly, in this process the

inherited, Israelite ways of looking at their own land were also taken over into the world of life as a whole, and the Israelite man or woman came to stand for mankind as a whole. For this critical adoption of a total perspective, Israel extended the validity of its own experiences as a people with the one, exclusively worshiped God Yahweh, to the whole sphere of the natural world, and to mankind in general. So far, all Israel's statements about creation are indivisible from the perception of Yahweh found in its statements of faith, even though Israel desired to say something about the creation of the world that was not merely valid for Israel, but had general application in view of the world's comprehensive order.[18] We must therefore avoid setting Israel's statements about creation over against its statements of faith.[19] On the contrary, "It is only through the identification of the creator with the God whom Israel encountered in its history that the concept of creation received its theological impress."[20]

On the other hand, although Israel now conceived the natural world-event as a totality, this concept could not simply be related to Israel's history of guidance in such a way as to give it universal scope. The world is not created merely for Israel; but mankind as a whole does not turn into Israel either. The creation of the world and Israel's guidance in salvation history are not the same thing. Israel clung to this distinction. But in defining the relationship between the two, it proceeded in different ways. One possibility was to put the universal perspective ahead of Israel's salvation history. This was what happened, as we saw, in the Yahwist's work, where the quality of creation in the world is strangely revoked, and Israel's salvation history is given universal significance. The Priestly Writing did the same thing in a different way. In both testimonies, the universal perspective of creation comprehends the universal starting point for all men, including Israel, and for all living things. In *J* the situation is ambivalent and has therefore to be mastered. In *P* it is permanent and basic. In both cases, it is a situation that is followed by Israel's salvation history. The other possibility was to integrate the events of Yahweh's guidance of Israel into his universal activity, as one manifestation of the creative power that forms the world, a manifestation in this case given to his group of worshipers in Zion. This is what we find in the Jerusalem conception. It is reflected in the psalms,[21] including Psalm 104, for example, and later in Deutero-Isaiah,[22] and probably also in the Wisdom tradition.[23] Yet Deutero-Isaiah shows that under the influence of grave, contrary experiences the creation perspective was drawn into a viewpoint based on salvation history, in expectation of new, supreme creative activity on Yahweh's part at the end and goal of Israel's history. And what is true of Deutero-Isaiah applies even more to postexilic prophecy and apocalyptic.

Thus the perception of the natural world in ancient Israel is not the same everywhere and at all times. It is rather in itself a historical process, determined by different preconditions and experiences of participation in the world-event.

It is obvious that when we are considering our theme world and environment, we must pursue the main train of thought found in the total perspective on the natural world in the Old Testament. But in order to recognize the forces, influences, and spiritual movements that dominate these texts, it is essential to see that an older, parallel line existed, one which handled the subject under an aspect limited to Israel and its own land, and this line, in its own earlier form and in its difference, gives profile to the universal trend.

If we consider the growing scope of the natural world in Israel's traditions (an expansion that also corresponds to an increasingly differentiated knowledge of the world), seeing it in the light of our present-day world, we seem to be brought face to face with a similarity or correspondence. This correspondence is related to the parallelism of the limited, everyday world that stamps our experience, and the rules or definitions which lie behind this world, which—though they are experienced simultaneously—are directed toward the totality, i.e., the endowments of the world as a whole, in its genesis, its development, its stability, and in the relations of individual natural phenomena as these reveal themselves to the inquiries of research and to the processes of education. This specifically

experienced view of the world and the total world picture of
science are certainly not identical for people today. Yet the
relation between findings in ancient Israel and our findings are
much less close, and the differences, both in the partial
perspective (which was concentrated on the Chosen People)
and in the all-embracing total perspective, are much greater
than seems to be the case at first. We shall discover this in the
aspects we are about to consider.

2. The Natural World and Environment as Creative and Initial Event

a. The connection between the following five sections

In arriving at its comprehensive perspective on the
creation of the world, Israel discovered a total view of the
natural world of life to which our theme world and environment
can be related, in the sense in which we defined it at the
beginning. The world (within the limits known at the time) was
accepted as being a total space for living, together with all living
things and the elemental factors that determine their lives; and
statements could be made about its existence and the
connections and links that constitute it. The three texts we have
taken as examples have already shown us this. The Old
Testament statements about the creation of the world must
therefore be given central importance in the framework of our
subject.

Our findings about the tradition justify this as well. Ever
since the development of the total perspective, ancient Israel,
early Christianity, and Christian doctrine as it has been
defined, have all clung, down to the present day, to the
statement about the creative quality in the natural world and
environment. This continuity of tradition certainly does not
mean that this statement has always been seen as an equally
adequate and equally accessible definition. We can discover
changes, even within the Old Testament tradition itself. The

difference between the Yahwist's work on the one hand (which denies the quality of direct creation in the world as we have it), and Psalm 104 and Genesis 1 on the other, became clear to us from the texts we took as examples. New perspectives developed even more clearly under the influence of new and contrary experiences of the world in the later Old Testament tradition, and this was even more the case in early Christianity, in the face of the coming of Jesus Christ and his life and death. These new viewpoints modify the statement about the direct quality of creation in the world and set it in new contexts. But in saying this we must notice that the historical, and also the factual, starting point, and the permanent basis of these transformations—a basis that was never supplanted—is the Old Testament statements which in their total perspective perceive a directly creative quality in the natural world and environment as we see it. We find these in the psalms, in Proverbs, in Job, and in the prophetic traditions, but also in the Priestly Writing. (The view that we ought to distinguish between the creation of the world and the creation of man in Israel's thought[24] does not seem altogether convincing, and we shall not be considering this theory here.)

We shall first turn to these fundamental Old Testament statements about the creation of the world and shall try to grapple with the complex of facts included here—i.e., the natural world and environment as God's creative event—considering them under different aspects in five separate sections. Our aim here is to take account of the central significance of the statements about the creation of the world for our contemporary world and environment theme, while also considering the difficulties of understanding we modern men and women are up against in thinking about these statements. After these five sections, we shall go on to develop aspects of creation as viewpoint or perspective and shall also discuss the transformations of this perspective in ancient Israel itself (section 7). The reader should therefore notice, in considering the divisions of what follows, that sections 2 to 6 belong together, as different aspects of one and the same Old Testament viewpoint, and correspond to the fundamental questions we discussed in the introduction: the

Israelite view which characterizes the natural world and environment as creation. The first aspect—subject of the present section—is: How does the natural world and environment as we see it appear, when we talk about it as a creative and initial event? The second aspect (section 3) is: What perception and knowledge of the world corresponds to this viewpoint? The third aspect (section 4) is: What elemental experience of significance underlies this view of the world? The fourth aspect (section 5) is: How far did Israel encounter Yahweh in this perception and experience of the natural world and environment, and encounter him in his divine relationship to the world, from which he is nonetheless distinct? The fifth aspect (section 6) is: How can we define the position of man, which is part of Israel's view of creation?

b. The aspects of the statements about creation that disturb modern men and women

The Old Testament statements about creation are bound to disturb people who are influenced by the modern world. They disturb them in two ways.

On the one hand, they are bothered by the weight of counter-experiences (either personal ones or experiences communicated by others), even in the sphere of the natural world and environment. These stand in the way when people try to connect statements about a world that is good and whose creation is deserving of praise with their actual experience of that world. G. C. Lichtenberg [the eighteenth-century physicist] already remarked that this world was so full of sickness, ill-fortune, earthquakes, storms, distress, and death that one was inclined to see it merely as "journeyman's work on the part of some subordinate spirit, who had but an incomplete understanding of what he was doing."[25] And Ernst Bloch gave eloquent expression to the same idea in our own time when he criticized statements that the world, which is really so inadequate, was a good creation, appealing to critical voices in the later biblical tradition itself.[26] Yet the biblical tradition already included these counter-experiences, the tensions in the natural world and its ambivalent phenomena, as well as the problem of man's use, formation, and modification of nature; and yet it still held fast to the assertions about creation—in what sense, we shall have to ask more closely in sections 6 and 7, as well as in the part of our book that deals with the New Testament.

What is more serious in the context of our present section is the disturbance caused by knowledge of modern science. Wherever we see the natural world and its phenomena—the planet Earth in the order of the cosmic systems of the heavens, the continents in their relation to the seas, meteorological and geological phenomena, the evolution of vegetable, animal, and human life—it is always a matter of complex, anonymous processes, subject to laws into which we can inquire, processes whose age can be counted in milliards and millions of years, with more or less hypothetically determinable beginnings.[27] The Old Testament—like the rest of the Ancient East—knew nothing of all this. It did not reach beyond individual empirical observations and classifications, and talked instead about God, who makes, creates, founds, or commands all this. Indeed, the Priestly Writing does not hesitate to say in Genesis 1 that this process lasted six days, and empirical days of twenty-four hours at that.[28] Does the Old Testament talk about the world as God's creation because it lacked the scientific knowledge of modern times? Because it came up against the limits of what can be discovered about the natural world much more quickly? Because the personally acting God had to be introduced as code-word for the inexplicable, which is yet imperatively in need of explanation if we are to find our bearings in the world, the inexplicable which has long since been explained? Are the creation statements of the Old Testament no more than historically understandable, naive early forms of science, which were bound to become statements of faith because in earlier times the limits of knowledge were much more confined? Or are the biblical statements about creation truths for faith which are still valid for believers as statements about human existence, untouched by, apart from and above, all scientific knowledge?

We should be distorting the Old Testament facts if we were to divide our contemporary knowledge, as the statements of reason, from the biblical creation texts, as statements of faith. For we have seen from the texts considered as examples that the creation texts also aimed to include the knowledge of nature which was available at the time, and which was based on reason and experience. Carl Friedrich von Weizsäcker has long since pointed out to theology that "a schism between existence and nature (in the sense, roughly speaking, that existence is the field of Christian faith and nature the field of the exact sciences) allocates too narrow a field to both faith and science—indeed a field that does not really exist at all in this form."[29] But we should be distorting the Old Testament facts no less if we were to discuss the difference between the viewpoints of creation and science merely from the aspect of science's more extensive knowledge of nature. On the level of the natural sciences this difference is indisputable, as is the judgment that in this respect biblical science, compared with our modern knowledge, is too simple, and that it has been superseded and indeed is simply wrong. That is so banal, so much a matter of course, that cheap feelings of superiority are just as superfluous as the touching and irritating attempts of the simple-minded apologetics which try to see the insights of modern science as being at least prefigured in the biological statements of the Bible, and which want to fill up the "gaps" in the Bible's scientific knowledge, so as to show that the Scriptures are "right" after all.[30] But the differences between scientific statements about the world and statements about creation go far beyond the initially disturbing level of our biological knowledge, and go far deeper. It is not that insights differ when the same questions are asked; it is the approach and the perspective that diverge. Someone standing in a different place perceives things differently. This is what makes these statements really disturbing.

c. *The starting point of the statements about creation*

For the average modern Western mind, the phenomenon which we have defined as the natural world and environment apparently belongs to a curious blind spot,[31] so that its essential importance for living escapes notice. Thanks to the mediation of scientific knowledge, "the world" today is already much larger, in terms of space, and its phenomena are considerably more varied than the sphere of the elemental world of life; even if science has at present ceased to insist on the universe's spatial and temporal infinity.[32] "World" is then an overriding concept that covers a multiplicity of scientific aspects and is detached from human contemplation and life as it is lived—cut off from the phenomenon of life. It is knowable and learnable, but its anonymous inconceivability makes it ineligible for orientation into life as it is actually lived. But this actual life as it is lived does not see itself as dependent on the natural world and environment for its elemental needs either. It sees itself as subject to a world set up by men and women, dependent on their formative activities in economic, political, and social processes, with initial circumstances that differ from one part of the world to another. According to this view, the natural world and environment is merely the self-evident presupposition and potential, in which the only important thing is the exploitable share which falls to the individual's lot (or ought to do so) in the political and social processes of distribution.

Israel was different. When, in its statements about creation, Israel penetrated beyond the phenomena of the political and social world to the totality of the natural world and environment, then (as the researches of Gerhard von Rad,[33] Claus Westermann,[34] and H. H. Schmid,[35] e.g., have shown) it did not merely encounter a curiously neutral, self-contained object of cognition, "nature," with its own genetic processes and inherent laws. And it did not encounter man as independent subject, beside nature and outside it, standing over against nature, disposing of it, knowing it, analyzing, it, modifying it, making it work for him, and exploiting it, in order to split it up into unnumbered partial fields of human questions and designs and to exploit it for man's self-imposed purposes—all the things he has to know and do in order to build up a human world that is ostensibly worth living in for the first time. When the Israelite observer perceived the natural world (and the same is true, largely speaking, of the

Ancient East as a whole) he did not exclude himself and direct his questions toward the investigation of something standing over against himself. On the contrary, guided by his presuppositions and his preconditioning, he began with himself, as it were, with the fact of his being alive, with his endowment with the essential conditions for existence. And he saw other living things, man and beast, as standing beside himself and similarly endowed. Everything living, everything before him and after him, was included in this elemental personal experience of life. His starting point in considering the natural world and environment was therefore the question of why he and other living things were alive at all. This "why" is not the neutral, analytical question about the essential conditions and reasons that make life possible. It is based on what is preeminently a question of values: the fact that I and every living thing should meet with the elemental good fortune and miracle of being alive. For Israel, at all events, the wonder with which it already perceived the miracle of its own existence spreads over the whole field of life and the equipment for living in general. "Astonishment over the fact that Israel *is,* when it might not be, is Israel's fundamental experience throughout its whole history."[36] Or, as Günter Altner puts it:

> God's actions in creation and salvation are experienced as the unexpected and unforeseeable. . . . God is the one who calls into being the thing that is not, or which feels that it is nothing. Whether this statement is related to the creation of the world, to the historical preservation of Israel, or to the putting to rights of stranded and hopeless lives—what it always means is the experience that existence is made possible, the sense of being permitted to live, which introduces a new stage in the nonpredictable future.[37]

Here, therefore, the most elemental of all experiences is not (as it is today) what is simply so self-evidently present that it can be passed over, but the essentials of life as such. This is the fundamental question that moves men.

d. The world seen from within in the creation statements

The other starting point has far-reaching consequences for the perspective from which the natural world and environment is viewed.

First of all, man sees his own position differently. He is the subject, not beside and outside an object "nature," but in the midst of the natural world, bound up with it in the experience of being alive and of being able to live.

Then, apart from the leading fundamental question, the natural world, with the living things in it, also discloses itself in a different way. In all the ways that animals are employed and that man uses the world's phenomena—cattle-herding and arable farming; fishing and sea-going; mining and time-reckoning; settlement and transport—the natural world and environment emerges under the aspect of elemental, always basic phenomena, living and nonliving alike, which are not at my disposal. They are givens for the existence of living things, and they make my own life, and all other life, actually possible. This world-seen-from-within, which is affected by our own existence and the existence of other life does not, for example, content itself with determining the principles of the metereological causes and conditions that bring rain. It asks why the vital rain really comes at the right time for me, for other living things. The essential thing about plants is not their analyzable order and internal genesis, but the way they continually grow and provide food. The goal of a perception of the world like this is not the geological development of continents and seas, but our continual experience of the permanent separation of the two, a separation that guarantees an unendangered living space for both man and beast. Interest does not remain concentrated on the geological and geographical phenomena of the earth, with their analyzable problems. It moves on to their quality as environments, which actually keep different living beings alive.

Further aspects of this perspective of the world-seen-from-within are directly connected with its focus on the elemental, basic conditions for life, which are not at our disposal. In this perspective the natural world and environment does not dissolve into a multiplicity of individual phenomena whose causation is to be determined in combinations of cause and effect, genetic series whose reciprocal relations are to be defined in causal connections, principles, and laws. Here the world and environment, together with all living things, remain a totality, beyond all detailed phenomena and individual appearances—the totality of the constitutive conditions that actually make life possible. And the goal of the perspective is to discover why this should be so. Such a viewpoint, which does not confine itself to detached analyses, but proceeds existentially from the middle of one's own and other life and from the actual insuring of that life, combines actual life and the possibility of life into a *unity*—a unity existing from the very beginning. It is therefore bound to grasp this unity and totality of all living things, with their actual, natural equipment for living, as a process. That is to say, the natural world and environment comprise something guaranteed, and not at the living things' disposal, something that is not a matter of course or static. It is an event of contingent, qualitative temporality, in which all life is guaranteed whatever is fundamental, nondisposable, and not autonomously achievable, but whatever is, on the contrary, ordained, bestowed, and conceded. According to this viewpoint, the most important thing is not that life is possible and explicable on the basis of this or that causal connection and law, but that life and the equipment for living should actually happen, come about, become event— that it has always done so, does so now, and will do so in the future. For example, naturalists in Israel were also quite aware of the fact that lions are dependent on particular ways of finding food. But the essential thing in the creation statements is that lions should actually get this food and so can live. That is why God asks Job, "Can you hunt the prey for the lion, or satisfy the appetite of the young lions, when they crouch in their dens, or lie in wait in their covert? Who provides for the raven its prey, when its young ones cry to God?" (38:39-40). [38]

In the statements about creation, therefore, the natural world and environment has for Israel the character of an event that continually moves toward the actual living thing, including man; an event which manifests itself in the miracle that all these things should actually be alive. And this event has the quality of powerful, life-conferring bestowal—the gift and concession of what the living thing never gives itself. Starting from the basic fact of the existence of its own life, Israel sees the natural world and environment in connection with the living, as an experience of power that includes man himself. This experience presents what the living thing itself cannot achieve but recognizes as being conceded, ahead of all its own actions, as the basic foundation of those actions, as the event of the gift of personal bestowal, placing at the disposal of living things whatever is elemental and essential. This nondisposable basis of all natural, living reality has to be grasped when Israel views the natural world and environment as an event which is God's creation.

Having said this, we must now go on to give these introductory remarks more precise form, in a number of closer definitions.

e. The natural world and environment as creative event

As we have just seen, Israel does not make its starting point a confrontation between man and nature. It begins with the personal experience of life as something not at one's own disposal, and something that has an evident meaning and value. Israel can see the phenomena of the natural world and environment, and the phenomena of living things within it, and not only in its actual and unquestionable existence. It rather sees in the statements about creation the fact that the world and its phenomena are continually conceded for the benefit of all life. Just because of that, all the ordained, elemental phenomena of the natural world and environment that have any relevance for life are perceived as an event, which realizes and gives effect to the basic conditions required for the fulfillment of every life. As the bestowal of nondisposable fundamental conditions, this is an event of continual turning toward the world on the part of God the creator.[39] It is he who confers on all existence what is bestowed and given at the same time as life itself, and what is not at the living things' disposal. He continually offers life, living space, life's necessities, and lease of life to everything that lives.

In this event bestowed on life, the natural world and environment, together with all living things, is conceived and adhered to as a totality that is constitutive for life. Accordingly the elemental conditions of life, and the living thing itself (including man), belong within the primal context of a continuous process that ceaselessly confers life—in the present. It is this present guarantee of actual, specific life to everything that constitutes the totality and unity of the world and the environment as the event of creation, and that keeps it continually present in experience of the world.

This unified and total event insures elemental meaning and value to all life; but this value and meaning is not at the disposal of the living thing itself. It is therefore the continual happening and experience of God's personal and powerful turning toward everything that lives. Seen in this perspective, therefore, experience of the natural world and of being alive becomes experience of God—experience of the power that is above the world and man, experience of what God can do and his goodness toward all life. Correspondingly, for Israel this event is only properly taken in when it is grasped as being the activity of God. This current life-conferring activity of God not only touches the actual gift of life for every living being, but also effects the continual and simultaneous gift of the endowments necessary for life. The fact that mountains stand, for example, or that the surface of the earth is stable or that vegetation continually springs up in the rhythm of the seasons is not a static finding. Because these things imply the equipment for living conferred on specific life, they are always a continual event that belongs to the miracle of the actual gift of life itself. In order to make clear this fact that the living actually find themselves now and at all times endowed with the necessary preconditions necessary if life is to be lived, the creation statements say that the whole elemental equipment for life in the natural world, not only every specific life, is created, made, founded, and commanded by God, and is founded on the acts of his will. The fact that the phenomena of the natural world and environment essential for life, and also the actual life of the living, are created by God is therefore a perception of the ground of experience to which personal experience of life corresponds. Seeing the natural world and environment as God's creation therefore means seeing it within an existential view of the world, in the context of the miracle of actually being alive oneself, and the equal miracle of other things' being alive too. This is the gift conferred on life in a continual event—an event that life never ceases to need and on which it is continually dependent.

In view of this, it is not difficult to understand why Israel was unable to use general terms like "world," "nature," and "cosmos." It did not merely avoid them because its language and thinking were limited. It avoided them for factual reasons. For these concepts represent a way of looking at things that objectifies and stands over against neutral, self-contained, total spheres, with inherent laws that hold them together,[40] and whose imminent and recognizable order would then have divine quality.[41] But this would mean screening off what is really the essential thing about the creation perspective. There the phenomena of the natural world and environment have to be seen in connection with the specific living thing and the fact of its being alive, and have to be seen, moreover, as an event and gift continually bestowed as the fulfillment of a will which is ceaselessly turned toward life. "The world was for (Israel) a ceaselessly sustaining divine activity which gave life its temporal span."[42] Significantly, Israel clung to this actual experience of the link-up between God, the world, nature, and life as a coherent event, even when it wanted to sum up the whole of the created world conceptually. The notion that the world's character is one of action and event is inherent in terms like "God's works" or "God's creations," just as much as it is behind the phrase "heaven and earth"[43] or even (in exilic and postexilic texts) "the universe, everything."[44] These words crop up in the framework of statements about actions involving creative activity. Von Rad accordingly stresses that

Creation is, in an ontological sense, something other than "world" in so far as it is, for the man who observes it, not a neutral object whose "meaning," whose advantages and disadvantages he could contemplate from the standpoint of an observer.[45]

In the statements Israel made about creation, therefore, the natural world and environment do not confront man as neutral spheres, in which man—and no one else—has to intervene formatively, in accordance with his own aims, to give them any meaning or value. In what Israel says about creation, on the contrary, man is completely included in the continual event of God's gift of life and the equipment for life, which as such bears within itself the meaning and value of the chance to live conferred by God. That is why it is very good, as the Priestly Writing says, "very good" meaning serviceable for life, reliable and absolutely trustworthy.[46] That is to say, under the perspective of the creation that makes life possible, which precedes and is at the bottom of all human formative activity, the world of life always has this quality. And this quality obtains in whatever is fore-given to actual human behavior; but this quality is not similarly present in man's shaping of life and of the world; for this activity is outside the perspective of creation, and tries to grasp the foundations which are not at man's disposal at all. The counter-picture of the creation statements is, accordingly, not the world man makes himself, but a world of phenomena that is not (or not yet) completely governed by the divine event of conferring life: i.e., chaos, that which has no meaning or utility for life, that which is unserviceable, as for example, an earth covered with water, as Psalm 104 describes it, or the state reported in Genesis 1–2.[47] In the process of creation that chaos is changed into what promotes life. It is changed once and for all, or again and again in the present, and loses its threatening quality.

f. The creation of the world and the scientific view

After these closer definitions, what we maintained at the beginning of this section would seem to be justified: a modern, scientific view of the world and the environment differs in its very approach and perspective from the Old Testament view, with its perception of creation.

In the questions and definitions of both classical and modern science (if we take the relativity of the questions and their dependency on their own time into account), the very aspects of the natural world and environment that are fundamental to the creation statements are ignored altogether: their existential perception of the connection between the world and life, including the inquiring man or woman, and their perception and adherence to the fundamental experience of a total and temporal conferring of the world on behalf of the elemental and actual existence of living things. We have already pointed out this difference from our present situation in the introduction, drawing on the work of Klaus Müller, Günter Altner, and Christian Link.

The relations between these two views—the natural world and environment, seen scientifically on the one hand, and as creation on the other—is not the relation between demonstrable knowledge and faith without reality, though this is the way it is often simplified. For although it is easy to push them aside in modern times, the creation statements, as we have seen, undoubtedly take their bearings from real and lasting experience. They consider the personal experience of the living thing in a fore-ordained world, which promotes life as an elemental and meaningful event, and they raise the question of its foundation. It is therefore true to say that modern science has ceased to have the same way of looking at the facts as the creation statements. The creation viewpoint has been forced out into the private and aesthetic field, where it is a matter of personal choice.[48] But in spite of this, the statements about creation are quite capable of absorbing the knowledge of nature open to inquiry by reason, although they absorb this information into their own perspective and go far beyond it. The biblical statements about creation already include all the science that was known at the time (the later the texts, the more the information): astronomical and meteorological phenomena, geography, botany, zoology and the processes of reproduction.

And in addition, there are highly rational regulations about the necessary stages in the building up of the world, information about the cosmos, the world's structure and statics, and so on. We have indicated this in connection with Psalm 104 and Genesis 1. The examples that could be drawn from ancient oriental texts, the Psalms, Job, the Proverbs, but also from later Wisdom literature and apocalyptic, are legion. Wisdom especially was concerned with recognitions of this kind.[49] This knowledge is by no means simply parallel to the statements about creation, let alone in opposition to them. It can and must be integrated, because the known phenomena, correlations, rules, and orders, though not indeed themselves divine, are also created by God, since they continually promote life, also in the present (as the personal experience of life-as-happening sees), and so have their function and meaning within the perspective of the world as creation. It is only in this framework that the real place, meaning, and value of knowledge of nature emerges.

If we want to give further distinctness to this fact, in consideration of our modern scientific knowledge, we shall have to differentiate. Because the creation texts start from the present world as it has always been, and focus only on the phenomena of the world as it is seen in life-promoting, nondisposable form, they perceive God the creator as the ground of their being. The processes and laws inherent in the world of life, as defined by modern science, are quite unknown in these ancient texts; and so is the slow and extended genesis of the cosmic, geological, and biological phenomena that first led to the world we see. This means that as regards their state of knowledge—the knowledge of nature accessible to reason—they are inferior to our present state of knowledge today; and they introduce God the creator into the process at too late a point, so to speak, i.e., only into the world of life as we see it.

Then according to what we know today, would God have to be brought into action much earlier for the statements about creation to be "correct"? Must he be predated, as it were, simply put back as "First Cause" or "Prime Mover" to the beginnings of anonymous genetic processes of development, with the laws that determine the world as we see it? According to everything we have seen—if it is permissible to draw such conclusions here for the moment—the Old Testament statements would categorically deny this. For according to their intention, the statements cannot be absorbed into quasi-scientific causal or genetic viewpoints, even though they are far from opposed to the possibility of this kind of viewpoint or to inquiry in principle. But they would criticize the striking deficiency of experience in such a scientific explanation of the world, when it exalts itself into being the sole truth that does justice to reality. They would urge that the inescapable elemental experience of life and the world of life is a nondisposable and continual happening that has meaning and value; an experience that must be absorbed into the statements telling us that it is God who creates, makes, and commands life and the world's fore-given phenomena essential for life. They would consequently describe all the phenomena of the natural world and environment that promote life as God's creation, and this would include all the details of their scientific evolutions. Nor would it exclude the long-term processes of development that build up to the picture of the natural world as we see it. The biblical statements about creation would accordingly regard a picture of the world dominated entirely by science as a gross curtailment of the real world of life.

The statements that God made or created this and that, or decreed it at creation, have, therefore, by no means a merely historical claim on reality, based on the ancient world's deficient knowledge and its religion—conceptions we have long since been able to transform and resolve into scientific insights. Their claim on reality is the experience, which is excluded by science, the experience of the meaningfulness of the life insured for all the living, which is a continual event taking place in the totality of the natural world and environment. Creation therefore does not merely take place, either in the existential sphere or in the cohesion of laws and contingency, chance and plan.[50] It is an event which revealed quite different characteristics in the natural world and environment to Israel: creation's self-testimony to the mystery governing it, in spite of all rational will to knowledge, and the wisdom intrinsic to it. Gerhard von Rad's investigations[51] have shown that it was Israel's "Wisdom" which thought about these things particularly.

g. The natural world and environment as creation in the beginning

We have attempted to give a closer definition of the view of the natural world and environment as creation, in light of our scientific knowledge; and the same definition may also be said to apply to the statements about creation that limit the divine creative activity in part (e.g., Psalm 104:5-9, 19) or as a whole (Gen. 1; also Gen. 2–3) to a fundamental initial period (which in Gen. 1–3 is prior to the history of Israel). For here too the question being asked is not concerned with the beginnings of the world and mankind in a strictly historical and unique sense. Successive genetic processes are not being defined in the light of their origin, nor is the development of the prototypes of particular world phenomena being fixed, as would be the case if this were a scientific, genetic approach. H. H. Schmid rightly says in this connection: "A consistent 'protological' understanding of creation is really only possible in the framework of what is in actual fact a sense of history; and we cannot presuppose that this existed in either the Ancient East or in the Old Testament."[52] Anyone who wants to understand the Bible's way of talking about the creation of the natural world and environment as an event "in the beginning" must therefore clear his mind of our historical questions about the initial beginnings of something, and must get away from scientific definitions of the evolutionary processes, genetic series, and processes of development which have finally led to the existence of natural phenomena as we see them. The mental position and way of looking at things that lead the Bible to talk about "the beginning" are different in kind.

Here we must notice above all (and Claus Westermann particularly has brought this out[53]) that this creative event "in the beginning" stands in the framework of an account of primeval history whose particular character we have already met with in considering that of the Yahwist and the account in the Priestly Writing. These descriptions of primeval history are not detached from the present and the world as we see it. They are not reaching out toward the beginning of things at certain historical points in time, by way of quasi-scientific genetic information about the origin of the natural world and its sequence of causes. What they are trying to do is rather to look back from the standpoint of the present[54] and, remaining on that basis, to grasp the guarantees of fundamental conditions that are still valid in the present world, and that have always been valid. The dominating interest of the creation statements "in the beginning" is therefore, in this method of narrative, to state the deeper dimension of the present world of experience, as it has existed from the beginning of time, and to expose the gift of these always-present, fundamental circumstances and conditions that guarantee life and have always been valid for the world and for man as a whole. Anyone who talks about the beginning of the world in the biblical sense is not simply fixing the causes of development and genetic processes and their impulses; he is asking about the origin of the present world as we see it; about an origin that already prescribes the vitally necessary whole, continuously present from the beginning of time, which represents the act of the deliberate conferring of what has been fore-given from time's beinning in the world as we see it and which is not at man's disposal. Anyone who talks biblically about "the beginning" is saying that he, like the whole world of life and the whole temporal existence of this world, derives from a permanently present, enduringly efficacious and experiencable origin,[55] in which this world, which is not at the living thing's disposal, is conferred.

That is to say, the biblical "beginning" is not a historical point in time that provides the initial datum, genetically speaking. Rather, this beginning means the event on which the specific world of life has been based as long as it has existed, i.e., that which living things today, from time immemorial, and in the future will never be able to create for themselves, but which is always fore-given, and given with existence. Christian Link makes the point excellently. "When we ask about the experience of creation, we are not asking about the date when the world began, but about something existing, something present, which through its presence creates its own recognition and validity."[56]

In these texts, therefore, Israel starts from its own historical position, perceives the event of the granting of its own and other life as an event existing since there has been life at all, and presents this, as it were retrospectively, as primal and initial event, on the basis of the experience of God and the world acquired in the present. And it does this in order to express what is fore-given and fundamental to all experience. To grasp creation as primal and initial event therefore means seeking for the given and always valid constituents of the present experienced world in its origin and foundation.

The seven-day event of creation in Genesis 1 is to be seen in this framework also. The seven days are not mentioned in the text simply because the Priestly Writing, in its ancient ignorance, thought of enormous periods of development as occurring genetically in these absurdly brief periods of time. They are there because an essential regulation of Israel's life, the sabbatical week—six days and the sabbath—was already grounded on the initial order of divine creative activity.[57] *P* is interested in the meaningful orders of the world of life, not in genetic derivations.

Of course, for Israel our scientific questions about cosmic and biogenetic processes and causes are also implicitly answered in these versions of creation as primal and initial event, although Israel did not put these questions in that form and did not have the "conflicting" scientific knowledge. But we must stress yet again that even though our scientifically based world picture today appears to be much more differentiated, and is very different in approach, the question about the founding and characterizing beginnings in which experienced life is conferred, with its elemental, life-promoting equipment, comprehends all the differentiations and changes in man's knowledge of nature, as does the answer to that question in the statements about creation. Indeed all natural science and all individual scientific research needs this viewpoint of fundamental and characterizing beginnings, which include the whole for all succeeding time. Science needs this because it is only in this way that the ordained, meaningful character, which has always been the foundation of all actual life ever since the beginning of time, can be grasped.

Finally, let me make one practical observation. Anyone who tries to make these Old Testament creation texts comprehensible must convey their particular approach and perspective. He must avoid a quasi-scientific misunderstanding of them on the one hand, and simple-minded apologetics on the other; for in their intention these statements are completely open for changing scientific insights. In illustrating the Bible and picture books about the Bible, and in preaching and teaching above all, the interpreter must avoid presenting these statements quasi-historically, like someone looking over the creator's shoulder "in the beginning," to see how everything was made. On the contrary, he must begin with present experience—the experience that for me (and for all living things since time began) life is not mere potentiality, but reality with the capacity for joy, a reality not at man's disposal. From here he must go on to the foundation of this experience, in which God the creator turns toward life, thereby comprehending all modern insights into biogenetics and the cosmos.

h. The framework and the unique character of the Old Testament statements about creation

The statements about creation concentrate on the fundamental fact, the elemental being-alive of the living thing, and its endowment with the essentials of life. Therefore, they see life, beyond biological survival, as a reality that is elementally capable of giving joy and that has meaning and value. But they are not closed to other positive fundamental conditions of human living, or to negative ones. As we have seen, the Yahwist's radius already reaches well beyond the statements about creation, and the same may be said of the Priestly Writing's primeval history. What God bestows in the natural world, in accordance with creation, is seen in close correspondence to God's equivalent gifts in the political and legal spheres of the social order and the conduct of life. (H. H. Schmid especially has recently developed this express aspect.[58]) The theological conceptions of the Jerusalem cultic traditions show this relation quite clearly in the psalms dealing with Zion, with the sovereignty of God and the king, and with the individual.[59] And Israel's Wisdom also gave serious consideration to this complex. The same Wisdom that characterizes creation also rules the field of human life in society, calling man to fulfilled, meaningful life in accordance with its moral and social orders.[60]

In this section we have concentrated on the approach and perspective of the Old Testament statements that see the natural world and environment as a creative event and are therefore in contrast to the interpretation of the world prevalent today, which takes its stamp from the natural sciences. Because this creation perspective has become so alien and has been pushed out to such an extent, we had to devote considerable space to a description of its basic features. The difficulties and differentiations, and the particular character of this viewpoint in Old Testament Wisdom especially, had to remain undiscussed; but the reader is recommended to read a late and masterly work by Gerhard von Rad, *Wisdom in Israel*.[61] In another respect, however, we have said too little about specifically Old Testament findings. The approach and perspective which point to the assertion of creation are unlike the modern viewpoint; but they are common to the Old Testament and the Ancient East, and are shared by other civilizations as well;[62] and this is an indication of the fact that here a fundamental experience in man's empirical dealings with life and the world is being expressed. What is peculiar to the Old Testament is merely the fact that Israel makes these statements about their ancestral God, Yahweh, who is the sole object of their worship, who confers the world of life and yet transcends it (and this is something which no longer by any means conveys anything to people as a whole). This is therefore a view of the natural world and environment as creation which is not prepared to put up with any dualism, which bans all chaotic "divinely" present counter-powers[63] and sets free a "natural" world governed throughout by Yahweh.[64] That is the reason for the rejection of all pantheistic interpretations of the world, which are extrapolations of life's value and nature's powers. For Yahweh is also the Will which can intervene in life, or diminish or end it.[65] That is why for Israel the view of the world as creation by no means excludes those features that threaten life, since Yahweh is not merely the power underlying positive personal experience, but is also the sole transcendent power underlying the whole world, a power that creates life and also puts an end to it.

Finally, because Israel talks about its ancestral God, who is experienced in its history and to whom its traditions testify as being the creator of the world and all life, creation cannot be a mythical event. It is a process in time, which is linked with Israel's history and includes it, which finds its appropriate form in the hymn of praise and thanksgiving. Christian Link puts it very well:

> For this is what distinguishes thanksgiving and praise . . . from all other forms of human perception: the fact that here we simultaneously experience how what is given to us as a gift ("made possible") can never be "established" by us as mere fact or clung to as something that is "established." Here we can neither claim anything nor, in thanksgiving, can we maintain our own rights. Anyone who thanks puts himself out of his own power, as it were. He no longer experiences being as firmly established positiveness but as an unfathomable, incomprehensible miracle.[66]

But we shall have to look more closely at the specifically Old Testament view of the creative event in our fifth section.

i. Summing up

The creation statements of the Old Testament express a view of the natural world and environment which, instead of dividing nature, as a neutral sphere, from questioning and formative man with his aims and goals, grasps nature and man throughout, from the very beginning, as being a total cohesion. This cohesion becomes visible in the perception of what seem all too easily to be matters of course but which are really highly realistic fundamentals, revealed when we consider the fact that we and everything else actually live and possess the elemental equipment for living, which is not at our own disposal. Like actual existence itself, the natural world and environment, which equips life for living, shows itself to be an experience (never at the disposal of the living thing itself) of God's mighty acts of bestowal as he confers life in the event of creation. Here the natural world and existence are absorbed into a single perspective which, with the preeminent experience "life," sustains that which cannot be made and that which does not come about inevitably as a result of the immanent necessity of law; but which, in all experience with life, is dependent on the realization of life that has been granted and which is always bestowed and given with life itself. This event, which includes the world that equips life and all living things, is consequently the event of God's gift. It is not contrary to knowledge and research, which change, but includes them. Creation is the natural world and environment, together with all life as the continual miracle of the natural insofar as it is given, happens, becomes reality for me and for other living things. We moderns view the natural world and environment primarily as the object of human action. Consequently the Creator hides himself, and the viewpoint of creation is pushed out, in spite of its elemental roots in experience. Israel, on the other hand, first of all perceived the bestowing hand offering and preserving the life that was not at its own disposal. Consequently it saw creation as a perspective valid for all time, a quality that belongs to the world and all life, springing from the activity of the Creator. The world as creation is the perception of a primal and fundamental totality. On the basis of the personal experience of human life's dependency, man and the natural world are seen in a primal unity which includes both. This unity reveals itself as the act of the divine gift of life. In the process of the creation event it points man and nature to a common future. Because the basic value, life, is realized for all living things in the event of creation, man—since he is included in the totality of the creative process—is directed from the very beginning to a given, overriding divine order of significance that is neither confined to man, nor takes place simply for his sake, but extends to all living things.

Although the Old Testament developed this view before modern scientific knowledge and the industrial exploitation of the world, there is no question but that we have here a perspective which has not simply been superseded by the circumstances of modern times. In its elemental relation to experience it is worth thinking about at the very point where man's present experience with his scientifically and technically exploited world (which has been so dangerously modified) brings him face to face again with the questions of the unity and totality of nature and man, their common cohesion or complex of life, and the values and limits that are fore-given. Here the Old Testament findings offer themselves as a basis for further self-critical thinking about our present situation, as we described it in the introduction, in our first basic question.

3. The Natural World and Environment and What Is Known of It in the World Picture

We have said that the Old Testament perspective, which perceives the natural world and environment (including man) as creative event, draws our attention to a grave deficiency in our modern attitude, a deficiency that is threatening us in the form of a survival crisis. But in that case the unique character of the perception of the world reflected in the creation statements calls for special attention. That is to say, we must consider the total picture of the natural world and environment perceived here, and the epistemological character of this perception of the world. For, as we saw at the beginning, the present discussion has defined the central problem of today's crisis as lying precisely in this basic attitude to the perception of the world and the environment. This discussion has criticized what we are accustomed to as a matter of course in modern times: our way of assessing the reality of the natural world and environment simply on the basis of the facts supplied by the scientific way of arriving at knowledge, and the possibilities of exploitation suggested by our awareness of how to act in technological and industrial affairs. That is to say, we see reality as part of a scientific and technological world picture, which—although it falls apart into so many individual images and features of unimaginable processes and developments that it is unsurvey-able—is seemingly the only one with the quality of scientific demonstrability on its side. In an attempt to control the crisis, the present discussion has linked this criticism to the question of an overriding perception of the natural world and environment in which nature and man are not divided as a matter of principle, but are linked together in a total and elemental sense, in a changed attitude toward the perception and picture of the natural world, which certainly includes the partial knowledge of science. We discussed this aspect of the present discussion in more detail in the introduction, in the second of our basic questions.

Accordingly, we shall now follow up the question about the view of the natural world and environment found in the Old Testament statements about creation as this touches on ways of perception—the perception which leads to knowledge. Active perception will be the subject of the sixth section.

a. The natural world and environment in the world picture of creation

Amused and superior, we can read today the reconstructions of the ancient cosmic picture that have been put together by historians with the help of ancient oriental evidence, as well as the statements of the Old Testament.[67] We notice their closeness to our own, prescientific ideas, which start from the position of man and the earth suggested by our senses, the result being a surveyable, limited pictorial view of the universe, with two or three storeys.[68] At the same time we notice how remote this picture is and how inferior compared with the features of our modern view, set up on the basis of scientific reasoning. This modern concept has nothing in common with that ancient world picture, which is also represented in the Old Testament creation statements. In our modern scheme, the earth and man are no longer the center and point of reference of cosmic phenomena. Our view is, on the contrary, "characterized by three absolutes: the infinity of space, the infinity of time, and the unbroken causal determination of natural events. The idea of a divine power which gives and determines meaning is pushed aside in favor of a view of nature as a whole which unfolds itself in causally determined processes."[69] "It seems to be man's task to get to know the structures and causally determined processes and to acquire this knowledge for the sake of dominating nature."[70] This difference is not affected by the fact that, in the wake of insights derived from the relativity and quantum theories, the scientific world picture can no longer be judged as being an objective picture of nature's reality; it represents merely a partial aspect, an extract, a historical and hypothetical interpretation that cannot be separated from the questioning and modifying subject. This is frequently stressed by scientists and has recently been summarily described by Joachim Track, among others.[71] It is true that as far as the state of scientific knowledge is concerned, the difference and superiority of our modern view is undeniable; the progress of knowledge is a matter of course; ancient notions about the genesis and form of the world picture have been superseded—though this does not mean that scientific insights could not be interpreted in terms of a theology of creation, as Wolfhart Pannenberg's reflections show.[72]

But in saying this—and today only fruitless biblicistic apologetics would have any reason to deny it—the meaning and truth of the ancient oriental and Old Testament world picture is by no means a closed chapter. Take the insights about ancient oriental concepts of the world that we find in the miscellancy *Frühlicht des Geistes*,[73] or recently in Stadelmann,[74] or—lavishly illustrated—in Othmar Keel,[75] as well as the—nonpictorial—Old Testament statements. If we put these beside modern reconstructions of these world pictures, we arrive at an important discovery. These reconstructions are themselves nothing other than "modern" curtailments, quasi-scientific descriptions of the ancient oriental world. Like the scientific picture of the world, they confront the world from a position outside it, like some static power; and it must be added that even modern insight into the relativity of this position has not led to a change of position. It has merely brought out the hypothetical quality of such pictures of the world, thereby excluding what is really the essential thing.

Keel especially[76] has quite rightly criticized these modern reconstructions. He has pointed out that the figures of the gods are to be found within the ancient oriental descriptions of the world, while cosmogonic texts also contain statements about God. Keel shows that these word pictures themselves, with their openness for various biological insights and ideas, have a far more comprehensive viewpoint than the reconstructions; for they take in the foundation, which is not at man's disposal, and thanks to which the world—always seen as a gift—allows itself to be experienced, always and in the present, as a stable and secure space for living. What is described here is therefore not something seen from outside, as an object, but an encompassing, experienced world. Not a world that can continually be repeated in constant laws and regularities, but the world than continually happens in the present. Not a neutral world that man first of all dominates and shapes in knowledge of its laws, but a world that in itself promotes meaning and value, that turns toward man, in his elemental dependency, instability, and with everything that promotes life.

Hartmut Gese has rightly pointed out how important and how permanently necessary this ancient world picture is, because it is the picture of the world communicated by human perception, a picture close to life itself. It is hence irreplaceable, if man's life in his world is to be lived fully and totally.[77] This world picture is not directed toward everything; it concentrates on what is elementally relevant in the world of life. It is a world that can be viewed as a whole, not out of naive ignorance, but because this viewpoint concentrates on what is graphically orienting and fundamentally essential—the natural world of our own, and of all, living existence. The natural world needs divine power, not only to be possible as a world that is stable and promotes life (because it is based on complexes of laws), but in order actually to happen, continually and in the present. This is what these accounts of the world express in picture or word. If we wanted to set against this a corresponding picture painted by modern men and women, then it would not only have to be the scientific world picture; it would have to be a picture of the world which attributes the general conditions of the world of life to natural laws and considers the world as favorable to life because it is at man's disposal. It would be a radically curtailed account, with all the dangerous results we see today.

The question about the world picture brings us, in the nature of things, to the same facts that emerged from the previous section. Notwithstanding their irreversible inferiority, scientifically speaking, as regards their knowledge of particular things, the ancient oriental and Old Testament statements about the world, with their graphically vivid ideas about the universe—have the advantage of us in a way that we have not yet made good and that has been positively suppressed. For these early world pictures are by implication opposed to the sole domination of our scientific and technological viewpoint. This criticism does not aim at reintroducing an ancient world picture in modern times, an attempt which would be quite illusory.[78] Its approach is based on a unique, realistic, total attitude toward reality that is screened out in the modern world and that is connected with a characteristic turn of mind where knowledge of the world is concerned. We must turn our attention to this in the following passage.

b. Recognition of the natural world and environment as creation

The ancient oriental and the Old Testament statements (compared with modern ones) are linked first of all by their different starting point in getting to know the world. In them, proved knowledge does not come about in the modern manner where man starts from the laws of his own autonomous thinking, uses them to put questions to a natural world that stands over against him as object, and thereby arrives at laws, structures, and processes until—at least in viewpoint or hypothetically—he comes to know nature by excluding whatever is individual, whatever is nondisposable as event, whatever is unique, and whatever belongs to the particular historical situation. With this knowledge he can go on equally autonomously to subject this nature to his own purposes.

The way the creation texts come to know the natural world, on the contrary, is fundamentally different, for there these presuppositions—presuppositions which are excluded today and which "belong to the blind spot which none of our sciences is able to see because of their own perspective"[79]—provide the determining starting point. Their fundamental experience can never be expressed in abstract terms, for it is the experience that actual, specific life is never granted to man or to other living things except in a way over which man has no disposal; and that the natural world and environment is no less a nondisposable endowment making it possible to live this actual, specific life at all. This means that cognition always takes place in a determining and permanent framework: the framework of the elemental experience of dependency, which is always deliberately kept in mind and which gives the name of "world" to the reality of one's own and other life, and to the specific equipment of life bestowed on oneself and others. Here the mind is continually conscious of what always accompanies human knowledge as its specific presupposition. Here the situation of the person who desires to know is not excluded. Here the inquirer does not assume an outsider's position over against nature. For here, it is held that the knowing person always encounters the natural world which is to be known, deals with it, participates in it, is affected by it, is included in it as life-conferring event, and is encompassed by its movement toward all actual living things—a movement that insures life. Here, therefore, what the natural world and environment really is can never simply emerge from an external perspective, which views and orders something that is given but is neutral toward man, and confronts him. It can never emerge merely out of empirical data and structural laws; never simply out of man's autonomous exploitation of the world as something to be used for his own purposes. On the contrary, knowledge of the world is encompassed by, and takes its bearings from, experience, one's personal experience of the life-insuring bestowal of the world. This experience is valid for all living things. And its result is that the world's phenomena can only be perceived in relationship to the knowing, living person. This relationship makes itself known only in encounter, and it cannot be pushed aside. As Link rightly puts it:

"Experience" and "thinking" cannot here simply be turned into methods of organizing freely selected (and hence workable) conditions. The sole point of both is simply *to allow* the world to appear under conditions—namely, conditions given by virtue of the very fact that man finds himself in a world that he has not designed and created. Really it is only in this recognition that Hebrew thinking—its "Wisdom"—is ahead of the Enlightenment. But it is sufficient to call fundamentally in question our modern Cartesian premises about the way in which we arrive at truth.[80]

Summing up, knowledge of the world according to the creation texts is based on the fundamental experience of the elemental fact that the natural event of the world, in the happening and fulfillment of actual life, is bestowed on the living. This is the experience to which the texts cling, and it extends to the whole of life. It rests on a way of dealing with the world that makes the receptive, existential situation of experience the foundation and framework of all cognition. Knowledge of the world, according to the creation texts, is therefore directed toward the phenomena of this world, which has from the beginning been turned toward life in this vitally relevant sense. And with this framework of experience, the inquirer asks about the foundation, the meaning, the order, and the goal of life and about the phenomena relevant for life—an event which is continually coming into being[81] and which is the fore-given condition for all human questioning.[82] In arriving at knowledge in this way, the questioner also arrives at statements about the divine creative activity, which allows the living—and the natural world for the sake of the living—to become reality.

Here, therefore, the goal of knowledge is not exhausted when the sectional and partial neutral laws and structural processes governing nature are understood; for within their framework man would have a completely free hand to form the world quite independently. The goal of knowledge is rather a more comprehensive one: to grasp the world phenomena, life processes, and orders that are bestowed on man as being in each case the actual, continual, contingent, nondisposable form which the processes of life assume—processes in which the knowing person himself participates. That is to say, this is the manifestation of the Creator's life-giving powers and the arrangements he has made for the purpose. This is a cognitive intercourse with one's own world, a cognition that perceives in it the ordained quality of creation, designed for the benefit of the living.

The reader who has followed all this will not fail to see that this kind of knowledge of the world does not merely encounter divine creative activity in the gaps that may be discovered in the objectively determined natural orders. We do not merely come upon creation at the beginning of cosmogonic, evolutionary processes. And it is not a matter of interpreting theologically, by means of some extravagant act of faith, that which has its quite natural scientific explanation. This knowledge of the world aims more comprehensively at dimension in depth, at the foundations of life's dependency, which we actually experience in the present. It seeks cognitively to find a reason for the reality that shows itself in our living dealings with the natural world as a whole, in all its vitally relevant phenomena. In other words, this knowledge of the world lays bare an elemental premise which affects—and affects permanently— the thinking of the knowing person in search of knowledge, before every act of cognition. Here faith and knowledge are a unity in the realization or achievement of experience;[83] so it is impossible in this framework to talk about the world in terms of knowledge without talking about it in terms of the divine creative activity.[84]

c. *The unique nature of the Old Testament's knowledge of the world*

What we tried to grasp here—and it was certainly by means of retrospective systematization—does not apply merely to the Old Testament understanding of the world. It is more or less true of all ancient oriental statements about the world, and of the statements about creation made in many religions; though this by no means reduces their critical energy and stimulating power in the problems of our situation. It is not difficult to see from these religious testimonies that their concept of the supporting foundation of the world of life in the event of creation is expressed in very varying forms—mythical, polytheistic, dualistic, and animistic.

Israel's understanding of the world shares the character of this ancient oriental approach, and also its development and goal. Yet it is characteristically different, as von Rad especially has shown in a series of investigations,[85] the last of which were directed toward the process and goal—as well as the accepted limits—of these attempts at knowledge in the thought world of Israel's Wisdom.[86]

What is important above all is the unique Israelite character of the starting point for achieving knowledge of the world. The fundamental experience is of a natural world turned toward the individual and all life, with power and the capacity to promote life, the actual event of being alive, with the equipment for life that is not at the disposal of the living. For Israel this basic experience is from the very beginning the

experience that comes from the side of its ancestral God
Yahweh, who alone is worshiped and who gives the vitally
relevant event of the natural world its individual stamp,
bringing it to event. This had serious consequences for the way
Israel came to know the world.

Consequently, Israel's knowledge of the world is by no
means without presuppositions.[87] It always starts from the one
God who was part of its experience of reality long before the
statements about creation, as von Rad has stressed several
times.[88] Israel therefore does not encounter Yahweh the
creator as the final conclusion drawn from the notion of a
transcendent foundation for the world of life and in the
framework of a completely rational will to know "as if there were
no God." There can be no question for Israel of knowledge of
Yahweh the creator for it is evident to reason and demonstrable
to every thinking person. A cosmological proof of the existence
of God is quite outside this kind of thinking.[89] It is true that
statements about Yahweh's creation of the world were not made
from the very beginning, but from the time when they existed
at all, they always already presuppose Israel's historical
experience with Yahweh and are primarily connected with that.
In presupposing Yahweh in its knowledge of the world,
however, Israel is not doing so in order to introduce the
premises of special events in exclusive fields of experience,
which are open *only* to faith, not to knowledge. Its purpose is to
seek the truth that proves itself in the real field of one's own
historical experience, and also in the extended field of one's
own historical experience, and also in the extended field of the
natural world existing for living things, which is presented in
the historical process. It is in this one factual and true reality
(which includes nature and history[90] and which is accessible to
every inquiry after knowledge) that Israel (bringing to bear its
experience of that reality) shows Yahweh to be the foundation
that guarantees its existence.[91]

Because Israel associates its own experience of the natural
world from the very beginning with the one God Yahweh, who
transcends the world, the whole field of knowledge of the world
presents itself in a unique way. On the basis of this approach,

knowledge of the world does not move in what is really a divinely penetrated sphere, one in which the objects of cognition are themselves divine phenomena and which compel people to an emanative, dualistic, or pantheistic interpretation and attitude. Israel's knowledge of the world belongs to a completely profane area of thought, especially in Wisdom. Here phenomena, and especially the phenomena of the natural world, can be inquired into with an objectivity that is in accordance with experience and perception. The wealth of individual biological facts included in the Old Testament creation texts is eloquent testimony of this. But von Rad rightly warns us against trying to rediscover our modern understanding of the world in this "spirituality which had detached itself radically from faith in mythical immanent powers . . ."

> This is a search for knowledge with which a keen rationality approached a demythologized world. But with this demythologization of the world, Israel only appeared to approach the modern understanding of the world, for to this radical secularization of the world there corresponded the idea of an equally radical domination of the world by Yahweh, that is the idea of the world as a creation of Yahweh.[92]

When Israel directed its will to knowledge toward the natural world and environment, in well-founded trust in Yahweh's creation of the world, then it was because of its unique approach

> Israel was of the opinion that effective knowledge about God is the only thing that puts a man into a right relationship with the objects of his perception, that it enables him to ask questions more pertinently; to take stock of relationships more effectively and generally to have a better awareness of circumstances. . . .[93]
>
> Faith does not—as is popularly believed today—hinder knowledge; on the contrary, it is what liberates knowledge, enables it really to come to the point and indicates to it its proper place in the sphere of varied, human activity. In Israel, the intellect never freed itself from or became independent of the foundations of its whole existence, that is its commitment to Yahweh.[94]

Where does a knowledge of the world that is bound up with Yahweh lead? Since it is directed toward Yahweh's governing power, which confers life and the world of life, it leads on the one hand to knowledge of the orders, connections, and relationships of the vitally relevant world phenomena. But these orders in the world of creation are not only the complexes of orders, neutral in meaning and value, which we call natural laws, meaning by this the conditions under which the natural happenings of the world can actually become event.[95] A misunderstanding of this kind would take us out of the existential, empirical framework of Israelite knowledge of the world. The orders in the world of creation that Israel traced in the process of achieving knowledge are very much more comprehensive, although, in terms of our modern perspective, they certainly include the natural laws that are the underlying conditions of physics and biology;[96] for in their reliability and validity they are perceived as institutions or regularities which the Creator has promulgated for the benefit of actual life in a world favorably equipped for living. Israel's knowledge of the world, therefore, does not here find itself confronted with neutral laws, which would undoubtedly be at the disposal of man's autonomous shaping of the world. What it finds in the world from the very beginning are ordering decrees, decrees of value and meaning, which insure the life that is fore-given and not at man's disposal. It is from these decrees that man's values take their bearings in insight, decision, and action. This is all the more the case since the orders related to the conduct of life, and which are perceived in Israelite Wisdom, are no different (see pp. 89, 147-48). To this extent Israel can say that a testimony to the Creator emanates from the world itself.[97]

But this is only one side of the matter. Israel's knowledge of the world is not directed solely toward conditions that make the world of life possible, but also toward the event of the granting of these conditions in actual experience. Consequently, it does not encounter only a lack of automatic, immanent necessity; to put it in other terms, it does not merely light upon the contingent, nondisposable occurrence of the coming-to-pass of a guarantee of this kind. It comes up equally against events that resist such an occurrence, detract from it, threaten it, or destroy it. As we have seen, Israel knew no dualistic way out. When it was faced with these features, it had to take them, consciously and in suffering, from the hand of the same God who as creator is active as the giver of life in the world.[98] This means that the recognized orders of the natural world always represent only a partial knowing. Beside the governing orders of Yahweh's stands his absolutely unlimited freedom of disposal in the granting of the world of life; and this is not the subject of fixed and demonstrable knowledge.

Wolfhart Pannenberg puts it as follows:

> For the people of Israel the God Yahweh was the true reality. Everything else, man and the world, had to be understood in the light of this God. That is the meaning of the Israelite belief in creation. The fact that God is the creator of the world does not only mean for Israel (as it did for Greek philosophy) that God is the hidden background of all things, standing unmoved behind them and manifesting himself in the unswervingly steadfast order of the world. On the contrary, the uniqueness of the biblical God is his freedom continually to produce something new, continually to intervene in unforeseen ways in the course of creation.[99]

Israel's knowledge of the world thus absorbs the dialectic of its experience of the world—the tension between knowable, partial orders and Yahweh's absolute power of disposal.[100] And in this way it sees itself, even in the field of the natural world that insures life, as being pointed to the encompassing mystery of God[101] and to the limits of human knowledge of the world.[102]

This unique character of Israel's knowledge of the natural world and environment makes it quite understandable (as von Rad has shown) that Israel should have been unable to talk about the world as a cosmos whose unalterable laws had a divine quality in themselves. And it was equally unable to talk about nature as a sphere which man sees as standing over against himself as we have already discussed. Knowledge of the world was for Israel the perception of the incalculable, nondisposable,

ordained event[103] of the life conferred (and also denied) by
Yahweh. To this extent it was a knowledge directed toward
given meaning and value, toward whatever promotes the life of
all actually living things—the features of the natural world
brought out in Psalm 104, Genesis 1, and the statements about
creation in Wisdom literature. In the wake of this knowledge
(which moves within the framework of personal experience of
the life that is dependent on Yahweh) the will to knowledge is
directed toward other living things too, toward their particular,
personally ordered gift of life and their equipment for living in
their own environment. It perceives all this, not as neutral,
natural phenomena, but as fore-given decrees of Yahweh's in
the coming-to-event of the natural world, imbued with
meaning and value. These decrees of meaning and value bind
and orient man's understanding and his formative activities in
the world (both in the experience of the life that is insured and
of the life that is threatened) and point man's understanding and
his formative activity to the mystery of Yahweh, which
comprehends all knowledge of the world derived from trust in
the Creator.

d. Israel's knowledge of the world and the present-day perception

It may seem a far cry from this description of Israel's
knowledge of the world and its world picture to the
fundamental epistemological problems of today's survival crisis
which we summed up at the beginning in our second basic
question. It is true that these Old Testament facts cover neither
the transformations that our modern consciousness has gone
through, nor the unguessed expansion of scientific knowledge
and formative activity, nor the picture of a world endangered by
scientific and technical domination. But in spite of all this, it
must make us pause when we remember what an important
part has been played in the recent discussions by precisely
these features of existential knowledge of the world, knowledge
always related to experience and the particular situation and
which sees the world as a temporal process in the framework of

a world-event turned toward life. The neglect of these features is seen as the essential reason for a dangerously truncated attitude toward the world on the part of man and is therefore held responsible for the survival crisis of our world; even as attempts are being made to overcome the scientific and technological perception of the world by way of critically constructive proposals for a comprehensive new orientation (see pp. 31 ff, 43 ff above).

As examples of this the reader may be reminded of the work of Klaus Müller (picking up the insights of Viktor and Carl Friedrich von Weizsäcker) in the second chapter of his book *Die präparierte Zeit*,[104] and in other publications,[105] where he stresses the dangerously narrowing effects of abstraction and scientific exclusion. We must also mention the writings of Christian Link and his new definitions of nature and the knowledge of nature (which he bases on Old Testament facts) in *The World as Parable*[106] and in his essay "The Experience of the World as Creation"[107] and finally G. Altner with his exemplary new definition of biological approaches.[108] It has been rightly stressed by Track that this contemporary state of affairs opens up the possibility and necessity of responsible discussion between science and theology. He also lays down guidelines for a dialogue of this kind.[109]

One insight is especially important, because it has been too little considered in the discussion. For the creation texts—according to everything we have seen—cognitive as well as formative perception of the world moves in a framework of meaning and value, based on experience, and fore-given by Yahweh to man and to all other living things. This framework is of essential importance when we consider the orientation of human behavior toward the world and environment. It is critically opposed to the autonomous exploitation (directed toward man's own purposes) of a world upon which man, like all other life, is always elementally dependent, and which he has not himself created. But we shall go into this in more detail in the following section.

4. The Gift of Life as the Basic Experience Which Gives Man His Bearings in His Perception of the Natural World and Environment

What we have said in the previous sections has shown that the statements about the divine creation of the natural world and environment in the Old Testament are not based on the perception of some special sphere of reality, which is only a certainty for faith and which lies beyond whatever is natural, reasonable, and open to general experience and to scientific inquiry and research. If this were the case, these statements would have no correspondence with man's experience in dealing with generally accessible reality. This may well be the situation and the dilemma of theological statements about creation today,[110] but in the Old Testament and even earlier in the Ancient East, things were different. As we have seen, the statements about creation speak of divine creative activity in the field of the natural world as we see it, the natural world accessible to reason, continually experienced, which satisfies the conditions of scientific laws. They talk about divine activity here in order to express the profound and fundamental dimension of this given world in all the wonder of its existence and its nondisposable elemental value (see pp. 128 ff). The fact that this is so—and this has already emerged—is connected with the particular framework of experience that always surrounds the perception of the one, natural, accessible reality in these statements. In this framework of experience, divine creative activity does not appear only as a conclusion drawn from "natural" knowledge of the world. On the contrary, this framework of experience is of such a kind that, on the basis of it, the one and whole natural world shows itself from the outset, from the beginning, to be a divine creation. Israel too did not merely introduce Yahweh into its experience of the world at a later stage, in the form of some retrospective interpretation. On the contrary, according to its determining field of experience, it saw Yahweh as being efficacious from the beginning in the sphere of the natural, accessible world; and it correspondingly perceived this world as his creative activity. We must first of all turn our attention to this framework of experience, which is related to the undistortedly natural, reasonable world and is open to general experience and investigation, and yet conscious of its character as Yahweh's creative event.

a. *Experience as the medium of a total encounter with the world*

If an approach by way of experience corresponds to Israel's view of the world and environment—if experience is the framework to which it is permanently related—then this means that a primal and direct plane of reception of the world is envisaged "which is given with the life of man in the world itself and which precedes every reflection."[111] That is to say, this is the level of a total, living relationship to the world, a level on which world and environment meet in totality and admit to an equal degree both the experience of the constant and the experience of the new. Experience in this sense grows up as life is lived, as a result of practical living in the "trans-scientific open-mindedness"[112] of concerned, encountering, self-involved dealings with the temporal event "world." Such dealing with the world is not afraid of entering into relationship, into dependency on what comes to meet it in experience—a dependency that is ready to learn.[113] This approach to reality based on experience is divorced from the special reservation of so-called "experiences of faith" by its unreserved and open relation to a generally accessible world. It is cut off from the frequently manipulated and maneuvered experiences of the modern world of the media by its relation to what is elementally evident to experience in the totality of its own life. And it is separated from the evidence of a scientific world's experience, which only grants the validity of the experience "acquired by treading a precisely statable path,"[114] because it avoids the exclusions that accompany such a view; and because it preserves the advantage that real perception of the world (which encounters that world in life as it is really lived) has over the curtailing and reducing experience of science. For "temporality and 'slovenliness' is the expression of real, concrete life; while the 'pure' truth conceived of in the eternal present of 'pure' timelessness reveals itself as the tragic illusion of Western philosophical reflection, which has had so mighty a historical influence."[115]

b. Life as fundamental experience

Now Israel's approach to experience, and the empirical framework of the creation statements, are not simply related to any and all experiences that can be had in the way we have mentioned. It is elemental experiences that are involved— those which emerge for man as being fundamental, ordained, and given simultaneously with all particular, individual experiences in dealing with the world. That is to say, these are experiences which show themselves to the reflective mind by way of many specific and individual involvements and through participation in the world of life as it is lived; experiences that lay bare the essentials of experiencing existence—for the individual, but for the existence of others as well—perceiving what always has been and always will be significant for existence, when it is existence at all. To be part of time, to be part of becoming and of passing away, could be called an elemental experience of this kind. What we mean, therefore, is what Eberhard Jüngel calls "an experience with experience,"[116] or following Track, we might call them "basic experiences" or "revealing experiences."[117]

The nature of the basic experience which gives Israel's approach (and its recorded framework of experience) its particular stamp as condensation and elemental foundation of its participation in the world, has already become clear in the texts we have considered and in the previous sections. Israel deduces first of all from its encounter with the world (considering the experiencing subject in the life he lives as elemental basic experience) the nondisposable, always fore-given miracle of living that is conferred with life itself. In addition it deduces the fact of being endowed with length of life, space for living, the means for food to sustain life, and the power of multiplying life. All these are things that actually precede human activity and are not at man's disposal either. The fact that all this happens—that it is a reality outside the scope of man's personal disposal—is the elemental, fundamental fact of one's own experience of life. It includes dependency, but in death and the threats to life it also includes, no less, the limits of man's own existence. It pegs out the space open for the active fulfillment of life. In this elemental experience of the nondisposable gift of life and its equally nondisposable withdrawal, the individual in Israel actively experienced Yahweh the creator as acting in the event of his life (Ps. 22:10; 71:5-6; 119:73; 139:13-15; Job 10:8ff; 33:4; 34:14-15; 35:10). Link stresses that in this connection "experience of creation is at heart the experience of being created oneself."[118]

This basic experience on the part of the individual, which takes up what is quite simply the most real aspect of his own life as he lives it and keeps it before him, is not confined to any particular individual, however. Its validity is perceived as applying just as much to other living things, whether man or beast, insofar as they live, have lived, or are going to live. According to this extended perspective, our basic experience is then logically related, in all-embracing temporal and spatial dimensions, to the whole natural world and environment with its living phenomena and also the nonliving ones that have any relevance for life. The natural world and environment reveals this basic experience on the part of Israel as the manifestation of the coming-into-being of a world of life that is beyond the disposal of the living thing itself, but in which living things and the indispensable world of life are continually bestowed by Yahweh himself. In the statements about creation, as well as in the wake of this fundamental experience, Israel gained its awareness of the most self-evident thing of all (something which is consequently all too easily suppressed but which, more than anything else, was really a matter of course for its orientation toward the world): the continual miracle that life and the world of life incessantly become what is in essentials a nondisposable event. Here Israel faced up to a fundamental datum of the experience of all living things; and it is certainly not by chance that in Israel statements about creation crop up only in direct or indirect relation to the problems of Wisdom.

> But the thinking of the wise men was never, from the very beginning, stimulated by signs of divine activity in history. Rather, they felt themselves stimulated above all by the much older question of humanity. In her practical wisdom, Israel was subject to the ancient stimulation of the world, that is, she asked one of the most elementary questions of human existence. She answered it in a way of which she felt capable, thanks to the particular form of her understanding of God and reality. [119]

Link may well be right when he maintains "that in the context of Wisdom especially, historical thinking reaches its most radical expansion, and pervades the natural *roots* of human existence." [120]

c. *The bearings and values conferred by the fundamental experience of life*

According to Israel's perspective of the world, the living man moves in this sphere of experience, one which was always sustained and kept in mind. Man could only ignore it at the cost of losing elemental reality. In this framework of the world experienced as Yahweh's creation, men and women are also from the very beginning given fundamental bearings for the conduct of life. Anyone who takes his bearings from these determining, fundamental experiences of his own life and the life of others does not align his interest in the natural world and environment simply toward everything in it that can be known and everything that can be done with it. He concentrates his interest on its quality as a world given to, and conferred upon, all the living. This is the primary and essential thing in his perception of the world, as we can see from the viewpoint and choice of subjects in the creation texts. Anyone who moves in this determining framework does not experience the natural world and environment of the living thing as a neutral sphere which man can unquestionably dispose in accordance with his own values and aims. Man's fundamental attitude to the world is different because he perceives the natural world and environment from the very beginning as a fore-given event with meaning and value, molded and stamped without any contribution of his, by the meaningful realization of the basic value life itself, in man's own existence as well as in the existence of all other living things with their elemental equipment for life. So it is understandable that within this framework of experience Israel can see no direct autocratic or exploitive relation between man and other living things (or the world's equipment for living). For other life, as for himself, man meets with the activity of Yahweh, which is not his to dispose. On the contrary, access to this happening has to be made possible and empowered by Yahweh, and this applies both to mental and spiritual dealings with the world[121] and to its active utilization for the purposes of life.

Keeping herds, tilling the ground, and eating vegetarian food, as well as killing animals to provide meat, must all have authorization given by Yahweh. The Creator of the world of life has to give express regulations about how to deal with blood, as the seat of life (Gen. 9:4), or with murderers, whether the destroyer of life is man or beast. For it is Yahweh who has life at his disposal, and he, the Creator of life, is the Lord who loves life (Wis. 11:26). Even the phenomena of nonliving nature are not excluded from this encounter wih the meaning and value of the world: they too are seen as phenomena in the framework of Yahweh's gift of life—mountains and the depths of the sea, cliffs and thickets, metals and minerals, all are qualified by their relevance for the living. The same may be said of the relationship between man and beast. In the framework of its formative basic experience, Israel perceives the fundamental and binding solidarity of the life granted by Yahweh—the ground shared even by man and beast alike, different though they are in their usefulness, their responsibility, and their capacity for hearing Yahweh's word. This makes it necessary for human dealings with animals to be authorized and regulated by Yahweh as well; it is not a matter for man's autocracy. This allows Israel to see animal life in the light of its elemental right to existence and its dependency on Yahweh's care (Ps. 104; Job

38–39; and elsewhere). In this context we should also remember the countless animal metaphors in both the Old and New Testaments; and we only have to read Psalm 23 to see what tender, intuitive sympathy for the needs of an animal belonging to the flock underlies the imagery of the text.

When we consider the character of Israel's basic experience with Yahweh on the elemental level of the individual life, it is impossible to estimate too highly its orienting power for determining the people's basic attitude toward the natural world and environment as a whole. It leads Israel to insights, evident to reality, with regard to man's limits and potentialities, which emerge from the framework of a world of life considered as a whole in space and time (and even in the future), a whole which the living themselves never created. It aligns life, as it is lived in knowledge and action, primarily and essentially toward an ordained meaning and value that Yahweh has from the very beginning built into the natural world and environment as the world of life. This is the finding of the Old Testament creation texts with regard to the third basic question of our essential conditions: Of what kind must man's experience of nature and of himself be, if man is to be aware of his vital link with nature and his position within the world and environment? What elemental content of experience must be laid bare if we are to achieve a broadly effective breakthrough and limitation of the subject-object confrontation between man and nature? In the theology of recent years the connection between experience and life, emphasized in this section in the context of the creation texts, has rightly come to the fore once more. The pioneer in reestablishing the connection was Gerhard Ebeling.[122]

d. Life and experience in the world of creation in the light of modern times

Here too, however, Israel's answer is not one that could be transferred directly into our contemporary world. A glance at the change in the point of departure shows this quickly enough. It is not only that the experience of life as basic value appears in a different light today, for many reasons; we have only to look at the actually existing and foreseeable overpopulation of the earth,[123] the manipulation and control of the genesis of new life, the high suicide statistics, and the extreme exhaustion of vitality in our modern industrial and bureaucratic world. The reciprocal relations between standard of living, population figures, limitation of living space and vital resources, and the potentialities for living in the natural world in accordance with the appropriate standard, are only derived from the problems of our modern society.

Consequently we have to note the conditions and qualitative determinations of meaning of Israel's basic experience of life as we find it reflected in the Old Testament. Israel's statements were made in the context of a society based largely on agricultural self-subsistence. Its vital resources were modest, but adequate for the population density, while requirements of minerals and raw materials were small in that preindustrial age. Accordingly, quite elemental conditions are in the foreground: undiminished, healthy living space as the equipment for life, which supplies the vital needs of the living—food, clothing, and shelter, and in addition a life-span reaching to a good old age, with numerous descendants.[124] The basic value "life" has an impress of this kind, based so closely on experience, when it includes a qualitatively satisfying and happy life, full of joy, not merely elemental survival. A sound order in the political and social world in which the person lives corresponds to this. So does conduct which is in accordance with the divine cohesion of order and value in the world of creation (and Wisdom aimed especially at the guidance and training for this proper conduct).[125] Vital power, free space to live in, justice, room for the development of life, externally and in the mind and heart, happiness, joy, respect on the part of one's fellows—all these things are accordingly named as tokens of a fulfilled life in Israel.[126] For Israel's particular kind of experience, the bestowal of elemental, natural equipment for living is fundamental in all this, and in this way it differs from the claims on life made by the modern world. At the same time, the fact that these elemental features stand at the center in such a determining way and give so decisive an impress to the perception of the natural world and environment as creative event, is not merely due to Israel's mainly agricultural world and its high degree of dependency on the natural world and environment, which were often a threat to existence. The importance of the elemental factors is connected above all with the fore-ordered meaning and value of the natural world and environment, as being the creation of Yahweh, the giver of all life. It was a value and meaning to which Israel did not shut its eyes. Consequently, Israel did not assign to the fulfilled life a position which over-reached the natural world in an autocratic, man-constructed standard of living, the achievement of which makes far-reaching interventions of man in an, in fact, insufficient natural world inevitable, and which leads to claims on that world that are today relativizing the world's creational equipment and increasingly veiling it from experience.

These differences between Old Testament and contemporary basic experience show how wide a gap we have to bridge theologically. But they do not diminish the importance of the elemental, Israelite approach, which starts from the experience of the miracle of being alive with all the equipment for living. Nor does it diminish the importance of the perspectives, meaning, and values which proceed from that approach—especially in a period when man's sole orientation toward a life successful by his standards is threatening to drive the natural world to its fundamental limits. Israel, at all events, molded as it was by the fundamental experience of conferred life, saw man and nature together. It did not see them in the framework of a world autonomously set up by man on his own behalf, but in the framework of an ordained quality of world which the creator bestows for the benefit of *all* life, and which is also the norm, measure, and limit of human dealings with the natural world. The next two sections will show this even more clearly on the basis of the creation texts.

5. Yahweh and the Natural World and Environment

Christian Link has written about our present situation:

> There is an experience which no one escapes: the era of "the death of *God*" has ended; what we are experiencing today is the death of the *man* who said, "God is dead." This death, which is threatening the foundations of human existence, because of the unrestrainedly exercised rule over nature (which has become simply an object) is revealing in a terrifying way the harsh truth of the methodical exclusion of God from the world of "knowledge."[127]

This insight coincides with the problem we came up against in the fourth basic question of our essential conditions: the problem of whether we could not replace our orientation toward autocratically determining and autonomous man—an orientation fraught with crisis—with overriding courts of appeal, foundations, values, and norms that would open up a way of escape from man's survival crisis. What is more obvious today than to find these things, the loss of which is so clearly felt in the crisis of our time, in the Old Testament's statements about God? For in these statements God is the quality proper to the natural world and environment; he offers the overriding standards that would secure the survival of the natural world of life because he is the criticism, limitation, and orientation of man, who is entangled in his own self-realization. That would mean interpreting the Old Testament's statements about God today as a cipher for the untouchable basic elements of the natural world. That would mean making Israel's statements about God in the creation texts plausible today as crystalliza-tions of the quality and content of meaning of the natural world. These crystallizations take precedence over all individual human interests, and even human interests in general, but they simply force themselves on anyone who considers the whole of the world of life rationally, if he draws the reasonable conclusions from the type of viewpoint, knowledge, and experience of the world which Israel points us to. Are Israel's statements about God in the creation texts, then, the exposition of what the world could be by itself if man allowed it, and the confirmatory expression of what a self-critical, reasonable human race, conscious of the crisis with which we are faced, must put a stop to if it wants to preserve the world's quality of life for itself and others, for the present and the future? Surely a majority, a consensus of opinion must be found here wherever people are reasonable and responsible?

Israel would emphatically reject this interpretation of the creation statements about Yahweh and his activity in the natural world and environment. It would not recognize Yahweh in modern judgments like these and would strip bare this way of looking at things as being the service of idols. It would do so because here Yahweh is being dealt with as if he were something deducible from our experience of the self and the world, out of forced consideration of the world's realities; because here Yahweh would be nothing other than part of the world itself, the projection of the quality which we desire and which is necessary for survival. But just because of that, the God of these reflections is not Yahweh as he revealed himself to Israel. [128] Link has rightly said in a theological interpretation of the prohibition of graven images: "The prohibition of images is therefore the criterion of theological talk about God, in the sense that it confronts the specific danger of every epoch, which is to form the concept of God according to the image of its own present and its needs and fashions."[129] This applies also to the ecological problems of our time and the need for survival. But how did Israel itself convey the relationship between Yahweh and the natural world and environment?

a. Yahweh—God, and not Israel's projective foundation

As numberless examples from the history of religion show, and also the very questions that weigh on us today, the creation statements about Yahweh's activity in the natural world and environment are undoubtedly related to a general human problem: the question about the foundation of a world as intact and unscathed as possible, a world favorable to life, which simply has not been put at man's disposal.[130] But statements about Yahweh still do not arise only out of an inner cogency, as it were, just because we are considering this problem in the light of the natural world, let alone in the context of a modern, secular perspective. Who Yahweh is was shown to Israel long before the people had taken in the sphere of the world, man, and all living things, because he had already been revealed in history, in the field of Israel's own history (see pp. 61ff, pp. 115ff, above). He was revealed, not simply as the demonstrable foundation of the positive needs of Israel's world, which were not within its own power, but as the one and sole giver of all the nondisposable happenings that determined Israel's existence—the elemental provisions for its life, its salvation and preservation on the one hand; but also whatever endangered and took away from it on the other. Even in its surrounding world, Israel saw itself as group and people, exposed to Yahweh as the sustaining event of its whole existence and as unconditionally dependent on him. It had therefore to talk about Yahweh's saving and life-insuring gifts as well as about what was unfathomable and incalculable in the experiences in which Yahweh showed himself in Israel's activities as the Hidden One. Israel did not see itself and its world in such a self-contained and surveyable way that it would have been able to define Yahweh as the projective foundation of that world.[131] It saw itself in its existence as exposed to a constant and unfinished event, reaching into the future as well as manifested in the past, in which everything essential must incalculably become event, because it is not at Israel's disposal but is fore-ordered and given together with its existence. Israel is completely dependent on the temporal and actual happening of everything essential—or on the absence or delay of these things. Israel is dependent on Yahweh, who himself leads the people in such experiences—in the guidance of Abraham as well as in Sarah's barrenness; in the deliverance from Egypt as well as in the privations in the wilderness; in the successful occupation of the Promised Land as well as in the menaces there; in his blessing on the fields, the fruits of the field, and the herds as well as in famine and necessity. From whatever period the Old Testament's statements may be dated, the First Commandment (which talks about Israel's exclusive worship of Yahweh[132]) and the Second Commandment (which forbids worshiping him in images[133]) express what was in fact the ancient and determining view of Yahweh in Israel; while the narrative traditions of Israel's history in its prenational period (which are related in the historical books of the Old Testament) are its early form. This perception of Yahweh revealed to Israel was of decisive importance before Israel laid itself open to the perspective of creation in its totality, and it was determinative for opening up this perspective as it is summed up in the Old Testament statements about creation. "The assumption that the Old Testament faith in Yahweh was also involved to a determining degree suggests itself from the very beginning."[134]

In this respect there should be a consensus of opinion, even in the present somewhat stereotyped, stylized controversy about whether the theological position of the Old Testament creation statements is to be defined in the light of Israel's experiences of salvation (von Rad's view) or in the light of the primal event which includes general elemental conditions (Westermann's opinion).[135] It cannot be denied that the creation statements reach beyond Israel's limited sphere of existence to the elemental plane of the conditions of all human life as a whole, as well as that of all living things; but it cannot be disputed either that this extension takes place as extension of Yahweh, who was known to Israel from its history and the events of that history. The texts we took as examples earlier showed us that the perception of Yahweh found in the primeval histories of the Yahwist and the Priestly Writing, as well as in the creation statements in the cultic poetry of the Psalms and Wisdom, presuppose, in their present form, the unique character in which Yahweh revealed himself to Israel before Israel extended its viewpoint to take in the whole world. We have only to think of the world view of the Yahwist's primeval history, which is so realistically ambivalent and which was intended to correspond to the universal viewpoint of Israel's salvation history;[136] or of the primeval history (and especially the creation account) in the Priestly Writing, in which the identity of God's activity in the universal sphere is measured against its correspondence to what he has done with Israel; or of the creation statements of a psalm like 104, with its Wisdom influence, which would be inconceivable in its present form without its attempt at bringing out the content of the First and Second Commandments. Describing Westermann's position ("creation as original event"), Link writes: "It is co-experienced in every experience—by all men, not only by the Israel of Old Testament history."[137] But this can be said of the Old Testament only in the sense of a general illumination of being, which Israel was given by Yahweh and promised by him; it cannot mean a statement accessible to all experience as such, independent of Yahweh's historical revelation to Israel.

If I see the matter correctly, there are two main problems about the relation between the creation statements and the statements that apply to Israel and its history.

On the one hand, what is the view taken of the relationship between Yahweh's universal activity in the natural world (with the divine activity that is related to all living things, including Israel) and the activity that is especially related to Israel? Here we find varying concepts, as we have already discussed. The Yahwist, the cultic theology centered on Jerusalem, and in its train, Wisdom and Deutero-Isaiah—each in its own way—gives to Yahweh's acts toward Israel creational dimensions which reach beyond Israel. The Priestly Writing makes the sphere of comprehensive, elemental order the basis, beside the specific regulations that order the relations between Yahweh and Israel. The Yahwist assigns the primeval history to the salvation history he is relating. Jerusalem cultic theology, on the other hand, makes Yahweh's manifesting acts of salvation for Israel part of the universal creative activity that sustains the world; and Wisdom (which expressly or implicitly presupposes the Jerusalem cultic conception) probably saw things in the same way. In both cases, however, the specific earlier forms of Israel's conception of Yahweh made themselves felt, and these prevented Israel's experiences of salvation from simply being integrated into an ancient oriental concept. Karl Barth's famous thesis about creation as the external foundation of the covenant and the covenant as the inner foundation of creation[138] would have to be discussed in the framework of this problem, in the light of the Old Testament facts.

The other problem, which we already touched on, has been critically raised in some important studies by H. H. Schmid, in which he disputes von Rad's view of how we are to define the relationship between the understanding of the world common to the ancient world as a whole, and the special, individual form it takes in Israel's concept of Yahweh.[139] Was Israel's special position already consolidated in the prenational period, thus influencing the people's absorption of ancient oriental creation themes? This was von Rad's view, and it is the one we are basically following here. Or does Israel's special character develop considerably later, and only gradually, out of a variety of the ancient oriental interpretations of the world, which Israel at first shared? This is H. H. Schmid's view.[140] This extremely important question can only be answered in detailed individual investigations of the development of the Old Testament's creation statements in the context of the history of religion. Here we must content ourselves with merely indicating the problem.

b. Yahweh—the God who transcends the world, and not the projective ground of an unscathed world

From the time when Israel became a nation, historical pressures and the inescapable confrontation with the civilizations surrounding it exposed Israel to the elemental world, no longer solely in the limited sphere of its own existence, but in the total sense that included all men and all living things on earth (see pp. 121ff above). In universal statements about creation Israel now laid itself open to the natural world and environment as a whole, as it was known at the time, though preserving the earlier character given to it by the proclamation of Yahweh in Israel's own, prenational history. Yahweh showed himself to Israel in this wider field in the same form in which he had already made himself known in the sphere of Israel's more limited historical experience, the form in which he was familiar to Israel. This had serious consequences for the definition of Yahweh's relationship to the natural world as Israel saw it. Let us consider this point in more detail.

As was the case with its more limited world, Israel did not see the field of the elemental natural world and environment, viewed as a wider whole, as something self-contained and surveyable, whose necessary orders and elemental gifts could be assigned a projective foundation in God, simply because they are outside the range of what is at man's disposal. The totality of the natural world and environment was also for Israel a continual event in time, reaching into the future. For that reason alone it was unfathomable and unpredictable. The essentials are not merely outside human disposal but have to come to event and are therefore, in both their occurrence and their absence, incalculable. Israel saw Yahweh's activity in the natural world and environment in this incalculable bringing-to-pass, or bringing-to-event, of what is not at man's disposal and yet is vitally essential. That is why for Israel Yahweh could neither be absorbed into the given orders of the natural world, nor into its calculable rhythms, though these were certainly not excluded from Yahweh's activity. On the contrary, the correspondence to the world's nondisposable temporality, seen through Yahweh's giving and withdrawal, shows Israel Yahweh's transcendence not only toward Israel itself, but toward the whole world as well. Yahweh's transcendence in the dependency of all things on the coming-to-event in time of the natural world and life cannot be surmounted in experience, knowledge, or any process of objectification. Its consistent expression for Israel is the prohibition of images. Von Rad showed that this was the real key to Israelite understanding of the world, [141] and it was recently emphatically included by Link in systematic theological discussions. [142] This transcendence of Yahweh's crystallizes into experience of the world, and yet is not totally absorbed by the world; and the Old Testament frequently expresses this transcendence over the natural world in its statements about creation as well as through its very avoidance of any attribution of divinity to the elements of the world of life—from the stars as "lights, lamps" (Gen. 1:14-18) down to Wisdom and the order it gives to life in the world— order being conceived as "a characteristic of the world, not a characteristic of God's."[143] It also expresses the divine transcendence in Yahweh's new, unexpected activity in the sphere of the natural world (even beyond his creative activity) in the form of manifestations and prophecies; and—from the Exile onward—in the proclamation of new creative activity as well. Israel sees itself exposed to the incalculable activity of Yahweh in the course of its history, and also in the realm of the natural world (which is itself in this way revealed in a historical sense). It knows that it must expect this also in the future, and realizes that in this way it is continually sustained and claimed by the activity of a transcendent Yahweh in its happy and unhappy experiences alike.

c. *Yahweh—the sole God of the natural world and environment*

Another factor is just as important. Israel accepted Yahweh as the one, exclusively worshiped God, and was shown this in Yahweh's revelation of himself through its historical experience. This revealed him to be the solely relevant God, who also had to be exclusively worshiped in the wider field of experience offered by the natural world and environment. Because of this, Yahweh also revealed himself to Israel as the sole, world-transcending God in the total world-event, both the political world and the natural one. The actual world of phenomena, with its riddles and abysses, is not a play of forces of different transcendent powers; even less are world phenomena themselves the emanations of different divine forces. The result was the view of a completely undemonized world, on the natural level, in which every numinous power of chaos is increasingly excluded. We can see this frequently in Yahweh's revelations to Israel in the Old Testament, especially through the prophets; and we have repeatedly seen the same thing in the creation texts. In a profane, "natural" world, man has to do with Yahweh and with Yahweh alone. This is Israel's experience of the "happening" of the natural world, its dependency on the experience and nature of the coming-into-being of its encounter with Yahweh, and with him only; for it is Yahweh who acts in the world, though he is not included in it.

Von Rad has pointed to two important results of this perception of Yahweh as he revealed himself to Israel in the world of nature. The world as the constant event of what is incalculable (because it comes from Yahweh) means encounter with the unexplorable, incalculable, which is only partially and incompletely conceivable through recognition of the various natural orders—Yahweh is free as regards these recognized orders too. Wisdom took the view that "to the extent, however, to which one was aware that God was at work behind the fixed orders, the world, too, which knowledge was endeavouring to control, was drawn into the sphere of the great mystery surrounding God."[144]

Rad writes in another place, the event of the world "much more within the sphere of the imponderable and immeasurable,"[445] and, "But she never found her way to the idea of a cosmos governed throughout by unchangeable laws. The process in which she found herself placed was too mysterious and too much a realm of the action of Jahweh for her to be able to do this."[146]

To this consequence drawn from Yahweh's transcendence of the world (a consequence which issues, so to speak, out of the Second Commandment, since this sets experience or knowledge of the world in the overriding framework of Yahweh's mystery and his hidden character in the world) is added the other result, drawn from the First Commandment. "Israel," von Rad writes, "naturally experienced also what was terrible and what was quite simply destructive, but she was unable to interpret this as being somehow independent, in some separate confrontation with Yahweh, or as being apart from him. She did not see it as something inherent in the world, which was at most kept within bounds by Yahweh. It was, on the contrary, part of Yahweh's direct action in the world. Israel, if one may so put it, paid a high price for her refusal to enter in any form into metaphysical dualism, for in the same degree to which she kept the world free from any internal divine strife or dualism, she imposed on her faith the burden of understanding and enduring this "dualism" as a phenomenon existing within God himself."[147] We may just add to this by saying that insofar as the antagonisms of the natural world are associated solely with Yahweh, and not with any counter divine power, human behavior toward Yahweh takes on the greatest importance. For what is unfavorable or painful in human experience of the world is not some fate imposed by some incalculable, arbitrarily acting god; it is connected with man's responsibility to Yahweh in the world.

d. Yahweh—revealed in the world, not deduced from it

We only have to put this Israelite perception of Yahweh drawn from the natural world beside the statements about the gods and the world made by Israel's neighbors in the Ancient East to see one thing immediately: to talk about Yahweh in this way in the context of the natural world is anything but a self-evident deduction which would be bound to be drawn, with inner cogency, so to speak, from every reasonable consideration of exierience of the world. The Old Testament's statements about Yahweh are not theoretical, analytical conclusions, even though they claim all-embracing validity. They are not deductions from natural experience, as it were. These statements had actually to be made *to* Israel, as the existence of the creation texts show. They are in their own sense *Yahweh's own revelations* about what is indeed experienced, what Israel—or man—does not know and cannot perceive by himself when he looks at the world. They are not demonstrable conclusions. Nor are they, even for Israel, deduced proposi-tions, drawn from the experience of history. They are proclamatory statements designed to guide Israel's experience with the world and to give it bearings. They had to be preserved by Israel in the pressing temptations of its environment, and they were intended to bring their critical, clarifying power to bear on Israel's view of the world, and on its knowledge and experience. What Israel knew about Yahweh it knew out of its experience of what Yahweh had bestowed on it. But this experience of what had happened to Israel in history, and in the universal sphere of the natural world, became evident to the people as the workings of Yahweh by means of God's proclamation of himself in his Word—that is to say in the Old Testament traditions.

e. *Yahweh's liberty in the natural world and environment*

In this section we have deliberately tried to describe fundamental features of Yahweh's relationship to the natural world and environment, without narrowing the world down to the world of creation. For this is the only way to show that Yahweh is by no means wholly absorbed by his relation to creation, and that therefore in the natural world, Israel not only encounters the Creator who confers life; it encounters Yahweh.

When Israel is shown the natural world and environment, including all the specific life it includes, as being Yahweh's creative acts, then the whole sphere only comprises one aspect of Yahweh's activity, as it were, which is that what is not at man's disposal and is already ordained and given with the event of actually being alive (together with the elemental equipment for all living things) is the act of Yahweh. It is Yahweh's activity, with the critical emphasis that in this event Yahweh alone is at work, for the benefit of life. The miracle of his constancy, his reliability, is bound up with this event, which grants the foundation of all existence. The accounts in the primeval history and those in the hymns and Wisdom all stress that this activity of Yahweh's has been valid since time immemorial, is valid now, and will also be valid in the future. In this way, they open up a perspective which has been tested by experience and is fundamental. And it is a perspective to which man and all living things can adapt themselves. It reduces the complexity of the natural world to its essentials—to the phenomena of the elemental gifts that make life possible. It also makes possible the confidence that living always needs. The creation statements, with their tested reliability, correspond to the promises of Yahweh, in which Israel saw its existence as guaranteed by him. This was the express reflective conclusion drawn by the Priestly Writing, as it worked out the identity between the signs of God's activity in the sphere of the world and in the sphere of Israel itself.

This reliability of the Creator's activities demands trust. But in spite of that, Israel was enjoined not to include Yahweh in this activity. Here too it had to expose itself to his transcendence over the world of creation. Israel met this transcendence not only in the limitations of its knowledge when considering Yahweh's rule in the natural world, but above all in actual experiences of the withdrawal or diminution of this creative activity in natural catastrophes, famines, droughts, sickness, premature death, or barrenness. Here too Israel was enjoined to see Yahweh, and Yahweh alone, at work—no other power. Yahweh is not only the life-creating and continually bestowing God; death is in his hands as well. Yahweh is not only the creator of the equipment of the world that promotes life; destructive world phenomena are also the volcanic expressions of his power. The contingent and actual gift of life, the space to live in, provisions for living, and an adequate life-span for all living things is for Israel the act of the God who transcends the world, whose divinity is not bound to activity of this kind, but is *free,* even behind the orders of his life-giving activity that are verbally experienceable, knowable, and perceivable in narrative and hymn.

We can see Yahweh's transcendence not least in the evaluation of natural life. The creation texts show an activity on the part of Yahweh that crystallizes into experienceable form in the gift to all actual living things of a world that promotes life and is prepared for the living. In this respect all life is pointed toward a fore-ordered quality of meaning and value which this gift implies. Man and the natural world are bound together in this meaning and value. It points to the orientation and norm set before man when he is acting freely and formatively in the natural world, distinguishing himself from nature. But because man is primarily directed not toward life, but toward the transcendent God Yahweh, this natural life—in the case of all living things and of man too—is not a numinous value of its own. It is not even a value of its own at all, which would be required for experience of God. Yahweh is not totally absorbed by the elemental experience of natural life. Yahweh is not the projection of the nondisposability of this value. He sets the value, in his creative activity, making it binding for all the living. But he himself is transcendent, above natural life as well. Consequently, Israel has to do with the one God Yahweh in one, single reality, even when life is withdrawn or diminished. Link has put it very aptly: "God is hidden because he is not absorbed by the being of the world that is realized in history. He therefore evades the conclusions of a logic which tries to think of him according to the pattern of that history, as being its prophetic ground. Because merely the experience of historical (and personal) crisis destroys the mechanism of these projections . . ."[148]

Consequently experiences which run counter to life-creative activity do not for Israel call Yahweh's divinity in question. They are actually experience's clues to his transcendence and to his mystery and hiddenness, both in the natural world and in the field of Israel's own history.

f. Summing up

The aim of what we have said has been to make clear that the Old Testament statements about the natural world and environment belong, for Israel, in the context of a proclamation of Yahweh that had far reaching consequences for the interpretation of the world. It means a criticism of, and a breach with, any theory about the divine as the projective ground of the world of life. It means challenging the capacity of human experience and knowledge of the self and the world to achieve any adequate statements about God with regard to the natural world. It means, on the contrary, that experience and knowledge are defined as the place where the proclaiming activity of the transcendent God Yahweh is revealed, and where knowledge of the world proves itself in its very dialectic of his hidden and yet revealed activity. To be exposed to Yahweh in absolutely everything; to encounter him, to find meaningful existence solely in orientation toward him, in what he gives and what he takes away, in his reliably revealed activity and in the activity that is mysteriously unexplorable—this was the determining background against which Israel perceived the natural world and environment—perceived it in experience, knowledge, and formative activity. This is also the context or background to the Old Testament statements about creation.

Seeing this background or context means seeing the deep chasm that has to be bridged if, in our present crisis of survival, we are to bring in the Old Testament itself, in its essential perception of Yahweh—not what is numinous and valuable in the world itself. Yet this is what we want to bring to bear, and not merely individual elemental aspects of the experience of the world and the self that belong to the ancient world, especially the world of the Ancient East, and that have entered into the Old Testament itself, aspects which have slipped dangerously away from modern people in their undue valuation of human autonomy.

The cleft with regard to man's active molding of the world and his modification is correspondingly deep. Israel had laid down for it the elemental quality of the meaning and value of the natural world through Yahweh's continual giving of life and the equipment for living. It was laid down for Israel's orientation, without implying any curtailment of Yahweh's transcendence, toward which man is directed and not toward values which he may describe as being divine. On the contrary, our situation is such that for far too long the unproblematical self-imposition of human claims on nature counted as values which had to be determined in resolving political interests. It is only recently, under the pressure of the survival crisis, that the question about overriding values has been raised again and that the fashionable, would-be progressive, depreciation of them (as being an encroachment on human freedom) has been challenged. To rediscover these overriding values, and to submit ourselves to them as something binding on us, is a necessary task if we are to survive at all. Whether we can find help from a theological viewpoint based on the statements of the Old Testament, with their pointer to these overriding values (which are not, however, merely the extrapolated values of the claims of a majority) is a question that cannot be divided from the essential, postulating Old Testament perception of Yahweh in his transcendence and uniqueness. We must remember this when in the next section, in confrontation with the present, we ask how the position of man in the natural world and environment appears in the Old Testament in the light of Yahweh's activity in the world.

6. The View Taken of Man and His Shaping of the Natural World and Environment

We saw in the previous section that the Old Testament sees man in the historical movement of time as constantly related to the one God Yahweh, who transcends the world. This is true of the political and social sphere, and applies no less to the elemental world of life. In this way man is always being pointed toward the unexplorable, incalculable coming of the divine activity, which is not at man's disposal. This activity requires clarification through Yahweh's actual Word, addressed to man in the present. But this does not mean that man is a being without bearings, a passive figure without responsibility or the power of acting formatively or of taking the initiative. He is not a pawn in someone else's game, a ball tossed about by Yahweh in the arbitrary events that make up the riddle of history. Yahweh declares himself to Israel in his Word, giving it bearing along the particular path for which it has been chosen, in dependable promises, in historical edicts, and in natural and social orders. By following these the hiddenness of God is clarified and removed from the apparent arbitrariness that merely creates fear. And in the same way, Yahweh's dependable creative event includes bearings for man's shaping of the world and environment, and the following of these bearings contributes to the Creator's dependability. We shall

be showing below how man and his shaping of the natural world
and environment are viewed in the creation texts.

a. The different situations providing the point of departure for the Old Testament and the modern world

The relevant Old Testament statements are admittedly
extremely difficult to understand today, because the points of
departure then and now are quite different. Thanks to his more
developed scientific and technical capabilities, the modern
person sees himself as being superior to nature in a completely
unparalleled way. He sees himself as having to perfect this
position even farther, and as having to preserve it by
compensating for certain negative experiences. In the Old
Testament, on the other hand, man finds himself in the natural
world and environment and has to come to terms with what he
can plan only to a very limited degree, and with what is always
elementally threatening and dangerous. Consequently the
security and success of human living in this elemental sphere,
including the growth of the population (Gen. 1:28), needs an
express guarantee and empowerment, which give his perception its bearings. Thanks to his technical exploitation of nature
and his industrial and economic civilization, modern man sees
himself (in fact or intention) as being capable of achieving a
quality of living that makes life secure, easy, and pleasant, and
that frees him to determine his form of living and his life-
expectation as never before. All this was denied to the men and
women of Old Testament times, and was something they found
inconce:vable, because the possibilities open to them were
much more restricted.

These different initial situations first come into contact
when insights begin to emerge about the results of our modern
way of living, with the potential crises and threats to existence
which were quite beyond Israel's horizon of experience. These
insights are making people ask once more about the elemental
foundations that give existence its bearings, bearings that will
keep the liberty of our modern shaping of the world in bounds
and that will withstand man's dependency—which is today

becoming obvious—when we consider the totality and continuance of the world of life. Here the Old Testament statements can have essential significance, even for modern man in all his self-determination, not of course directly, but certainly indirectly.

b. Man's position within the event of creation

Let us keep in mind what we have already seen in considering the texts we took as examples, and their thematic aspects.

The Old Testament statements begin at a much earlier and more elemental point than does the modern mind, and this applies to man's dealings with nature as well. The correspondence to the experience of simply being alive (oneself and other things) as something conceded and not at one's own disposal (any more than the equipment for living provided by the elemental world of life is at one's disposal) opens up a basic perspective of determining importance. In the formative framework of a view of the world seen from within, a view which is close to experience and deeply affected by life itself, man sees himself as included in the event of the gift of life, an event which neither he nor other living things has any control over, but which Yahweh freely brings about—has brought about from time immemorial, and will continue to bring about in the future. This event does not apply to man alone, but to all living things. Consequently, when man moves about in the natural world and environment, experiencing it and acting in it, he is not moving in a sphere that can be viewed as being at the disposal of primarily human purposes and claims. It is man who, perceiving his actual and special world of life, can make the transition to the totality of the natural world and environment; but he thereby sees the living and the phenomena relevant to life as being willed by Yahweh and granted for the benefit of life; and he thereby perceives that other living things have in principle the same right to live as himself. According to this framework, which ultimately determines the whole viewpoint, there can be for the Old

Testament absolutely no direct relationship between man, *seen by himself,* and the external world of nature (together with nonhuman life) seen by *itself* alone; even if this is in contradiction to our arrogant (and, at present, somewhat terrified) domination of nature and exploitation of life in modern times. According to this Old Testament perspective, man, like all living things, is primarily related to Yahweh the creator, who ensures his life and the life of all things. It is only on this level that we can see relationships within the world of creation, between man and nature (see pp. 107-9).

This means a fundamental difference from our present-day outlook. Where modern man, impelled by his own claims and his potentialities for shaping life, takes an external view of his exploitable and utilizable material (whose existence is taken unquestioningly, as a matter of course), the creation texts reduce the complexity of the world to nondisposable manifestations of Yahweh's activity. Accordingly, they confront man (both in the phenomena of the nonliving natural world that have a bearing on life and on everything that lives) primarily with expressions of a fore-ordained will, which extends to everything that lives—has extended to it from time immemorial, extends to it now, and will do so in the future; and to this will man also owes his existence. In this fundamental framework there is no special position marked out for man over against other living things. There is only the confrontation between Yahweh (who transcends the world and brings life and the equipment for living to event) and his nonliving and living creations, which he has formed for the benefit of all life. In the Old Testament, therefore, man's position in the framework of the event of creation is in principle a position of participation in the elemental and primal dependency and relatedness of all created things to Yahweh the creator.

c. *Meaning and value for man within the event of creation*

But for the Old Testament creation statements this creative event of Yahweh's, which moves also toward man and includes man in itself, is not merely a neutral, causal event bearing on the nondisposable origins of every specific existence (which would put the actual shaping of existence itself completely in the hand of man). Nor is it simply the making available of the nondisposable elemental conditions with which man would first have to build up what gives life meaning for him. If, indeed, to be alive and to be equipped for living is experienced as the elemental, meaningful event per se, and as the fundamental elemental value, then the creative event of specific life in the natural world and environment is, in its totality in time and space, already in itself and in its fore-given character, a highly qualitative event which confers meaning and value and which has a binding power of orientation. Therefore, the elemental world of the gift of life conferred by Yahweh also points man to a meaning and value which he himself does not determine in the first place, but which Yahweh promulgates, preceding all man's interventions, alterations, and actions. It is always something already conceded and given, together with Yahweh's will to grant life to the particular living thing, whether man or beast. Therefore, the primal relationship of man to Yahweh is from the very beginning the relationship to a higher, preceding will which endows the whole world of life with meaning, value, and elemental quality, and which also primarily and fundamentally gives human behavior its bearings in the world. So wherever man meets with what has an elemental relevance for life, he meets something fore-given and meaningful, derived from Yahweh's creative activity, which from the very beginning sets an elemental limit to the autonomous, intervening actions of man.

d. Man as an actively modifying civilized being in the event of creation

If we stopped short at what we have said hitherto, taking it to be an adequate rendering of the Old Testament facts, we should be misjudging the matter. For we should be implying that they intend a naive incorporation of man, as a purely natural being, in the elemental world of life, without any further distinction; or that they aim at an illusory reintegration

of man in nature.[149] What we have just described is the
fundamental, determining framework. But the Old Testament
is very well aware that not only animals have to intervene in
other animal life, killing to preserve life for themselves (cf. Ps.
104:21; Job 38:39). It is equally aware that, if he is to achieve
length of life for himself, man can by no means remain passively
in a state of nature. He must laboriously plan and reshape the
natural world and environment given to him by Yahweh, in
order to make active use of it as the equipment of living given to
him: he has to till and plant the ground, lay out gardens, fell
trees and process wood, build transport and irrigation systems,
mine for minerals and process them, breed and tame animals,
make use of animal products, slaughter animals for food—to
give only a few illustrations. Thus the elemental world of man is
created by Yahweh from the very beginning for work, through
which man cooperates in forming and modifying the world of
life; turning back to our illustrative texts, we may think of Psalm
104:14-15, 23, or Genesis 1:28-30. For the Yahwist, even man's
original paradisal existence is characterized by labor (cf. Gen.
2:15[150]). Indeed, in the Old Testament view Yahweh offers the
elemental gifts necessary for modifications of this kind, and in
this working relationship to the world of life (where it is in
accordance with creation) that includes an objectification of
what has been fore-given on the part of the working subject as
well. It includes the development of techniques, tools, separate
working processes in the mining and processing of metals, but
also in trade and commerce, and the like. Thus far the creation
texts see man in his character as created being (a character he
shares with everything that has any relevance for life), not
simply as a *natural* being like everything else, but also as
civilized being distinct from other living things, though the
ambivalence of this does not go unrecognized, especially in the
Yahwist's primeval history.

According to this view of man as civilized being,
technology and industrialization, with their eminently positive
effect on the quality of human existence,[151] certainly belong
within the viewpoint of the biblical creation statements in spite
of the reshaping of nature involved. And this is all the more so

because in his creation Yahweh grants, not merely what is elementally necessary for survival, but also whatever "gladdens the heart of man" (Ps. 104:15).

e. The criteria and limitations of man's special position

And yet—the Old Testament statements about creation do not see this reshaping of nature, which is conceded to man for the purposes of his own life, as simply impelled by the continual urge to perfect what man can do of himself—what *he* wants, the claims *he* makes, or the purposes *he* has. This is the essential difference between the Old Testament view and the threatening picture that human reshaping of nature has meanwhile come to present in modern times. For the Old Testament, this reshaping of the natural world and environment for the purposes of man's life, granted to man and affirmed in creation, stands permanently and constitutively within the predetermined framework of meaning and value of Yahweh's creative activity, for the benefit of *all* life. All reshaping of the natural world and environment, which man has within his power for the benefit of his own life, is therefore subordinated to the meaning and value that provide a point of reference, directing man to the criteria and standards which are binding on him. It is not man who sets up this meaning and value as point of reference; it is Yahweh, as the giver of all life. This point of reference, giving meaning and value, is not merely related to the world of human life; it includes the world of all the living. It does not depend on externally doctrinaire, and hence alterable, edicts, but corresponds to elemental experience in respect of all life. It is not exhausted in perspectives relating to the present but—in accordance with the enduring and dependable constancy of Yahweh's creative will—covers the all-embracing guarantee of the whole world of life—from time immemorial, now, and in the future.

Within this given framework, the activity of man in the world created for him is not directed in the creation texts toward his own autonomous goals. His activity is directed toward what Yahweh has empowered man to do in observance of his whole event of creation which is designed for all the living. These authorizations are the point of orientation, not merely for man's perception, but also for whatever he does in order to utilize or modify nature and indeed to liberate himself from nature altogether. This can be pointed out quite simply, without any reflection about the difficulties that arise through conflicts of interest. That is the case in Psalm 104, where man is assigned his sphere, with his work in the fields and with his herds, *parallel* to other spheres that exist for other living things. It can be pointed out with as much consciousness of the ambivalence of the cultural differentiations of human activity as we find in the Yahwist. It can finally be done as reflectively as in the Priestly Writing's primeval history.

According to the Priestly Writing, in the wake of the event of creation Yahweh took into account the problem presented by the common sphere of earth, shared by the terrestrial animals and man; and blessed only man, giving him alone the capacity and authority "to fill" this sphere through increase (Gen. 1:28). Yahweh did this without diminishing the terrestrial animals' independent right to exist as part of creation in the same sphere—a right which was to be valid *forever* (1:24-25). In accordance with this, Yahweh also included the problem of the conflict between living things in the food sector, settling it by allocating vegetarian food to both man and beast (1:29-30); later (in order to insure that the danger from animals should be successfully controlled) he gave man the right to eat the flesh of animals (9:1 ff). In accordance with this, Yahweh finally took up the problem of breaking the ground for the purposes of cultivation. Here again he blessed man and gave him the capacity and authority to make the modifications necessary to make the earth serviceable (1:28).

Of course, these divine authorizations of man's activity in forming the world in which he lives are—both here and in other passages in the Old Testament—restricted entirely to what is elemental, because of the period at which these writings were composed; they could not even guess at a human world of such complexity as the one we see. At the same time, certain criteria are at work in man's active perception of the natural world and environment, just as they were in his cognitive perception of it;

and these criteria are by no means tied solely to an agrarian way of life. They are of fundamental importance for the Old Testament. Since Yahweh, the creator of all life, gives these bearings to man in his work and formative activity within the world of creation, these authorizations belong within the whole framework of creation Yahweh had laid down. Everything is thrown open to man in his dealings with his natural world and environment that can preserve his existence and make life pleasurable: everything which, in the first place, does not destroy, for other and future people, the fore-given quality of creation of the world in which they live, down to inanimate nature; and everything which, in the second place, preserves for other living things, both now and in the future, the life and possibility of living created for them by Yahweh in their independent and legitimate right to exist; and everything which, in the third place, restricts the killing of nonhuman life to life's elemental needs and to the defense of man against danger.

These criteria are therefore no negation of the needs, interests, and joys of fulfilled human existence. But they take their bearings from Yahweh and from the experience he has thrown open to men and women of the elementally fore-given gift of the world of creation as a whole; and this includes the common origin and common future of all the living, of man and nature, in their world of life. Even if it lies beyond the imaginative possibilities of the Old Testament period—human claims on the scale of the present, which lead to an alteration and draining of the natural world and environment and to the actual destruction of the elemental foundations for life, and especially future life, is definitely rejected according to what the Old Testament has to say. The *liberty* given to man in his shaping of the natural world and environment to his own world of life—a liberty conferred through his bond with Yahweh the creator and Yahweh's definitions of significance—finds its *limits* in man's responsibility toward the given world of creation as a whole, including the phenomena of inanimate nature that have any relevance for the living.

On the basis of this total view and perception, the world

picture of the Old Testament creation texts, which provides the
bearing for both knowledge and action, must necessarily be a
theocentric one, unlike the curtailments of our modern
scientific world picture, which is only partially superior; and a
geocentric and anthropocentric sphere of human responsibility
for creation is bound up with this theocentric view.

The Priestly Writing defined this responsibility of man's
for the natural world and environment, for its quality as the
creative event designed for life, not for the sake of mankind's
existence and continuance. It defined it according to man's
qualification and special position as "the image of God" in the
world of creation. According to this, as we have seen, man is the
earthly representative and steward of God the creator. Bound
to God and taking his bearings from God, he acts as ruler with
the aim of preserving the continual realization of the meaning of
the creative event in the relations of created beings—including
the preservation of the endangered animal world. Quite
rightly, the double relation of man[152] in his total dependency on
God and in his sovereign position toward the animal world is
put side by side with these statements. Psalm 8 is expressing
this idea when it says:

> When I look at thy heavens, the work of thy fingers,
>   the moon and the stars which thou hast established;
> what is man that thou art mindful of him,
>   and the son of man that thou dost care for him?
> Yet thou hast made him little less than God,
>   and dost crown him with glory and honor.
> Thou hast given him dominion over the works of thy hands;
>   thou hast put all things under his feet,
> all sheep and oxen,
>   and also the beasts of the field,
> the birds of the air, and the fish of the sea,
>   whatever passes along the paths of the sea. (vv 4-9)

The Priestly Writing interprets both man's lordship over the
beasts (Gen. 1:26, 28) and his subjection of the earth (the
much-invoked *dominium terrae*, v 28) as being a purely positive
aim, which is in accord with creation and is enjoined by God, its

aim being to preserve God's "very good" world of creation.
This was already clear in the context of our consideration of
the Priestly Document's primeval history. The notion that
the *dominium terrae* was already seen ambivalently in *P*, as
people frequently maintain today,[153] must be categorically
disputed, if only because of the whole layout of Genesis 1[154]
(see pp. 107-8 above). To make this biblical statement, in its
original meaning and its genuine intention, responsible for
the dangerous domination and exploitation of nature since the
beginning of modern times is completely erroneous; here
Günter Altner has put things in their correct light.[155] It is
another question whether critics such as L. White, Jr., G.
Kade, C. Amery, and J. B. Cobb are not right insofar as the
Jewish and Christian tradition of Genesis 1:28 did in actual
fact act as a legitimation of this kind. Here we need detailed
studies on the history of the text's influence. The beginnings
have been made, as regards the early period, by D. K.
Jobling[156] and D. A. Yegerlehner,[157] and these have been
taken farther in an essay by Gerhard Liedke especially.[158] But
Altner rightly points out that a misunderstanding of the
dominium terrae in the sense of man's exploitation and
despotism—a misunderstanding fraught with such serious
consequences—goes together with the secularizing sever-
ance of man from the fore-given, binding relation to Yahweh
the creator and his ordained decrees of significance for the
world of creation as a whole.[159]

How are we to grasp conceptually this responsibility
assigned to man for the existence and continuance of the given,
elemental world of life as a whole, as it touches on human
activity today? We have already come up against this problem
in the introduction.

A concept such as "co-creatureliness" is not a term that
provides "maxims of behavior"[160] but, clumsy though it is, it
may, even exegetically, represent correctly the criterion of
action drawn from the overriding framework of significance of
the whole of creation, in which, as we have seen, human activity
is bound to move, according to the creation texts. Its

disadvantage is that it does not express the special position of man as the Bible sees it.

Far more problematical exegetically are the concepts attempting to overcome the exclusively autonomous relation of man to a world that is purely material and at man's disposal and which therefore define the relation between man and nature as "partnership" or "cooperation." These concepts, though the intention behind them is good, go to the other extreme. At all events, they by-pass the exegetical facts, because they encourage a pseudo-personalization of the relation between man and nature and (not without a sideways glance at what can be made plausible in an atheistic world) deny that in the framework of creation to which the Bible testifies there is only one determining, personal relationship for man which defines responsibility and guides personal relations—the relationship to Yahweh, man's creator and the creator of all things. Accordingly *man is not nature's partner*. As we have seen, the Old Testament defines this relationship much more soberly and objectively, though it still expressly brings out man's responsibility to Yahweh for this sphere too—in order to insure the continuance of the whole of creation. *Even less is man the partner of Yahweh the creator,* since he himself is created and elementally dependent on his Maker. He is Yahweh's representative, steward, and executive for the preservation of the world's character of creation in time. This means that cooperation with nature is not an adequate term either, because it excludes the question of criteria and does not consider the fact that to overcome the view of nature as mere object, and to assess the need for man's work in reshaping nature to preserve the permanent right to existence of other life and the natural equipment for living (based on creation), one depends on orientation toward Yahweh, in whose creative activity man is supposed to act, both for himself and for the whole. It we make the biblical statements our basis, the constitutive, primary orientation toward Yahweh is indispensable. The meaning and value of the human life that comes after us and its elemental equipment for living, the meaning and value of nonhuman life and its equipment, and the meaning and value of an elemental world of life as totality would otherwise lose their binding justification.

f. Summing up

If we look back, we can see that the Old Testament's creation statements present clear rules for the formation of man's viewpoint and for his shaping of the natural world and environment. It presents them as both man's *authorization* to shape his world on the level of the elemental foundations of creation, through use and modification; and his *responsibility*, not only for himself and his descendants, but for the whole world of creation (including its future quality), since man, and only he, is the living being who knows Yahweh, the creator of the whole, and is addressed by him. Man has reponsibility because it is to man and man alone that the meaning of the whole of creation has been made known; a responsibility manifest in its most direct form today, since it is only man who recognizes the present danger in which the world of creation as a whole stands.

This viewpoint preserves the creaturely incorporation of man in the world of creation and the common future of both, just as much as it preserves man's freedom and self-confidence in his special position, which find expression in his distinctness from the natural world and his creative planning and technological reshaping of the world and environment.

Two interconnected conditions are of decisive importance for the Old Testament. They are quite elemental and a matter of course, but they are also existential and are kept always in mind: the framework of the creative event as a whole, in which all human shaping of the natural world takes place, but which embraces all living things, not only man; and within this framework, the perception (communicated by experience) of one's own life and of all life in its relationship to Yahweh the creator of man's existence, which is not at his disposal.

When man acts in relation to the natural world and environment and the life in it, these conditions provide him with the fore-given fundamental attitudes, models, behavior and orientations of value destined for him. They are directed toward the meaning and quality of the whole world of creation, which have been determined by Yahweh, not man. They form the foundation for the specific decisions and considerations presented to man in ever new groupings for each new situation. This framework of action also embraces, locates, and tends to limit our modern objectifying processes of knowledge and action, as well as man's technological and industrial shaping of the world. But it radically criticizes an attitude in which man in his autonomy makes himself the framework. It unmasks the view of a seemingly insufficient natural world in which man suppresses the most elemental experiences of bestowed life and the equipment for living that is guaranteed in advance, and—under the sole impulse, not of necessity, but of self-determined aims and continually expanded claims on life—increasingly relativizes the creative, fundamental equipment of the world, destructively calling it in question.

For the Old Testament the framework of the primal relationship of human life to Yahweh the creator (a relationship based on conscious experience) provides the valid goals of human knowledge and action as regards the natural world and environment. And these goals override all changes and transformations. The goal of knowledge is not merely the objectifying inquiry into sectional, partial, natural laws and processes in nature, necessary though these may be in their proper place. The aim—overriding and limiting these as merely partial goals—is the understanding of natural world phenomena, life processes, and orders as the contingent, conferred event in the gift of life and the equipment for living, which is not achievable by the living themselves. Natural phenomena and life processes are, in fact, seen as the form taken by the life-giving will of the Creator. And the goal of action for man is to build a serviceable world that gives joy and also, without doubt, to build it through a reshaping of nature by labor. This also includes a redistribution or adjustment of goods for the benefit of the socially underprivileged, so that men will not lose the elemental experience of creation because of the

burdens imposed by their social situation (Prov. 14:31; Job
31:13-15). But in building his world man must preserve, as far as
is at all possible, the right of non-human life to live; and the
inviolable proviso is the preservation of the permanent quality
of the world of creation as a whole. The problem presented for
human responsibility, accordingly, is to balance out the
elemental needs of man and his autonomous claims, distinguishing between what is necessary if his life is to be fulfilled
and what is desirable and achievable, but deleterious for
creation as a whole. This balancing out must be guided by the
criteria we have mentioned and must take its bearings from the
whole of creation in its temporal dimension. It is in deciding
this problem that man asserts the special position and dignity
assigned to him.

Will man conform to all this? The creation statements of
the Psalms, the Wisdom texts, the Yahwist's primeval history
and, above all, the Priestly Writing lay down provisions,
without idealizing reality. Since threats to the world of life in
the demon-freed world of the Old Testament testimonies are no
longer caused by numinous counter-forces, but only by the
living themselves (and preeminently man), *man* becomes the
essential problem for the existence, form, and realization of the
world of creation. The Yahwist's primeval history has a
ruthlessly realistic viewpoint with regard to man as he really is
(see pp. 69ff above). The pessimistic thesis of the psychosomatic expert R. Bilz that man is the being who is capable of
madness[161] already finds its confirmation and definition in the
Yahwist. The only negative element named in Psalm 104 is the
endangering of the creation event by sinners and the wicked (v
35), and even the Priestly Writing sees the original world of
creation as flawed or fractured by the phenomenon of violence,
though this is admittedly absorbed into the regulations
embodied in the blessing to Noah (Gen. 9). The fact that the
world of creation and the empirical, natural world and
environment are not fully congruent must therefore continue to
be of concern to the biblical tradition. The question is already
considered in the Old Testament itself in the face of all the
counter-experiences that Israel and the individual met with; it

is thought about in the context of man, in the context of Yahweh as creator, and in the context of the future and total reality of the world of creation. We shall see what this means in the next section.

7. The Problem of the Natural World and Environment as Creation in the Face of Counter-Experiences

As we have already explained, the following section has an importance of its own among the thematic aspects of the Old Testament's statements about the natural world and environment. Its subject is the changes in the view taken of creation in ancient Israel, changes which came about in the wake of counter-experiences. We shall also be considering how this became a problem, especially in the later and post–Old Testament texts, and how it affected the world behind the New Testament as well.

In contrast to this, the previous five sections belong together, as we have already said. They reflect the same Old Testament facts under various aspects—the perception of the natural world and environment as creation. This is of the greatest importance in view of our present situation and cuts across all differences in the political, economic, and social systems and circumstances. But if we want to do justice to the Old Testament itself, one thing must not be overlooked: the views taken of creation, with their own concentration on the naturally given world and environment, and on the fact that man and all living things are alive at all, certainly provide a perspective that takes in whatever is elementally essential. In this sense, it is of permanent and fundamental importance as long as there is life at all. But even in the course of the Old Testament tradition itself, it was not a viewpoint that satisfied all sides and made everything else superfluous. For man does not belong only to the history of the event conferring the natural world and environment, with the concomitant elemental circumstance of actually being alive; he belongs no less to a world of life that varies, that is subject to change, and that is partly shaped by man himself, since it is determined by the political, social, and mental factors that are involved in man's historical involvement with a community of people. It is unnecessary to say again that the Old Testament always kept this complex of facts in view, seeing itself just as continually exposed to Yahweh's activity in the historical field of its political and social events as in the elemental and natural sphere. We have frequently pointed this out in the previous sections.

But within this complex of facts we must notice a difference in trend between that society and our own, because of the difference in the challenges presented. As we noted at the beginning, today the elemental problem of the relationship to the natural world emerges as the problem of survival; it runs through the different forms of man's political, social, and mental world and compels us to adopt views and make regulations that affect the political, social, and mental fields. Israel, on the other hand, like the whole of the ancient world, was not as yet confronted with the problem of the survival of the natural world and environment. Here the center of gravity lay firmly on the other side of the complex. The changing and vitally important events of Israel's political, social, and intellectual world, and Yahweh's workings in these events, constituted the problem that stood in the foreground. That is to say, people were mainly concerned with their experiences of the difference between creation and Israel's history of salvation, between creation and actual life as it was, between the empirical world (especially Israel's) and the world of creation. These experiences, which Israel endured and suffered, showed the nation a special activity on Yahweh's part in the present. These incalculable experiences threw up the whole question of Yahweh in relation to his creative activity, and the question about man as he was designed to be according to creation, and as he was in his actual behavior. In this way they led away from the experience of Yahweh in political, social, and intellectual events and cast a retrospective light once more on changed aspects of the natural world and environment.

If we were to trace the testimony of the Old Testament

here with the required thoroughness, we should have to do nothing less than to write a theology of the Old Testament; for here enduring, fundamental experiences are under discussion. But we must lower our sights and must content ourselves in what follows with merely indicating these extensive movements of thought, and must concentrate on the changes in the view taken of the natural world and environment.

a. The continuity of the view taken of creation, in the face of Israel's experience of Yahweh in political and social life

For the Old Testament, the natural world of life and political and social events belong together as fields of the given, goodly order of the world arranged by Yahweh. They declare themselves to be the total, coherent context of experience to the extent that human behavior in political institutions and social orders moves within the framework which Yahweh has set for them.

In the prenational traditions and in those dating from the early national period, this coherent context is brought out, where it affects Israel as region, without any consideration of serious contrary experiences. Its dimensions are extended in the comprehensive conception of the cultic tradition centered on Jerusalem[162] above all, as well as in Wisdom writing, which was closely bound up with the same conception. Contrary experiences stemming from the natural world, such as drought or dangerous illness, but also from attacks by foreign nations or injustice in law or social life, were seen as temporary, isolated cases. They are due to the mistaken behavior of individuals, can be coped with by means of the institution of the Royal or the Individual Lament (examples are found in the Psalms), and do not call in question the total context of a visible world that has been well ordered by Yahweh in *every* respect. Even the Yahwist starts from the reality of a world that is well ordered on every side, even if (faced by a world of creation seriously spoiled by man) he sees this goodly order as proceeding—in a newly initiated divine action—from the political existence of blessed

Israel and spreading to a whole world in need of blessing.

At all events, from the middle of the eighth century B.C., the correspondence in experience between perception of the natural world as the life-giving work of Yahweh, and the goodly order of the political and social world, which finds expression in Yahweh's saving acts on Israel's behalf, broke down. From here on Israel lost the unfettered scope to develop its own life, something a power vacuum in the political world had hitherto made possible. Israel and its world came under the foreign rule of the Assyrians,[163] the neo-Babylonians.[164] It lost the liberty of its own country, its own national institutions, and, through deportation, its common life as a people. These losses, with their grave economic and social results, were not really affected when, in the later Israelite period, the neo-Babylonians were followed as Palestine's overlords by the Persians,[165] the Ptolemies, with their mainly economic interference,[166] the Seleucids,[167] and finally, after a brief ambiguous independence under the Maccabees/Hasmonaeans,[168] by the Romans.[169] For Israel, both in the country itself and in the Dispersion, it was a period of great upheaval, not only mentally and theologically, but above all politically, economically, and socially.

We must dispense with a historical account here, but the interested reader should turn to recent studies of the period from 300 B.C. to A.D. 100, especially—for example, the work of Martin Hengel,[170] and the volumes of *The Jewish People in the First Century*, edited by S. Safrai and M. Stern (I, 1974; II, 1976; and VI, *World History of the Jewish People*, ed. A. Schalit, 1976).

It is not surprising that throughout this extensive period Israel was moved above all by the question of the intention, reasons, and goal of Yahweh's activity which it encountered in these political, social, and economic experiences. At the same time, Israel in this period did not withdraw from the total range of the natural world and environment which it had meanwhile won through to, reducing it to the pressing field of experience of its own natural world alone; though here exceptions can of course be found, under the weight of other influential Israelite traditions, for example, the outlook in Ezekiel's "draft constitution" (Ezek. 40–48) or the deuteronomic promises of blessing, and the things said about the land of Israel in Deuteronomy, Jeremiah, and elsewhere.[171] Seen as a whole, however, Israel did preserve the total range of the natural world and environment, still seeing Yahweh the creator at work in this sphere, which precedes all political and social shaping of the world and all differences of experience and which is permanently given to man per se. In this way it stood up to every temptation to give way to a dualistic explanation of the world or to a demiurgic depreciation of it, even when experience changed.

This can be shown from a long series of Israelite creation texts, from the deep cleft in experience caused by the Exile in the sixth century B.C. to the end of the late Israelite period in the first century of the Christian era. They are to be found in the Old Testament and in the Apocrypha and Pseudepigrapha, which date from the period between the testaments. Here are a few examples.

We must of course mention the Priestly Writing, which belongs to the period of the Exile, but we must also draw attention to the numerous statements about Yahweh as creator of the natural world in Deutero-Isaiah, the prophetic writing that has come down to us in Isaiah 40–55 (40:12-31; 42:5; 45:11-13, 18-25; 48:12-15; 51:9-10, 15-16), or in prophecies such as Jeremiah 31:35-36, 37; 32:17, 27; 33:25.

Coming to the postexilic period, we must point out that the earlier creation texts in Genesis or in the Psalms were assimilated into later traditions, though we must also draw attention to the numerous statements that were made in this period for the first time. For example, postexilic psalms, such as 136:145-48, but also Psalms 90 or 139; or the great penitential prayer in Nehemiah 9, which begins with Yahweh's bestowal of creation (v 6). Then, in the context of Wisdom, come the varied statements about creation in the great dialogue section of the Book of Job (5:8ff; 9:4ff; 28:25-26; 31:15; 32:22; 36:26–37:18; 38–39), occasionally in Ecclesiastes (3:11-12; 11:5) and again more extensively in

Ecclesiasticus (16:26–17:9; 39:12ff; 42:15ff). We then find them in apocalyptic texts (Ethiopian Enoch 2:1–5:84; Jubilees 2ff; 4 Ezra 6:38ff; 8:44; Syrian Apocalypse of Baruch 14:18-19, as well as elsewhere[172]); and finally, deriving from hellenistic Judaism, apart from the Septuagint (the Greek translation of the Old Testament), with its interpretative reproduction of the creation texts,[173] and the great treatise *De opificio mundi* by Philo Judaeus, we have special testimonies such as Wisdom 11:17; 13:1-10 and 2 Maccabees 7:28.

In some of the late texts Yahweh's creative activity is proclaimed in a world in which angels and demons are also visible.[174] This had integrating causes—reasons belonging to the history of religion. Like the appearance of Wisdom as person at creation (Prov. 8:22ff; Job 28:25ff; Ecclus. 1:9; Wis. 7–9),[175] it only seemingly surrenders Yahweh's sole creative activity in a world freed of demons, or gives up man's responsible position in the world of creation, which we had to consider in dealing with the creation texts. Right down to the late period, the natural world and environment is seen as the act of Yahweh and of no other person.

This intention, however, had to be preserved by integrating it into knowledge of the natural world that was becoming more extensive and more precise. This is clearly shown by the details of the creative event, with all the variety of the biological, meteorological, astronomical, and geographical phenomena in Job, Ecclesiasticus, and the apocalyptic writings, especially Ethiopian Enoch. The same kind of integration was needed in the confrontation with the conceptions of the world and nature that made themselves felt in late Israel from the hellenistic sphere of intellectual influence. It was a critical preservation of Israel's point of view. Ecclesiastes holds fast to the tradition in its own way,[176] but even more so does Ecclesiasticus;[177] while hellenistic Judaism plays its part in the Wisdom of Solomon, for example, and above all through Philo. H. F. Weiss has pointed this out in a comprehensive study.[178] The doctrine of *creatio ex nihilo* ("creation out of nothing") is the best-known expression of this preservation of biblical aspects of creation as the biblical view came to terms with the hellenistic mind and with the correlation between the material and the spiritual principle that was of essential importance there (2 Macc. 7:28; different, however, Wis. 11:17);[179] whereas the biblical texts, which belong to a different intellectual world, express the divinity of Yahweh the creator as the power and liberty of Yahweh's acts (Gen. 1, 2, and 3) but do not yet see them as carried out in freedom from a material principle.

b. The changed direction of the creation outlook in the face of Israel's experience of Yahweh in politics and social life

Changes in outlook and knowledge of the world followed on greater information about the world, as well as on new ideas; but important though they may be in their own place, they are not really the essential thing that characterizes the statements about creation from the exilic period onward, compared with the creation texts that we have noted. If we consider the texts we have just mentioned, we shall notice that in the statements made about creation from the time of the Exile onward, the life-giving activity of Yahweh in the natural world and environment, and among living things, retreats strangely into the background, considered as the real aim of the statement. We only come across it in the usual way when some saving activity on Yahweh's part is perceived in the present political and social world of postexilic Israel. That is to say, we meet it in the postexilic psalms, which presuppose a positive judgment on the postexilic temple theocracy,[180] and in the Priestly Writing, which sees the reality of salvation in Yahweh's pure, cultic community, quite apart from the political and social conditions existing in Israel, or even enjoyed by the individual.[181] It is true that here and there passages can also be found that bring out the relation of the creation event to life (e.g., Isa. 42:5; Neh. 9:6; Job 31:15; 32:22; Ecclus. 16:29-30; 39:16, 22, 25-27, 33; 42:23-25). But if we notice the particular contexts and the trend of what is said, we see that on the whole this stress no longer has a primary function, but is rather indirect and auxiliary. Apart from Ecclesiasticus and texts deriving from hellenistic Judaism, the statements about creation no longer have the goal of illuminating the elemental experience of the natural world and environment as something well ordered by Yahweh which guarantees life. Their goal is rather to make statements about God, tested by experience and touching on problematical areas of life, so as to come to terms theologically with the current events that seem to run counter to divine activity. Elemental experiences, tested by life, and contemplation of the natural world were to make it plain to Israel, in the face of these counter-experiences, that Yahweh's power was still unlimited (Deut.-Isa.; Jer.; Neh. 9); that his word and commandments were still really valid and efficacious (Deut.-Isa.; 4 Ezra 6); that he was still bringing about a well-considered order in his world of creation which gives meaning to everything (Ecclus.; Eth. Enoch); and that in spite of everything, he was of a surpassing preeminence which man, indeed, cannot grasp because, in the words of Job 26:14, he only reaches "to the outskirts of his ways."

Why was there this shift from the perception of the natural world and environment in experience, knowledge, and action as the divine activity of Yahweh that guarantees life, to the need for stating in a strictly theological way what is effectually and assuredly true of Yahweh, where statements about creation only perform an auxiliary function? The reason must be seen in the fact that, at least from the breakdown of the Israelite state onward, the cohesion of a comprehensive goodly order in Israel's world, an order sustained by Yahweh, fell apart. This cohesion is no longer visibly intact, and the experiences that run counter to it are not merely exceptions that can be coped with in the framework of the total conception. Israel's experience now forced it inescapably to call their whole cohesion in question, and with it God himself. Tension was felt between the event of creation in the natural world and its imperfection in individual life; the correspondence between Yahweh's act as creator in the world and his saving gifts to Israel's actual political and social world was no longer apparent.[182] Let the world of creation be what it will, Israel's existence politically, socially, and nationally is one of disaster and judgment. Let the world of creation as a whole be what it will, there is a puzzling cleavage between the idea that life is providentially guided, and what actually happens nationally and individually. The innocent suffer, the wicked flourish. Because this connection between Yahweh's activity in the natural world (which guarantees life) and his saving activity for Israel and for individual destiny has become a problem, Yahweh himself becomes a problem. He is a problem because his will toward salvation was vouchsafed to Israel in its political and social existence, but it has now been withdrawn. This comes out in the prophetic texts particularly. But the perceptibly just ordering of the world is also a problem for the Wisdom texts in view of what actually happens to the righteous and the wicked, and for the apocalyptic writings where this question is linked with the difficulty of Yahweh's now-suspended will toward Israel's salvation. Following H. H. Schmid, U. Luck has impressively worked out the way this cleft between a just world order and actual contrary experience of the world appeared to Israel and to the Israelite who felt bound to Yahweh's ordinances.[183]

Because life is more than the elemental equipment for living and the world is more than the given natural world and environment, the creation texts were drawn, from the period of the Exile onward, into this whole problem—the problem of Israel's contrary experience of the world, as nation and as individual. Imperfections in the natural world (we may remember the Yahwist's primeval history; see pp. 65ff above), danger from wild beasts (e.g., Isa. 11:6-9; Syr. Apoc. Bar. 73:6); as well as lives spoiled by suffering, disease, and death, all become a problem (e.g., Isa. 25:8; 26:19; 35:5ff; 65:17-25; Zech. 8:4; and passages in apocalyptic literature[184]); though this does not mean a denial of the quality of creation in the existing world as Yahweh's act. Rather, Yahweh's undisputed creative activity in the existing world is seen together with these areas of contrary experience which Israel and the individual have to endure. It becomes a part of the problem of Yahweh's fulfillment of salvation in Israel and in the life of the individual. But moving the creation texts into this complex means distorting their function, since they are called into service in an attempt to master these problems by raising a strictly theological question about Yahweh and his all-embracing activity, which sustains all areas of life in Israel and in the world.

It is highly significant that in the face of this, all solutions were forbidden to Israel that would have led to any limitation of Yahweh's uniqueness and his sole efficacy, or that would have called into question Yahweh himself because of these contrary experiences, as if he were merely the exponent of the happiness man desires. Nor was there any depreciation of the existing natural world. Even in considering the problems which Israel's experience now forced it to consider, postexilic Israel proclaimed Yahweh as the one, sole, transcendent God, on whose contingent, free disposal the world and man remain dependent for the guaranteeing of the natural world and for the event of a just world order that would realize the promises of salvation made to Israel, in the political and social sphere as well as in individual life. The abolition of the difference experienced and suffered, and reconciliation between the actual world and Yahweh's activity can therefore be an event which only Yahweh himself brings about, in the sense of bestowal of quality of life in all sectors of the world. Thanks to his autonomous, independent initiative, man is separated from Yahweh and is incapable of shaping these sectors in a positive way, either in the given natural world or in the political and social sphere or in individual life. The Yahwist, but still more the scriptural prophets and the deuteronomic and deuteronomistic writings, with their far-reaching influence, see man himself as the reason for the cleavage and difference between Yahweh's life-conferring activity and the real world as we see it; for man's activity is in fact opposed to Yahweh, and Israel has departed from Yahweh's precepts. The problem of the innocent who suffer (Job) and the question of whether Yahweh is recognizable in his acts in the sense of providing bearings for the way man lives (the Wisdom teaching of Ecclesiastes) remain without any clear solution. They are grasped as being problems that, indeed, are not open to any apparent solution at all and that bring us up against the mystery of Yahweh's rule.

We have first of all indicated the trend of the whole problem into which the statements about the creation of the natural world and environment have now been drawn. The solutions which emerged for Israel from the exilic period onward are highly varied. We shall look at them in the following pages, considering them under the headings of prophecy, Wisdom, and apocalyptic.

c. *Experiences that run counter to the natural world and environment in the testimony of the prophets*

In the prophecy of exilic and postexilic times, the problem that makes Israel's real world a world of suffering is not the fate of the individual. It is the political and social world of the people of Israel in the community of the nations. For this was marked by the withdrawal of Yahweh's tokens of salvation because of Israel's guilt and by the wicked and aggressive attacks of other nations. In the face of this the prophets of the period proclaim Yahweh's renewed bestowal of salvation on Israel. This can also include the whole world of man, and will lead to a world saved in all realms of life, including the natural world and the environment.[185] This proclaimed world can only be Yahweh's act. The proposition applies both to the time when it will come and to the power that will bring it about. For the damage to the world of life, in all its sectors, is the work of human activity which men and women experience in Israel and the world in general, and it is therefore confirmation that not only the natural world and environment, but the political and social world of man also, needs Yahweh's fore-given ordering warranty to give human behavior and actions their bearings. Here, in the prophets, therefore, the world is included in a perspective of a qualified, contingently nondisposable future, which Yahweh means to bring about. In other words, it is a future that goes beyond the constancy of divine creative activity in event and quality as Yahweh's *new* acts. In the fact of Yahweh's interrupted saving activity in the world of man, the view of the continual guaranteeing of life by the Creator is now bound up with the view of a world corrupted by human guilt. But this existing world points prophetically to a future salvation, which is not immanent, which does not have to be progressively developed, but which will be brought about by Yahweh and will efface all man's harmful wickedness.

In this perspective opened up by the prophets for Israel, and by association, therefore, for the whole world of the living, the statements about Yahweh's creative activity (still bestowed in the existing natural world and environment) play an important part, as we have already indicated. They are the justification, tested by experience, of the mightiness, preeminence, and real power of the divine Word, with which Yahweh is also able to bring about the proclaimed future of salvation. We see this, for example, in the prophecies in Jeremiah 31:35-37; 32:15-44; and 33:25, and in the prayer in Nehemiah 9:6.

But we find this train of thought, above all, in Deutero-Isaiah. In this prophet's discussions, Israel is pointed to Yahweh's creative activity as the essential reason why he is willing and able to put into force the worldwide saving activity on Israel's behalf which the prophet proclaims.[186] But not only that. In magnificent theological concentration, Deutero-Isaiah takes in Yahweh's whole activity in world events, past and future alike—in Israel's earlier salvation history as well as in the new saving activity on its behalf, in the natural world, and even in the suffering imposed as punishment, and in the disaster that has come upon Israel because of its trangression and the wickedness of the world of man; and he shows all this to be Yahweh's creative activity which manifests his unity in all that he does.[187] Deutero-Isaiah can actually proclaim of him: "I form light and create darkness, I make weal and create woe, I am Yahweh, who does all these things" (45:7). It is only here, in this all-comprehensive expansion, that creation can be seen as an eschatological term covering the whole activity of Yahweh, even the activity that is new and belongs to the future. But in Deutero-Isaiah this activity is no longer constitutively bound up with the natural world and environment but bridges the difference between Yahweh's creation in the present world and in a coming eschatological event, through its grasp of the whole divine activity in general.[188] Deutero-Isaiah certainly directs this proclamation toward the new saving activity of Yahweh for Israel in worldwide dimensions; the creation statements, insofar as they touch on the existing world, are auxiliary to this; but—unlike the salvation history which has been withdrawn in an act of judgment—they display a manifestation of Yahweh's all-embracing creative power that corresponds to experience. In the wake of the imminent total and comprehensive realization of salvation, this all-embracing creative power of Yahweh's—seen now without any restrictions—will be directed as new activity toward the natural world and environment as well, and will surpass the continuity of creative activity as man normally perceives it. Here Deutero-Isaiah is thinking especially of Yahweh's abolition of the unfavorable conditions of countryside and vegetation in the desert, for these were in the way of the people returning home to Zion from Babylon (e.g., Isa. 41:18-19; 42:16; 43:19-21).

Other prophecies envisage salvation for Israel's natural world as finding its realization in the quality of the soil, the provision for water and agricultural yield (e.g., Hag. 1–2; Zech. 8:12; Ezra 47; Zech. 14:8); or in man's dependency on the heavenly bodies (Isa. 60:19).

In the context of Yahweh's future realization of salvation in the political and social field in Israel and among the nations (and with an eye to the natural world and environment that is involved), still other prophecies proclaim even more funda-mental renewals in this sphere, renewals which go beyond existing creative activity. So the famous prophecy in Isaiah 11:6-9 does not promise control and expulsion of the wild beasts (cf. Hos. 2:18; Lev. 26:6; Ezek. 34:25-28); it looks for their pacification, thanks to a universal recognition of Yahweh, which will ensure that domestic animals, people, and wild beasts will be able to live together without danger. Or there is the elimination of handicapped life for the blind, the deaf, the lame, and the dumb (Isa. 35:5-6), the ending of premature death (Isa. 65:20, 23), and of death in general (Isa. 25:8; 26:19). Indeed, in accordance with the future, total, and comprehen-sive realization of salvation for Israel, Yahweh's activity can actually be extended to the renewal of the whole natural world and environment (in contrast to Deut.-Isa., who extends Yahweh's creative activity to his universal, comprehensive activity in all spheres), for where prophecy remains within the outlook of the generally accepted creation tradition, there is talk of the creation of "a new heaven and a new earth" (Isa. 65:17; 66:22).[189] This was not given specific worldwide form, however, and the eschatological renewal of the natural world was not bound to expectation of the end of the world, beyond the winding-up of this world's conditions in Yahweh's judgment (cf. e.g., Isa. 24:1–27:13; Zech. 12–14; Joel).[190]

What is the intention of these prophecies? In exilic and postexilic prophecy alike, Yahweh shows himself in the way already familiar to Israel, as the one God who acts in the dimension of the world and yet transcends it. Israel, the world, and men are fundamentally dependent on his fore-given activity. Moreover, he shows himself in this way even in the face of Israel's experience of withdrawn tokens of salvation, and even in spite of the deprivation and depreciation experienced in the natural world. Because, for the prophets, these contrary experiences do not call Yahweh into question; they are themselves Yahweh's acts of punishment and judgment toward Israel and the world of man.

This is the starting point for these prophecies, and they proclaim a new activity on Yahweh's part: this is the expression of his liberty, which is far above the world, and of his faithfulness toward what he has done. His saving activity for Israel was not dependent on Israel itself, so it cannot be ended by Israel's guilt, or by judgment either. Yahweh freely desired to bestow a just and good world on the living, in the natural world and in social and political life; and in the same way his will to salvation will now be a total one and will also include the whole natural world and environment in the renewal. This is what these prophecies proclaim. They are not consolations for the future, along the lines that Israel had inherited from its fathers in the perception of Yahweh.[191] They are the expression of Israel's definite knowledge—proved in salvation history and in the elementals of life—that the world in all its sectors is an event ruled by the purposeful activity of Yahweh, directed toward the bestowal of life in its highest quality. This is true, even if in the existing world the goal has been spoiled by human guilt, and—as has been proclaimed by Yahweh's dependable Word—will only find its universal realization in the future.

These prophecies state that Israel will have to wait for the all-embracing realization of this goal for it will come about through Yahweh alone. In a world still created by Yahweh, in spite of all man's culpable destruction of it, the essential thing is to do what is in accordance with Yahweh's will, trusting his promise and with no illusion of being able to bring about independently what the world can only experience as something fore-given by Yahweh. For the realization of this goal also includes a renewal of man which cannot be achieved by man himself but has to be created by Yahweh (Isa. 2:2-4; Jer. 31:31-34; Ezek. 11:19; 18:31; 36:26; Joel 2:28-32; Ps. 51:12).

d. Experiences that run counter to the natural world and environment in the testimony of Wisdom

Matters present themselves in a different light to Jerusalem cultic poetry and to Wisdom in the postexilic period, for their starting point is not serious counter-experiences on Israel's part which have relevance for theology. The creation statements are not drawn into the problems of the still-unfulfilled and expected realization of salvation for Israel. On the contrary, in these texts, postexilic Israel sees its existence in a cultic community centered on the temple as being Yahweh's realization of salvation in the present. It is in line with this that the creative activity of Yahweh in the world is lauded as in preexilic times. We have already drawn attention to the psalms that belong here.

The questions do not emerge in the field of salvation history, with Israel's political and social existence; they are initiated by the fate of the individual. The problem is individual suffering and premature death, in contrast to Yahweh's activity in the world of creation as a whole, which guarantees life. But it becomes increasingly hard to come to terms theologically with this contrast as being a deserved requital for wickedness, or as a fate that is merely set aside by Yahweh when he saves the

person from his distresses. The contrast turns into a problem
particularly when suffering and premature death threaten the
innocent.

   In the postexilic devotionalism of the Psalms, this tension
certainly does not call either Yahweh or his activity as universal
creator in question, but it does change life's perspective.
Yahweh's acts of bestowal can now be distinguished from the
guarantee of life in all its fullness; and in the face of such
contrary experiences, the fact is stressed once more that
Yahweh was always perceived as being transcendent, even over
life. The reaction of the three men to Nebuchadnezzar's plan to
throw them into the burning fiery furnace makes this plain, for
example (Dan. 3:16-18). Fellowship with Yahweh can now exist
beside and beyond the experience of an innocently spoiled or
prematurely ended life. The man who prays puts his hope in
Yahweh, but death, the limit of life, is no longer seen as the
limit of a living relationship to Yahweh. As von Rad has
shown,[192] grace and life are now distinguished from one
another. The two do not coincide; and the living fellowship with
Yahweh conferred on men by him is not abolished even by
death (e.g., Pss. 16; 63; 73). In the later statements about the
resurrection of the righteous,[193] this stepping beyond the
natural world through man's fellowship with Yahweh, beyond
the experience of elemental fate during his lifetime with all its
problems, is then linked with the eschatological expectation of
salvation.[194]

   The problem of the cleft between the individual fate of
the innocent and Yahweh's life-guaranteeing activity in the
world of creation is taken up with much rigor in the dialogues
of the Book of Job. For the Job of the dialogue poetry,[195] the
traditional interpretations of suffering (as due to guilt or as
aimed at tempering the soul) perish on the rock of his
innocence. Yahweh the creator is himself called in question in
the context of Job's fate. Job curses his birth (3:1ff), he loathes
life (10:1ff), Yahweh has robbed him of his true deserts by
bringing suffering down on him (27:2). Thus in the Book of
Job, Yahweh's gift of life and a just world order break sharply
asunder because Job's conduct has by no means conflicted

with this universal order of Yahweh's; on the contrary, it has
been in complete accordance with it. He is righteous and is not
conscious of any guilt. Justice—indeed Yahweh's credibility in
his world order—is now at stake. But what answer is Job given
when he challenges Yahweh? He is not pointed to something
new, some third fact, lying between the creation of the world
and his own personal fate—some superior aspect of Yahweh
which explains everything. He is pointed to the activity of
Yahweh the creator in the world (Job 38–40), but not so that he
may perceive his own life and that of all things as conferred in
goodness after all. The purpose is so that he may perceive the
preeminence of Yahweh, unattainable by all the human senses,
which is nonetheless the order-conferring mystery of this
activity in the world; and so that in this mystery he may find
with Yahweh the answer to the riddle of his own fate as well. [196]

The dialogue poetry of the Old Testament Book of Job
dares to say the most extreme things that can be said about the
problem of theodicy. But it is still not enough for the preacher
Solomon. In Job it was impossible to discover a divine order
which surpasses the world and individual destiny; there
wisdom and the way to wisdom was known to God alone (Job
28), [197] and something supervening was to be found only in the
mystery of the unattainable preeminence of the divine
ordering activity. But for the Preacher world events and the
orders that orient and clarify experience and shape life now
diverge completely. [198] He too supposes that in world events
and in Yahweh's creative acts a planned event, full of
goodness and beauty, is being perfected, where everything is
to be fulfilled at the time appointed for it (Eccles. 3:1-15). But
man, with his need for bearings, with his questions about
meaning, set in time and in the future by all he does, finds no
help in this divine activity, because he cannot recognize its
totality, its order, and its relation to time. The point of time
when things happen, and when he has to act is concealed from
him (3:11; 11:15). All events are determined and ordered by
Yahweh, and man is completely dependent on this divine
activity, but it is an activity that is completely obscure. Justice
in the individual life and in social relations cannot be

discovered; the future is dark; death, the leveler, is inescapable. Yahweh's acts in the world—in the natural world and environment too—the joyful, elemental fact of life conferred, the meaning of this activity and its bearings on conduct—all these were things which earlier Wisdom had pondered upon. But now they are drawn into the obscurity of God's inscrutable rule. The personal relationship to Yahweh disappears; a definition of the meaning of all human life, drawn from his sovereign rule, gives way to total nothingness; knowledge, experience, and Yahweh's activity all remain dumb. It is man's part to enjoy what is open to the senses in the individual experiences of happiness which life offers (3:12-13, 22; 5:17); but the reason for these individual experiences and their place in the world as a whole are completely obscure.

It has rightly been said that the Preacher is not representative of Israel's late Wisdom. He is an outsider, a lone wolf.[199] Influenced by the hellenistic spirituality of the Ptolemaic period,[200] he views the attempts of Wisdom to arrive at knowledge as fundamentally questionable; without any relationship of trust toward the external world and toward Yahweh—without any living relationship at all—he establishes facts rationally and thereby loses the total meaning of world events and his own life. Is this not the very reason why he appeals so much to modern man, in all his perfection of scientific and technical knowledge and all his pessimism and gloom about the possibility of perceiving determinations of meaning, and norms that are evident and binding?

Israel's late Wisdom did not pursue the path taken by the Preacher. That was really a dead end. It did not accept either the total hiddenness of Yahweh in what he does in the natural world and environment; or the impossibility of taking bearings for living from fore-given orders; or of understanding the course life takes. But it does share with Job and the Preacher in shifting the function of the creation statements. Their purpose now goes far beyond clarification of the natural world of life, serving to illuminate the problems cast up by the fate of the individual— and of Israel itself.

This is shown by the Wisdom of Jesus the Son of Sirach (Ecclesiasticus). [201] Ecclesiasticus is a book (dating from the Jerusalem of the beginning of the second century B.C.) whose hellenistic connections and anti-hellenistic attitude are equally notable. [202] For this book, the order existing between Yahweh's rule in world events, in the world of order existing between Yahweh's rule in world events, in the world of creation, and in the destiny of Israel and the individual is by no means beyond our reach. On the contrary, there is an overriding order which is quite recognizable and which makes it possible to see world events, Israel, and individual destiny as the realization of Yahweh's righteous activity, conferring meaning and significance—the order of Wisdom. This Wisdom characterizes the world of creation, and accordingly Ecclesiasticus stresses that Yahweh's creative event is the realization of a well-considered order which gives everything its meaning (1:1-10; 16:25ff; 39:12ff; 42:15ff). But this Wisdom, which rules throughout the world of creation, has taken up its habitation nowhere but in Israel, in order to shape its life and clarify its significance. This Wisdom takes the form of the Torah, as the famous text Ecclesiasticus 24 stresses[203] (cf. also its earlier history in Job 28 and Prov. 8). The teacher of Wisdom explains this identification in Wisdom between Yahweh's order of creation and the Torah through what he knows of cosmology and salvation history, as well as in his ethical precepts. It binds the elemental bestowal of life in creation and the guarantee of orientation and significance to Israel and the individual into a unified divine event, which is, above all, accessible. Significantly enough, Ecclesiasticus already talks about the godly gift of the commandments in the context of creation (17:11ff; cf. too the tasks of the teacher of Wisdom, 38:34ff), and it interprets those phenomena of the natural world and environment that are the enemies of life as Yahweh's acts directed against the wicked, inside and outside Israel, who do not permit themselves to be guided by the Torah, as the teacher of Wisdom sees it (39:24-34). [204] This is the way in which Ecclesiasticus counters the experience of the imperfectly fulfilled life of the righteous and innocent individual.

The book opposes contrary experiences of this kind even

more emphatically with regard to Israel. For Ecclesiasticus the interpretation of the eschatological prophecies is one of the tasks of the teacher of Wisdom, and it is in line with this that he sees the Israel of his time as experiencing Yahweh's righteousness in the urgently prayed-for future of salvation (36:1 ff).

In Ecclesiasticus, therefore, we come upon a conception which moves Yahweh's activity in the natural world away from its original function in the creation statements and includes it in the pressing problem of theodicy—the realization of God's righteousness in world events as a whole, in Israel's life and the life of the individual in Israel. The identification between Wisdom and the Torah in the framework of this conception has admittedly a serious consequence. It intensifies Israel's fundamental conviction that Yahweh's activity in the world does not force itself on every reasonable person as Yahweh's activity, but has to be proclaimed. And it heightens this view into the thesis that anyone who wants to understand the order of the world must belong to Israel and lead his life according to Wisdom, i.e., in accordance with the Torah.[205]

e. Experiences that run counter to the natural world and environment in the testimony of apocalyptic

The apocalyptic texts that date from late Israel start from this view of things, Ecclesiasticus having prepared the way. They present a combination of the worldwide perspectives on the prophetic proclamations for Israel with their universal scope, on the one hand; the Wisdom viewpoint of a world order, on the other, a viewpoint that is directed both toward world events as a whole and toward individual destiny. Many attempts have been made along well-trodden paths, to define, more or less superficially, the phenomenon of apocalyptic at the end of the late Israelite period with all kinds of seemingly characteristic "isms." Luck, on the contrary, has rightly stressed that here extensive knowledge was mobilized in the new strenuous attempt to understand the entire world-event, in all its dimensions of time and space. Taking account of the

injustice and wickedness experienced in the world, the aim
was to understand Israel's fate and the fate of the individual as
a comprehensive process in which God's righteous order is
fulfilled in spite of the experiences that run counter to it.[206] It
is this insight offered by apocalyptic that can preserve the
deeply shaken trust in God and his righteous world order, an
order required if life is to have direction and find
fulfillment.[207]

It may be said in this connection that we can only
appreciate the unique character of apocalyptic when we
notice that it is confronted with problems of experience which
Ecclesiasticus was not yet up against, and in the face of which
that book's conception was no longer sufficient. For events
after the period of the Seleucids caused a split within Israel.
The Law—the Torah—was itself exposed to persecution.
Altogether the events of the Jewish War in the Roman period
meant contrary experiences in a world lacking order and with
disorder and destruction increasing to such dimensions that
the Torah, which had been given to Israel, and the prophetic
writings (understood in the sense in which Wisdom
understood them) no longer offered the clarifying bearings
which they had been able to do in Ecclesiasticus' perspective.
The Torah and the prophetic writings became questionable
for the person—even the Israelite—who, because of the
catastrophic fate of his nation, was unavoidably involved in sin
and violations of the Law. This is the position which Ezra
discusses.[208] In this utterly enigmatic, obscure, and negative
experience of the world, the apocalyptic writers now go
beyond Jesus Son of Sirach, the teacher of Wisdom, and make
a final attempt to show that for Israel the order of world events
is a just one and that there is good reason why the people
should take their bearings from the Law. The attempt was
now made to reveal the wise and hidden order of the whole
(and hence also the true meaning of the Torah and the
prophetic writings) by means of revelatory writings, which
were given the authority of Enoch, Moses, Baruch, and
others.[209]

The creation statements about Yahweh's acts in the

existing natural world were adhered to and were undisputed as regards the facts they stated, but here they acquired their function only in the comprehensive context of the totality of world events, and in the framework of the apocalyptically revealed plan of divine determination and of the order of the times. This was to clarify the whole world order, which had become obscured through contrary experiences. The plan is directed toward the undiminished realization of God's righteousness in the future; for this future the devout had to wait patiently in faithful observance of the Law.

So in Jubilees 2ff, for example, creation functions to underline through revelation the dignity of the Law's ordinances, especially the sabbath commandment, which was in considerable danger at the time the book was written.[210] In Ethiopian Enoch 2–5, the preservation of the order of creation, embodying the meaning of the whole, is contrasted with the way the wicked ignore the Law, this being the proof of their wickedness and future fate. In the petition to leave the devout remnant for the eschatological turning point, Ethiopian Enoch 84 appeals to the power of God in his continual creative activity. Finally, in 4 Ezra 6, the prophet concentrates the creation event entirely on Yahweh's marvelous and authoritative activity, in order to set something against the absence of this power in Israel's destiny. His aim is to explain the divine paradox found in the tension between the mighty realization of God's Word in creation and the incomplete realization of his Word for Israel.[211]

Originally Israel perceived harmony between the event of creation in the experience of the elemental, natural world of life and experience of the world-event as a whole. This link had now been completely lost. The world-event is marked by wickedness in an intensity that has corrupted the creation ever since Adam's transgression (cf. e.g., Jub. 23:18ff; Eth. En. 84; see what the seer has to say in 4 Ezra 7:11-12). The world-event is therefore bound to end in divine judgment. The devout—those who base their lives on the Law—will survive, however, because of Yahweh's divine faithfulness, though their journey through the world will be marked by suffering. They will enter into a "new creation" (Jub. 1:29; 4:26; Eth. En. 72:1; 91:16; 4 Ezra 7:75; Syr. Apoc. Bar. 32:2, 6; in the Qumran texts I QS II.4-25) which God will bring to pass.[212]

And what about man? Taking Ethiopian Enoch[213] and 4 Ezra[214] as examples, Luck has shown what solution apocalyptic offered on the threshold of the New Testament.[215] In its temporal, spatial, political, and social dimension, in Israel's salvation history and individually, the world is stamped by such human wickedness—is so wholly alienated from God and his order—that Yahweh's activity in the natural world and in world events is no longer perceptible as part of an overriding divine order of significance. Wisdom, Law, and prophecy in their traditional form can no longer throw light on God's righteous activity in this event or on the meaning it confers. This illumination is only given through the esoteric, revelatory wisdom of the apocalyptists, who show the purposeful plan of a righteous divine activity, even in events which corrupt the world of creation through their wickedness. The extent of the wickedness can no longer be checked, according to this revelation, and it will bring the world-event to an end in judgment and annihilation. At the same time, a general punishment for sin and the inescapability of a senseless life in a world empty of meaning is emphatically rejected. The proclaimed plan of the divine realization of meaning in the world is a motive for the devout man or woman to keep Yahweh's Law even in a wicked world, in faithfulness to God's ordinances, even when this is contrary to appearances and there is no visible sign that the Law will effectively change the world. Here the devout person is urged to understand and endure life in this world as a suffering transition to God's future, undiminished, and just world where salvation will be fulfilled. Actual experience of the world and the experience of God are admittedly more and more mysteriously separate in this conception, and the cleft can only be bridged through esoteric revelation. Man's significant relationship is now directed toward God apart from the existing world, as he looks toward the divinely revealed plan and commandment in the future world, which is really the only one having meaning.[216]

In this way, apocalyptic also sees the orientation and behavior of man as the central problem for the state of the existing world and for human experience of the meaning given to life, meaning conferred by Yahweh. The question which concerns us, How men and women can behave toward the natural world and environment in accordance with creation? is not discussed by the apocalyptic writers at all. In their conception, this problem would be part of the faithfulness of the godly toward Yahweh's Law, which has to be practiced in life. But the person guided by apocalyptic no longer takes his bearings simply from Yahweh's creative activity in what he experiences, perceives, and does. He looks toward the comprehensive plan and cohesive order which the apocalyptic writers reveal. In this way, however, Yahweh's creative activity in the existing world is now merely a theological argument to show up an overriding divine activity, which will issue in the new creation. Yahweh, and Yahweh alone, will bring his new creation about, since for the apocalyptic writers, man, even the devout man, has no power to create the quality of life of the natural world. The experience of the natural world as part of meaningful life, still remains for Israel the experience of a given world, the event of a power above man, and Yahweh's turning toward the world in his gift of life—even if his creative act will only be fulfilled in undiminished quality in the future.

f. Summing up

There is no need to suspect that these postexilic theological trends were indulging in groundless speculation as they dealt with the statements about creation. These are testimonies intended to proclaim Yahweh's activity even in the face of real and serious counter experiences in the political and social world. They go far beyond the elemental experiences of the created, given, natural world of life, and necessarily give these experiences a different function and new dimensions, and in so doing they preserve the uniqueness and sole efficacy of Yahweh in his activity conferring life and giving it meaning. It was to this activity that Israel always saw itself directed, in spite of a world that is mysterious and bereft of significance in the face of man's destruction of all meaning and the abyss of titanic obsession and constriction found in the person who has cut himself off from Yahweh. These theological trends do not detract from the special importance of the older creation statements—with their elemental, natural closeness to life—for a period when the acts of man irrevocably threaten the natural foundations of life. But they do show from the course of biblical tradition how inappropriate it is to isolate these statements about creation in aid of a modern orientation. The trends in the later testimonies of the Old Testament indicate horizons for man's responsibility to nature too. To overlook or disregard them would reduce attempts at saving the world and environment to a naive and specialist game, and a game in which the main problem would be suppressed. For the real problem is man and what determines the things he finds significant; man, and whether it is possible for him to have the confidence in the world that makes action possible. The New Testament shows this even more when it testifies to the coming of Jesus Christ in the acceptance and breakthrough of these horizons.

B.
THE NATURAL WORLD AND THE ENVIRONMENT IN THE NEW TESTAMENT

If the subject of the natural world and environment is to be confronted with the biblical findings because it is the serious challenge of our time, then we cannot restrict ourselves in a biblicistic way simply to the statements which touch directly on the natural world and the life in it. That is to say, we cannot stand still at what the Old Testament has to say about creation and at a few statements in the New, torn out of their context. We have already had to reach out farther than the Old Testament in order to make the essential connections of the subject clear. Moreover, there are reasons of principle, for the Christian church and its members take their bearings in experience, thought, and action from the Bible, fundamentally speaking. The Bible has this significance in all its testimonies as a whole. Consequently, its importance for the challenges of the present are not determined by particular thematic correspondences in selected extracts from the biblical testimony, picked in accordance with the topical themes. The decisive thing is this testimony as a whole. Its capacity for exercising critical power in the present and its outlook, which breaks through the current way of looking at things to give a new orientation, can make themselves felt at the very point where strict thematic correspondences are not to be found.

The previous section on the end of the Old Testament period showed that Israel, from the Exile to the late period of its apocalyptic writings, was primarily concerned with the perception of Yahweh's proclamation in the fields of world history and the history of salvation, and in the sphere of individual destiny. But out of this it gained new ways of looking at the natural world as Yahweh's creative act, new ways of seeing its ambivalence, the suffering that constitutes its character, and its future hope.

This applies even more to the New Testament and its testimony to, and perception of, the new proclamation of God in the coming of Jesus Christ, which is his final revelation. The natural world and environment are now also perceived in the light of this event, and the Old Testament sayings are surrounded and encompassed in their decisive Christian sense by the coming of God in Christ to which the New Testament witnesses. Eberhard Jüngel has recently developed this programmatically in a series of theses:[1] "The identification of the truth with the person of Jesus Christ is constitutive for the Christian understanding of truth." And this means "hermeneutically that there is no true knowledge of God which is not as such brought about through Jesus Christ—in whatever way—and which is not related to Jesus Christ as its subject—in whatever way."[2]

Of course this does not mean that the Old Testament has been superseded by the New in the Christian church. Witness to God in the sphere of the present, even with its new and special challenges, takes place in the Christian church on the foundation of both testaments. The Christ-event to which the New Testament witnesses is certainly the yardstick of Christian theology. But the Old Testament with its dimensions and embodiments of God's activity helps to define the Christ-event theologically in the face of present-day challenges in a new and hitherto unformulated breadth, so that Christians may find their bearings and motivations for their responsibility for the world. This applies particularly to the theme of the natural world and environment, which is considered very extensively in the Old Testament, unlike the New.

If the Christ-event to which the New Testament testifies is the yardstick of all Christian orientation, then this alone provides the reason why we cannot confine ourselves in what follows to the scanty New Testament statements in which the natural world and environment and the life they contain are the direct subject and aim. We must also draw on the other viewpoints and contexts to which these statements belong; for it is against this background that they throw light on the Old Testament findings. In view of the space available, this can only be done briefly, and often only in the form of hints or indications. But in considering the facts we may remind ourselves that it is not the task of this New Testament section to solve in advance the problems that must be settled by the various theological disciplines. We do not have to determine here the form of Christian truth for confronting today's environmental problem. The task of explaining theologically the whole intention of the biblical statements in the light of specific present-day problems is even less soluble in an exegetical and historical account; because the biblical texts— not only the Old Testament ones, but the New Testament ones too—knew nothing of the world and environment theme in the sense of a survival crisis. They did not expound their testimony in that light and did not expressly take account, as problem, of the measure of responsibility facing man here, especially in view of the prophetic and apocalyptic expectation (shared by wide sections of the New Testament) of an imminent turn of events in the world to be brought about by God.

This New Testament section is also divided into two main sections. One of them gives an account of the textual findings in the context of their time. The other gathers together thematic aspects that have a bearing on the question of the world and the environment. Of course, this New Testament section continually casts back to the Old Testament part, either implicitly or expressly.

I. Some General Guidance About the New Testament's Textual Findings in the Framework of Their Time

1. Living Conditions in New Testament Times

The setting in which the New Testament statements about the natural world and environment were made (in the first Christian century and the beginning of the second) was no longer purely agricultural; and the same is, of course, true of the people who made these statements and to whom they were made. This was already the case in the late Israelite period, in the Dispersion particularly, although the viewpoint and the dependency of these people on their agricultural surroundings cannot be compared with the highly indirect relationships existing in modern industrial and economic civilizations. Even in Palestine, the home of Jesus' message and the Jewish Christianity that grew up there, trade and commerce had for some time provided additional ways of making a living and had a great influence on society.[1] This was even truer of the Christian congregations that belonged mainly to the towns and cities of the eastern and northern Mediterranean area, as far as Rome, where missionaries had carried the hellenistic-Jewish Christianity of Palestine, and where Paul and his co-workers especially then founded churches based on a Gentile Christianity, free of the Law.[2]

Of course, there were important distinctions between the different areas. We can see the world of the country people of Palestine "from the pictorial material of Jesus' parables into a vivid panorama of farmers, shepherds, fishermen, and tenant farmers, with absentee landlords, and their slaves in administrative positions in the background."[3]

This world certainly looked very different (see the books cited on page 178) from society in a hellenistic town or city, inside or outside Palestine, with all the manifestations of its varied ethnic and cultural groups and its special problems of social integration.[4] Perhaps this is the reason why we can find in the traditions of the first three Gospels a more direct relationship to features of the natural world and environment than in the other New Testament texts.

Yet the different form in which the New Testament expresses the coming of Jesus in relation to the natural world is integrally connected with the different mental and traditional background summoned to help define the "new thing." The Old Testament writings are always drawn upon, but by no means exclusively so. The different living traditions in the theological perception of the natural world and creation which we encountered as prophecy and apocalyptic and as the Jewish-hellenistic stream of tradition, in the last part of the Old Testament section, are of essential importance for the form of the New Testament statements, while in Paul the two traditions come together. H. H. Schmid rightly says of the New Testament that "the given background of thought was the only possible criterion for integrating new experience; though in the process of this integration the framework of thinking expanded and was modified."[5] A glance at relevant New Testament texts dealing with the natural world and environment may help to make this clearer.

2. The Findings of the New Testament Texts on the Subject of the Natural World and Environment

a. The ministry of Jesus and the testimony to it in the first three Gospels

There are frequent references to the natural world and environment in the ministry of Jesus and the testimony to that ministry found in the first three Gospels. (A differentiation between historical sayings of Jesus and later tradition would require a detailed analytical account, for which we have no room here.) These references cover both man and beast[6] and are especially frequent in the parables, as we have already said. We may take the following examples from the Gospel of Matthew (to which the references apply unless otherwise stated): the dependency of everything on sun and rain (5:45); the eye as the light of the body (6:22); the birds, whom God looks after, and the glorious lilies in the fields (6:25ff); man's inability to determine how long he will live (6:27); his dependency on food (6:31ff; 7:9ff et passim); thorns and thistles, contrasting with grapes and figs (7:16); tree and fruit (7:17ff); the house that is properly built in accordance with soil and weather conditions (7:24ff); the foxes' dens and the birds' nests (8:20); clothing, and the storing of wine (9:16-17); sheep and wolves, the wisdom of snakes and the doves (10:16); the sparrows (10:29); tilling the ground (13:1ff, 24ff; Mark 4:26ff, et passim); fishing (Luke 5:1ff); the shepherd's life (18:12ff); eagle and carrion (24:28); the fig tree (24:32).

Here the natural world is treated quite realistically, even where it is imperfect or unfavorable (e.g., fishing in vain, Luke 5:1ff; unsuccessful building, Matt. 7:24ff; unsuccessful sowing, 13:1ff; endangered animals, 9:36; 10:16; 12:11; 18:12ff; storms at sea, 8:23ff). Losses that have to be sustained are considered too, with poverty (6:1ff; 19:21; 26:11; Luke 16:19ff), and above all sickness and premature death (cf. the miracle stories in all four Gospels).

There is no doubt, however, that the natural world, which is there to provide for man and beast, and the gift of life itself are seen, entirely as a matter of course, as God's creative activity.[7] People know how to give good things to their children, so how much more will our heavenly Father give good things to those who ask him (7:11); the sparrow's life is in his hand (10:29-30); referring to Genesis 1:27; 2:24, Jesus says that from the beginning (creation) God created man and woman (19:4-5); Jesus praises the Father as the Lord of heaven and earth (11:25); other statements talk about the beginning of creation and the foundation of the world (Matt. 24:21; 25:34; Mark 13:19).

The sayings about anxiety or worry in Matthew and Luke are particularly significant in this context, and we shall look at them more closely.

Digression: The sayings about worry, Matthew 6:25-34 (Luke 12:22-32)

The purpose of considering these sayings about worry is to give at some point an example of the individual dynamic of the statements about the world in the synoptic proclamation of Jesus. We may assume (following New Testament scholars) that these statements are largely based on sayings of Jesus, even though in their present form they are grouped together in the wider setting of "man in the context of anxiety"[8] and are also furnished with the special theological emphases of Matthew's Gospel, as Dieter Zeller has recently shown in a detailed analysis.[9]

Therefore I tell you, do not be anxious about your life, what you shall eat or what you shall drink, nor about your body, what you shall put on. Is not life more than food, and the body more than clothing? Look at the birds of the air: they neither sow nor reap nor gather into barns, and yet your heavenly Father feeds them. Are you not of more value than they? And which of you by being anxious can add one cubit to his span of life? And why are you anxious about clothing? Consider the lilies of the field, how they grow; they neither toil nor spin; yet I tell you, even Solomon in all his glory was not arrayed like one of these. But if God so clothes the grass of the field, which today is alive and tomorrow is thrown into the oven, will he not much more clothe you, O men of little faith? Therefore do not be anxious, saying, "What shall we eat?" or "What shall we drink?" or "What shall we wear?" For the Gentiles seek all these things; and your heavenly Father knows that you need them all. But seek first his kingdom and his righteousness, and all these things shall be yours as well. Therefore do not be anxious about tomorrow, for tomorrow will be anxious for itself. Let the day's own trouble be sufficient for the day.

If we look at this passage together with the Old Testament statements about creation, we are especially struck by the direct closeness to life and experience with which Jesus' words appeal to people. This is particuarly noticeable compared with what we met in the Old Testament from the Exile onward, where the creative event has become overlaid because the relationship to Yahweh has itself become problematical in other sectors of life. Here it is not the esotericism of hidden, apocalyptic knowledge of a secret, divine plan in a mysterious world that motivates the essential obedience to the commandments for a future world. No, Jesus shows God within the actual elemental experience of the world that man has in life and that Jesus brings out once more.[10] Indeed, since man has been rather left to himself in elementary things by the encroaching theological conceptions of his time, he is concerned quite simply with the fundamentals necessary for living—with eating and drinking, with the essential nourishment; he directs all his activity toward insuring this, so that he may have it in the future as well, as if it all depended on him, on his anxiety and his trouble.

Here, therefore, in contrast to a sated modern society, people are quite conscious of their dependency in principle on the elements of the natural world and environment that are essential for life; but their character as gift which is not at man's disposal has been nonetheless pushed aside; and paradoxically, worry actually turns these things into something that man can dispose, as if there there were not God and no creative activity. Jesus does not introduce God into this basic attitude as if he were really outside such obvious experience. In this elemental reality of the world of life, which is apparently free of God altogether, Jesus shows him, not in what is theological or future or inward or personal, as in the midst of it all—a concept entirely in accordance with the Old Testament creation texts and the unique character of their perception of nature."[11] He does this by pointing man to what is fundamental, given, and practically always suppressed in his own experience. The fact of being alive at all is not something over which man can anxiously dispose; it is a gift of God to man, and it is conferred and is to be valued (vv 26, 30)—a gift made to man, who could not of himself extend his life by a single ell and who could not even make a single hair on his head white or black (5:36). And the same may be said of the provisions for living that are given to everyone who is listening to Jesus—food: look at the birds of the air! They show no anxiety in what they do, as if there were no God. "Your heavenly Father feeds them" (v 26). Clothing: look at the lilies in the fields! How gloriously God knows how to clothe them in his overflowing munificence (vv 28-30)! On Jesus' lips the phrase "God the creator" is not a theological proposition or a theoretical deduction. God the creator is again the revealed, illuminated, elemental experience of life in our dealings with the world, in which Jesus shows God the Father and his fatherly goodness in the midst of the world—the Father who knows very well "that you need all these things" (v 32), so close, so present, so tenderly providing is God, the fatherly creator, in the midst of the elemental world of experience. Thus expressed, the experience of creation is no longer the theological argument for an actual encounter with God in some other place; nor is it another way of expressing the encounter with God in Jesus. Creation, on the lips of Jesus, is man' involvement in the experience of the loving, ever-present God in the elementals of life as it is lived.

What conclusion does Jesus draw for men and women? It is this: we are not to introduce counter-experiences, not to escape into fields of experience where man, cast on his own resources, has to get along without God. It is not the assertion of evil or of undeserved suffering or the reality that there are good and wicked in this world, since God the creator lets his sun rise on them all, the evil and the good, and the rain falls on the just and the unjust alike (5:45).[12] Man does not have to cling to order, contrary to appearances, by means of Wisdom, the Law, or apocalyptic knowledge. Jesus has simply one, no less elementary condition for man, based on the experience of creation that is directly drawn from life: to trust this elementally manifest God, proclaimed by Jesus in a way close to experience, knowing his loving closeness to life and our own vital dependency. That is to say, we must live on the foundation of our own life, instead of being "of little faith" (v 30).

Jesus' specific conclusion in our text is to let worry go, because it is contrary to nature and based on an illusion; to stop trying to secure the elemental things of life for the future, as if they were at our own disposal, and instead to trust the God who has proved himself a loving God, as he now comes near to us in Jesus; i.e., to give a new direction to our impulse to make life secure, and to take our bearings from the kingdom of God, which is imminent in Jesus (v 33). This is the meaningful future of man, graciously opened up for him in Jesus and conferred by the God who has also given, and still gives, the foundation and sustenance of life. This orientation toward the God who in creation is lovingly and universally present to all life, and who in Jesus has come close to us for our salvation, is the proper direction man must take to secure the future of his life. So when man takes the bearings that give his life meaning from the divine future opened up in Jesus, this in no way diminishes the value of the natural world and environment in which he moves. Jesus shows it to be the sphere, evident to experience, of God's loving nearness, from which the proper human way of living emerges, a way in line with the future of the kingdom of God. If he makes this his orientation, man (who is reached and held fast by God in his elemental world especially) will not walk beside his world thoughtlessly and given up to planless illusions. He will live in his world on the foundation of creation, looking toward the imminent coming of God in Jesus. The admonition not to worry (vv 25, 28, 31; cf. v 34) does not exclude responsible and well-considered behavior but, like the creation texts earlier, it does dispense with the illusion that we should feel and act as if life is something that is at our own disposal.

And what about the counter-experiences? They are not argued away, in the view of things which Jesus shows us; but they are seen in a different perspective. Life, high though its value is, is something created by God (vv 26, 30), and that value is not exhausted (as in the creation texts) in length of life in undiminished form and in life's goods (7:19ff; 16:26). It takes its new quality from its relation to the kingdom of God, which has been brought close to man (vv 25, 33). In this relationship even death does not set a limit to life's fulfillment any more (7:14; 10:39; 16:25). This relationship also determines what man really needs, what the criterion really is by which he judges quality of life. It distinguishes actual need from desire and from what is suggested as desirable. And what about suffering? Tribulation through the existence of good and evil in the world? In Jesus' ministry the kingdom of God stands open to all in the midst of the given reality of existence, therefore, Jesus' proposal based from the unrestricted goodness of the creator God and the way he behaves in sending the sun and the rain on the wicked and the good alike is "Love your enemies!" (5:44).[13]

So in Jesus' words and in his ministry of miracles[14] and parables,[15] the fatherly goodness of God the creator and redeemer, who is now approaching in his kingdom, becomes reality in the midst of the world, through the actions and behavior of Jesus' followers. Jesus and the rule of God that dawns in him has taken the place of Wisdom and Torah, and the world of creation opened up in loving-kindness through the approaching rule of God has replaced a world mysteriously governed by God. The clear evidence of Jesus' coming has replaced an esoterically revealed world plan, and the discipleship of Jesus[16] in the midst of the accepted and surmounted ambivalence of elemental existence has replaced the apocalyptic demand for obedience to God's commandments in a world that conceals God.

The fact that, in spite of the sayings about demons and Satan,[17] this ambivalence in the existing natural world, with all its imperfections, is not the fateful work of divine counter-forces but corresponds to the wickedness of man that corrupts creation, is shown by Jesus' critical ethics in general, as well as by the saying in 19:8. But it is equally clear that this existing world is also seen against the background of the world's impending turning point at Christ's second coming (24:3; cf. 19:28) and the breakthrough of the kingdom of God which in fulfillment will bestow life (7:14; 10:39; 16:25-26; 18:8-9; 19:16-17, 29; 25:46) and the provisions for life (8:11; 22:1ff) with

God.[18] The fact that final judgment and the complete breakthrough of the kingdom of God also mean the end of the existing world is obvious and is stressed by Matthew particularly (24:3; cf. 19:28 and 13:36-43). How we are to conceive of the process is not developed, however.[19]

Whereas these texts must be seen against the background of Old Testament and late Israelite statements, in other New Testament texts matters are more complicated because we have to reckon with complex influences deriving from the traditions of the hellenistic world.

b. The Gospel of John

The natural world and environment is not one of the subjects treated in the Gospel of John.[20] Natural phenomena are picked up in what is already metaphorical form (light, life, living water, bread, shepherd, flock). In the miracles of healing, the feeding of the five thousand, and the raising of the dead, Jesus' actions have to do with these things, but no statements are made about them for their own sake. The fact that God the creator is active in the existing world is presupposed rather than developed. In 17:24 we hear about "the foundation of the world," and especially in the prologue to the Gospel, Jesus is termed the Logos (against the background of later statements which described Wisdom as a person[21]) who "became flesh and dwelt among us" (1:14), thereby coming to his own, because everything was made by him, since in the beginning he was with God (1:1). "All things were made through him, and without him was not anything made that was made. In him was life, and the life was the light of men" (1:3-4).[22]

This retreat into the background of the assertions about creation is connected with the way John's Gospel sees "the world." Apart from a few general and neutral passages, this existing world is described with theological precision as the world of man—subject to evil, dominated by the devil and by the wickedness of human actions, which take their bearings from the world and misjudge, reject, and hate Jesus the bringer of salvation. It is marked as whole by its orientation toward itself, not toward God and Jesus, the one sent by God to save the world. That is to say, it is marked by sin and is hence without any meaningful future, but is given over to perdition and judgment.[23] If God loves this world and sends his Son into it, if the Logos becomes flesh (3:16-17; 1 John 4:9; John 1:14), then it is not in order to save this world itself but in order to free believers from being determined by this world and to save them from becoming the victims of its corruption (17:15). It is in order to draw them to himself (12:32), who is not of this world (8:23) and whose "kingdom is not of this world" (18:36), one who confers life, eternal life,[24] and who is himself life.[25] If believers are liberated from this world and, as believers, already enter into eternal life, it is certainly not so that they may flee from the world. They are no longer determined by the power of the world, they are in it as a world of suffering, a world of affliction, sadness, and hate,[26] but they are active in love of the brethren and in keeping the commandments, the words of Jesus.[27]

The phenomenon of the natural world and environment takes on wider scope again in the Acts of the Apostles, even more in Paul, and then in the later Epistles.

c. The Acts of the Apostles

In the Acts of the Apostles[28] the natural world and environment are seen in the framework of statements about creation—apart from a few individual cases, the most striking of which are perhaps the healing of the sick (3:1ff; 5:12ff; 9:32ff; 14:8ff) and Paul's voyage and his behavior during it (27–28). The prayer in 4:24, "Sovereign Lord, who didst make the heaven and the earth and the sea and everything in them," appeals to the power of God the creator to make the path smooth for the apostolic proclamation in word and deed. In Stephen's address, which again picks up Old Testament phraseology, the creative activity of God is used in argument against the idea that God dwells in houses made by human hands (7:49-50). More important, however, are two passages from the missionary sermon to the Gentiles. Under the influence of hellenistic Jewish views, non-Jews are pointed to their experiences in the natural world and environment as signs of God the creator to whom the proclamation of the gospel testifies: "Turn from these vain things to a living God who made the heaven and the earth and the sea and all that is in them. In past generations he allowed all the nations to walk in their own ways; yet he did not leave himself without witness, for he did good and gave you from heaven rains and fruitful seasons, satisfying your hearts with food and gladness" (14:15-17). The same is true of the famous Areopagus address.

> What you worship as unknown, this I proclaim to you. The God who made the world and everything in it, being Lord of heaven and earth, does not live in shrines made by man, nor is he served by human hands, as though he needed anything, since he himself gives to all men life and breath and everything. And he made from one every nation of men to live on all the face of the earth, having determined allotted periods and the boundaries of their habitation, that they should seek God, in the hope that they might feel after him and find him. Yet he is not far from each one of us, for "In him we live and move and have our being"; as even some of your poets have said, "For we are indeed his offspring." (17:23-28)

The fact that the goal of the statements is to bring people to the gospel is as clear as the fact that Acts just as much as Luke's Gospel, has in view an eschatological goal for life in the future of the kingdom of God (Acts 1:3; 8:12; 14:22; 19:8; 20:25; 28:23; on the resurrection: 1; 17:31-32).

d. The Pauline Epistles

The way the natural world and environment are assimilated theologically in the Pauline Epistles is of great importance. It is, of course, completely bound up with the whole Pauline proclamation, though we cannot describe that here in even the broadest terms. We must content ourselves with brief indications. For a fuller account of Pauline theology the reader should turn to Günter Bornkamm[29] or W. G. Kümmel.[30]

We have to remember that Paul was taking over a tradition which contained both the prophetic-apocalyptic strand and the hellenistic-Jewish element. For him, as for the New Testament as a whole, the natural world and environment and the life in it is the work of God the creator. This is already shown by the references to Old Testament creation texts. Genesis 1 is taken up in Romans 4:17 and 2 Corinthians 4:6; Psalm 24:1 in 1 Corinthians 10:26; Genesis 2:7 in 1 Corinthians 15:45 (cf. on the creation of man also 1 Cor. 11:8-12). This means a rejection, here too, of any dualistic, demiurgic depreciation of elemental existence and its natural equipment for living. This is seen in the rejection of other gods (Rom. 1:20; 1 Cor. 8:5-6), while in the latter passage—which takes up late Wisdom utterances—Christ is also included in the creative activity (cf. above John 1:3; also Col. 1:16; Heb. 1:2; cf. also Rom. 11:36). Indeed Paul can say, in statements similar to those in Acts 14 and 17, that God the creator has proclaimed himself also to the Gentiles in creation: "Ever since the creation of the world his invisible nature, namely, his eternal power and deity, has been clearly perceived in the things that have been made. So they are without excuse; for although they knew God they did not honor him as God or give thanks to him, but they became futile in their thinking and their senseless minds were darkened" (Rom. 1:20-21). But Paul, unlike Acts, does not say this in order to link knowledge of this kind directly with the proclamation of the gospel, but in order to explain—on the basis of the gospel—the inexcusability of man who makes himself subject to wrath because, in spite of knowing all this, he cuts himself off from God, perverting himself and his world (vv 22ff). The Jews' situation with regard to the Law is the same (Rom. 2–3). All this manifests the entanglement of all men and women in the power of sin, and the fact that people make themselves the center instead of God (Rom. 3:9; cf. vv 10ff).[31]

Consequently, when he is treating the event of creation Paul talks about God the creator, or the creation of the world (Rom. 1:20), or simply creation (1:25; 8:18ff); but he does not talk about the world as creation. For Paul the concept "world" is defined, not from the event of creation, but out of the perspective opened up by Christ's sufferings and death. It is the

sphere of man's existence, which man molds and which molds
man (and in this respect the Pauline concept resembles that in
the Gospel of John). "This world" is the sphere of influence of
sin that shuts out God and has dominated it since Adam—not as
fate, but as the actual act of each individual and the power that
enslaves him at the same time (Rom. 5:12ff).[32] This guilt, which
has to be answered for, brings death in its wake for everyone as
"the wages of sin" (Rom. 6:23). So because of the general
character of human sin, this world is for Paul the sphere of death
and destruction; it passes away (2 Cor. 4:18), being molded by
man and yet dominating him through "the elemental spirits of
the universe" (Gal. 4:3) as the sphere of power of the "God of
this world," Satan (2 Cor. 4:4), remote from God.

We are reminded of the concept of 4 Ezra, and yet there is
an important difference. Whereas, there the way of salvation
was pointed out in the apocalyptic revelation of the plan of
salvation and in obedience toward the Law, to which this
revelation gave fresh motivation, for Paul salvation is not
opened up by the proclamation of esoteric Wisdom, and the
Law is rigorously excluded as the path of salvation.[33] For Paul
salvation is offered through the coming, death, and resurrection of Christ, as God's gracious (Rom. 3:24; 5:2, 15; 2 Cor. 9:8;
et passim) and loving (Rom. 5:8; 8:35, 39; 2 Cor. 5:14; Gal. 2:20)
bestowal of the divine righteousness to sinners,[34] as the
reconciliation with himself which God grants the world (Rom.
5:10-11; 2 Cor. 5:18-19). This gift is without the works of the
Law; it is offered to faith, as the trusting and obedient
acceptance of the salvation that is conferred and brought close
to us.[35] For Paul this means that the believer is included in an
event which certainly does not take him out of this world as the
place of his existence, but which does—in the warranty of
Christ's resurrection—point him hopefully to the imminent
coming of the risen Christ in glory (Rom. 13:11; 1 Cor. 15:50ff;
Phil. 4:5). Then (and this is linked with the resurrection of the
dead and the Last Judgment) the believer "in Christ" will have
thrown open to him unimperiled fellowship "with Christ," life,
glorification with Christ, and immortality. This world will then
have passed away (1 Cor. 7:31), death will be destroyed, the

powers of the world, whose power is taken from them through
faith in Christ, will be set aside, and God will be all in all (Rom.
11:36; 1 Cor. 15:28). This is what Paul proclaims by means of a
whole number of different concepts and individual variations. [36]

What does this mean for the existence of the believer
who—though he is incorporated in the church and led by the
Spirit[37]—is still in this world? For the Christian—liberated
from the powers of this world, which determine the world and
man, and freed from sin and from guilt through the
Christ-event—the determination and orientation of believing
existence and action and their place in the world cleave
asunder. In being and acting, the believer is liberated from his
direct relation to the power of the world cut off from God. He
has been delivered from it (Gal. 1:4), detached from its
standards (1 Cor. 1:3). Like the apostle, he is "crucified to the
world and the world to him" (Gal. 6:14). The world is no longer
a power. It is merely the place where the believer lives—hence
the demand, "Do not be conformed to this world but be
transformed by the renewal of your mind" (Rom. 12:2).
Wolfgang Schrage[38] has rightly pointed out that for Paul this
conferred liberation from the power of this world and from
one's own self, and transforms the world from sphere of
existence to a sphere of liberty for the believer, who has no
further need to detach himself from it, either through
libertinism or asceticism. It is transformed into a sphere in
which its conditions can be accepted as they are, in which the
flesh offered to idols is merely based on a numinous illusion,
because the earth is the Lord's with everything in it (1 Cor.
10:26). There is nothing impure about it (Rom. 14:14, 20), and
even the power of the state has its necessary function as long as
this world continues to exist, a function which has to be
respected (Rom 13:1ff)[39]. He can now say, "All things are yours,
whether Paul or Apollos or Cephas or the world or life or death
or the present or the future, all are yours; and you are Christ's;
and Christ is God's" (1 Cor. 3:21-23). Apart from this liberated
way of dealing with the world, the altered position of the
believer in it is shown in three ways.

It is shown, first of all, in the bearings that determine what

he does. The action of believers—free from the Law and from
the compulsion of having to determine what is significant and to
bring it about by themselves—is the concrete form taken by
conferred salvation in the relationships of the world. The
exhortations in Paul's Letters show various evidences and forms
of Christian action, for example, the kind of freedom that does
not stand on its rights but can give way for the benefit of the
weaker person (1 Cor. 8:1ff; 10:23ff; Rom. 14–15). They have
their fundamental definition in what Paul calls love *(agape)*,
which is a conceptual compression of what he means. [40] For the
believer, who has experienced God's love for the person who is
opposed to him (Rom. 5:8ff), it is the determining and
unrestricted power of his activity (Gal. 5:6, 13-14; 1 Cor. 13)
that is opened up in God's bestowal of salvation. Thus the
believer's actions are by no means confined to the limits of the
church or congregation; they are in fact directed to the
proclamation of salvation in the world—in the apostolic
existence in which Paul has become "all things to all
men"—Jews, Gentiles, the weak, in order to save some of them
(1 Cor. 9:19-23)—and also in the acts of believers (1 Cor.
14:23-25; Rom. 15:7ff) as "children of God without blemish in
the midst of a crooked and perverse generation among whom
you shine as lights in the world" (Phil. 2:15).

The second aspect of the changed position of the believer is
his detachment from the world. This does not mean
unworldliness, a depreciation of the world, or asceticism. It
means that the existence of the Christian in the world is seen in
the light of the fact that this world passes away because Christ
the Lord is coming again. [41] That is why Günter Bornkamm
says, "According to Paul, the life of the Christian is as far
removed from subjection to the world as it is from flight from
the world. Faith liberates us for independence of the world, yet
at the same time gives us the obligation to prove ourselves in
it." [42] And he goes on, referring to 1 Corinthians 7 in contrast to
the views of the ascetic enthusiasts in Corinth, "the apostle is
not concerned with the conditions which have to be changed
first of all—in themselves, they have no significance for
salvation; he is concerned with the behavior of Christians in

those circumstances. The keynote and yardstick of Paul's directive is simply the relationship of believers to the coming Lord."[43] When faith draws its interpretation of the world from the salvation conferred in Christ and his second coming, this means a change in the believer's evaluation of his own life too. The well-known words in the Epistle to the Romans makes this clear. "If we live, we live to the Lord, and if we die, we die to the Lord; so then, whether we live or whether we die, we are the Lord's" (14:8).

The third aspect, finally, affects the suffering which constitutes the character of Christian existence in the world. Since the turning point of salvation, which has already come about through Christ (1 Cor. 10:11; Gal. 4:4), will take place in this world that passes away; until his coming again, the believer too (although he is liberated from the determining power of this world) is still exposed to its resistance, its frailty, and its depravity. He is exposed to it in enmity, persecution, weakness, and frailty, in sickness, suffering, tribulation, the threat of death, and death itself. In this respect Paul can talk with emotion about the suffering of the apostolic office (1 Cor. 4:9ff; 15:30ff; 2 Cor. 1:4ff; 4:7ff; 6:4ff; 11:16ff; 12:1ff; Phil. 1:20-21),[44] but equally about the suffering of believers (Rom. 5:3; 8:17ff, 35ff; 12:12, 14; 1 Cor. 12:26; 15:24ff; Phil. 1:28-29; 1 Thess. 1:6; 2:14; 3:3-4), sufferings that are simply the form life takes when we are in Christ, his suffering and cross. This belongs to life in this world and will pass away with it; for "I consider that the sufferings of this present time are not worth comparing with the glory that is to be revealed to us" (Rom. 8:18).

After these hints at Paul's theology, we must come back again to what the apostle has to say about creation. It is noticeable that he by no means only talks about God's creative activity in the context of the existing world (apart from its enmity to God as this world). Paul can also describe God's bestowal of salvation in the coming of Jesus Christ as being itself the act of God the creator. In Romans 4:17 (cf. vv 23-25) faith is directed toward God, who makes the dead live, who has raised Jesus "for our justification" (v 25), and who in this way, as Paul puts it (picking up Gen. 1), "calls into existence the things that do not exist." If Ernst Käsemann is right in interpreting this to mean that here Paul is seeing the Christ-event, justification, and the resurrection hope as the workings of God the creator;[45] perception of the salvation event in terms of creation terminology is even clearer in 2 Corinthians 4:6: "For it is the God who said, 'Let light shine out of darkness,' [Gen. 1:3] who has shone in our hearts to give the light of the knowledge of the glory of God in the face of Christ." Here the apostle's proclamation of faith is also included in God's creative activity.

Does this have consequences for the interpretation of the existing world as it is revealed through Christ? The insights of recent Pauline scholars (E. Käsemann,[46] P. Stuhlmacher,[47] G. Bornkamm,[48] F. Hahn,[49] and others) are of essential importance here. According to their view, in Paul the event of salvation goes beyond its anthropological and ecclesiological scope and has a universal dimension. W. Schrage sums up this view. "[Paul] corrects a soteriology which is oriented solely toward the individual and the redemption of the individual—indeed, he rejects a purely anthropologically directed soteriology in general. . . . For Paul the essential thing is the sole eschatological lordship of God—his lordship over the whole world. . . . This rule of God over the whole world is more than the new existence and hope of the individual. . . . Christ is now already, not merely the one to whom the individual Christian and the church belong, but the one to whom the world belongs . . . the still hidden cosmocrator, whose lordship the church has to proclaim now, and must testify to by obedience in the still rebellious world"[50] (Phil. 2:10-11; 3:20-21). If this is so we can go on to consider with Schrage whether, for the believer who has been liberated from this world's power and alienation from God, the world in which he moves shows itself once more as the world of creation, freed like him from the power of sin—at least as far as the believer's existence and behavior are concerned, though certainly not as regards his suffering. Schrage sees examples which suggest that Paul held this view, but he himself points out that Paul's thinking is not entirely covered by the viewpoint that "for the Christian, life in a cosmos newly understood as creation is again made possible."[51] And he gives reasons why in Paul it is not enough "to draw the line between the 'nay' to the fallen world and the 'yes' to the created one, become once more manifest as creation. And it is evidently not enough because this would reduce eschatology to restitution, and new creation would only be conceived in the framework and context of creation. It is probably not by chance, however, that the word *kosmos* is avoided by Paul and the rest of the New Testament in describing the future world and the new creation."[52]

This is confirmed by the two statements in which Paul terms the sphere of being in which believers in Christ already find themselves as "new creation" (Gal. 6:15; 2 Cor. 5:17). As Stuhlmacher has shown, in both passages the term is by no means merely a statement about believers.[53] In the formulation in Galatians 6:15, "For neither circumcision counts for anything, nor uncircumcision, but a new creation," the world (6:14) with its differentiation into Jews and Gentiles (a prerogative belonging to salvation history) is contrasted with the new creation opened up in Christ as the sphere of existence of the church, "the Israel of God" (6:16). Second Corinthians 5:17 tells us that "If any one is in Christ, he is a new creation; the old has passed away, behold, the new has come." As F. Hahn has shown, Paul is saying here that with the inclusion in the Christ-event, given for the believer in the church and open to everyone, the reality of the new creation has already dawned. In this reality sins are forgiven, the destructive world power of evil is broken, old things have passed away, and salvation and the life of Christ as "the new thing," penetrate and transform the earthly sphere. Something final and ultimate is dawning here, something that has universal significance, beyond the sphere of the individual and the church.[54] The new creation "as Romans 8:18ff shows, aims at the renewal of the whole existing cosmos."[55] The new creation "as the becoming-present of eschatological salvation is a reality that takes in the whole world."[56] So "although it is only dawning, it is no "less" than the cosmos, it is "more," and more comprehensive than the cosmos, because everything earthly is included in the divine reality of salvation. The eschatological proviso does not abolish the presence of the salvation of the new creation."[57]

Digression: The inclusion of nonhuman creation in the event of
          salvation, Romans 8:19-22

The eighth chapter of Romans shows how Paul depicts the
present and future of this new creation with a universal scope
reaching beyond the context of man: the certainty, even in life's
suffering, that "in everything God works for good with those
who love him" (v 28); that no opposing power of any kind can
separate them from the love of God (vv 31-39); and the view
according to which all created things will be brought into the
liberty of the salvation planned by God for the future. Paul
expounds this viewpoint in 8:18-27 and more particularly in
8:19-22, and we must analyze it more closely, even if we can do
no more than indicate an approach. For details the reader
should turn to the great studies by Käsemann (1973),[58] H. R.
Balz (1971)[59] Henning Paulsen (1974),[60] and Peter von der
Osten-Sacken (1975).[61] We shall be following the last of these
particularly.

In the wider context of the whole theme of Romans 8 ("the
question about the reality of salvation in the face of suffering and
death"[62]), Paul takes up the problem of how suffering with
Christ can be fitted in here (v 17*b*), how it is a reality, and how
the goal of this suffering with Christ is glorification with him.
After the "transition" in v 18,[63] he develops this in three
sections, considering creation (vv 19-22), Christians (vv 23-25),
and the sighs of the Spirit (vv 26-27).

The first of these development passages is the most
important for our present context. "For the creation waits with
eager longing for the revealing of the sons of God; for the
creation was subjected to futility, not of its own will but by the
will of him who subjected it in hope; because the creation itself
will be set free from its bondage to decay and obtain the glorious
liberty of the children of God. We know that the whole creation
has been groaning in travail together until now." Here Paul
asserts that the whole nonhuman creation (vv 19, 22[64]) is
waiting longingly for the revealing of the sons of God—for their
future liberty, which will be conferred on them with their glory
in the form of immortality (v 21). This longing expectation on
the part of the whole creation is due to the fact that, without

having done anything itself, it has been drawn by man (v 20; cf. Rom. 5:12ff[65]) into the slavery of decay or transitoriness, under which it has suffered, sighed, and groaned from Adam until the present (v 22). But Paul stresses that this subjugation of the whole creation is "in hope" (v 20) because creation too is to be freed from its subjection to decay and is to enter into the liberty of the glory of believers (v 21). In pointing out that the condition of creation has up to now been one of hope and therefore this is itself a time of hope, Paul (whose concept of hope is an extremely precise one) also includes creation in the saving event of Christ's resurrection. Creation is also to emerge from the suffering of its bondage to death and, with believers, is to achieve the liberty of glory, showing—by its suffering hope for participation in glory—the connection with what has been touched on in verse 17b. Käsemann stresses the parallelism between verses 19-22 and the saving event for men. "In our verses the justification of the godless is given a cosmological variation, as salvation for the fallen and groaning world."[66]

Verses 23-25 develop the subject of verse 17b as it affects believers, bringing out the parallelism and the difference between nonhuman creation and the world of men. Believers also sigh, since they have the Spirit; but they are not subjected in hope, as creation has been subjected up to now (v 20); they are saved for hope (v 24) in patience (which is the form taken by suffering with Christ),[67] waiting for the final turn of events when salvation will be fulfilled as the reality of being glorified with Christ.

Finally, verses 26-27 develop the theme as it touches on the Spirit, for the Spirit sighs in believers in their weakness, because of the sufferings of this world, thus interceding for believers and their salvation.[68]

In this whole train of thought the first development (which is related to creation) is not merely an example taken to illustrate a theme that is really directed at and restricted to believers.[69] It includes nonhuman creation too—living things and the world in which they live—in the saving event opened up in Christ. Here man and the world of creation belong together, in the depravity of the world of creation and also in the participation by the world of creation in the glory of the children of God.

What is striking here is the different perspectives under which Paul is able to see the existing natural world and environment of all living things, including man. He sees it (a) as God's creative activity; (b) as "this world," which has been depraved by man and is dominated by the power of sin and death; (c) as creation which still has to hope for glory with believers, even in this depravity, and opens itself up for believers in its behavior as liberated creation; and (d) as new creation, already dawning in believers, which manifests itself in the midst of a still groaning world; for according to Romans 8 the whole of creation will be included in the salvation to come. Paul does not say that before the eschatological turn of events anything will change fundamentally, or can be changed in the existing suffering of nonhuman creation for which man (who is himself a part of creation) is responsible (Gen. 1:26ff; cf. 9:1ff). Indeed he rejects this possibility. The patience of Christians in the present corresponds to the waiting and sighings of creation, as the form assumed by hope.

If we look back to what we discovered about Paul's Letters, we are struck by the fact that he confines neither creative activity nor the world of creation to the divine bestowal of the elemental world as it actually exists. For Paul this bestowal can comprehend an event which covers, even in time, the universal dimension of the world in its creation, in the Christ-event, and in its future glory. We may remember that in Deutero-Isaiah the event of creation similarly took in the totality and unity of Yahweh's acts, including his new, final activity, and this suggests itself as being a theologically comparable process. Of course, even in the Epistle to the Romans creation is not treated as if it were the sustaining, fundamental conception behind God's whole activity. But we must point to this new viewpoint, which Käsemann[70] and Stuhlmacher[71] have introduced into Pauline scholarship with their interpretation of justification as a creative event,[72] and their view that the event of salvation has a dimension that includes the world. This view has been given

Old Testament support by H. H. Schmid.[73] Objections to it[74] (some of them historical) cannot be followed up here, though we may mention that doubts have been raised as to whether the word "creation" is not used here in an extended sense for the more comprehensive concept of an unscathed, righteous world, *including* the elemental natural world and environment, which is really bound up with the concept of creation.

e. Additional aspects in other New Testament writings

In going on to look at other New Testament writings and what they have to say about the phenomenon of the natural world and environment, it is impossible to consider the total conception or the details of what all these different writings have to tell us. But though we have to bear this in mind, we must first of all mention the Epistle to the Colossians.[75] The much-discussed[76] hymn to Christ in Colossians 1:15-20 (exhaustively analyzed by E. Schweizer[77]) is the reworking of an earlier fragment of tradition. Two of its verses talk about Christ as the preexistent mediator of creation, "the image (this is not derived from Gen. 1:26, 28) of the invisible God" and "the first-born of all creation" in whom, through whom, and for whom everything was made; and it also talks about Christ as the redeemer, "the first-born from the dead" who reconciles the universe through the cross. In Colossians, therefore, the whole activity of God in creation and redemption is seen as christological event. In this it differs from Paul, being a discussion about, and defense against, a different and distinct counter-position with regard to a redeemed and unscathed world.[78] In creation, too, Christ is the manifestation of God, so "that one can only understand God's creative activity when it comes face to face with Christ,"[79] and only in the light of its connection with the event of redemption. Accordingly, in Colossians redemption has a cosmic dimension that goes beyond the world of man. It is directed toward the continuance of a reconciled world, in correspondence to the new man whose nature "is being renewed in knowledge after the image of its creator" (3:10).

Again the word "image" is a reference to Christ, not to Genesis 1, which describes man as the image of God.[80]

We met this assertion of Christ as the mediator of creation in John 1 and in Paul (1 Cor. 8:5). It shows the influence of Wisdom and of Hellenism,[81] and we find it again in the Epistle to the Hebrews (1:2-3, 10) and in the Revelation (3:14), each of which gives it its own particular emphasis. It is intended to take in the unity and complete cohesion of the event of God's total gift to the world, and hence to bring out the connection between the creation and the redemption of the natural world and the life in it, from the point of view of God's revelation of himself in Christ, which is now experienced. Unlike Deutero-Isaiah and Paul, Colossians does not express this unity and cohesion as the event of creation, but as the Christ-event, which proceeds from God and has a universal scope both in time and space. Here hellenistic concepts about the unity of the universe through the God who rules it all are taken up and yet broken through. Here the character of event in the divine universal activity is brought to bear in the Old Testament sense; this is the act of the incalculable God, who transcends the world and initiates something entirely new. As in the Old Testament, his activity can be perceived retrospectively, from the point of view of what is new but which nonetheless reflects on the whole. This whole is now seen in the light of the redemptive coming of Christ into the world. Thus in its own way the statement about Christ's mediating office in creation preserves what the early Christian testimonies all express theologically in their various ways. Since the coming of Christ, God has made known what the natural world and environment as God's creation really is—its meaning, its condition, and its goal—solely in the light of that redemptive coming, which opens up the future of salvation. Yet this eschatological finality, which is inherent in the event of creation from the very beginning, is not expounded in any detail, either here or anywhere else in the New Testament. Pannenberg has rightly pointed this out.[82] As we have seen, even Paul in Romans 8 applied it only to creation, which is enslaved "in hope."

Apart from statements about the creation of the world through Christ, the late New Testament writings also contain statements about the creation of the world by God. These assertions are found in brief, predicative phrases in the context of a christological or soteriological statement—e.g., Ephesians 3:9 ("God who created all things"), Revelation 4:11; 10:6; 14:7—or in admonitions that commend believers (as men and women liberated from other powers) to the existing world and the proper use of their natural span of life, contrary to ascetic tendencies aimed at the achievement of salvation (cf. Col. 2:20-22, where there is no direct reference to creation, and 1 Tim. 6:3ff, where there is such a reference).

A final additional aspect touches on statements made in the later New Testament writings about the end of the present world and its future new and redeemed form as the sphere for living, beyond men and women and their eschatological future.

We have seen that both Paul and the Epistle to the Colossians do not confine the event of salvation to men and women, but also relate it to the whole world as the sphere of all created things. This is in order to preserve the comprehensive framework of divine activity, even soteriologically and eschatologically. But it is not because the elemental connection between the living thing and its world has to be made apparent in salvation's consummation as it was apparent in creation, thus constraining the development of concrete notions about the living, especially believers and their redeemed world. The New Testament dispenses with detailed information about the way we are to think of the replacement of the existing world of creation by the eschatological new world. Paul has nothing to say about this, in his statements about "the new creation" or in Romans 8 or anywhere else; and neither has the Epistle to the Colossians. This is also the conclusion which A. Vögtle comes to in his extensive study on the New Testament and the future of the cosmos.[83] This world, which is evil's sphere of power and a depravation of creation, will pass away (1 Cor. 7:31; 1 John 2:17); the word of Jesus is more enduring than the passing existence of heaven and earth (Matt. 5:18; Mark 13:31); the kingdom of Christ is not of this world (John 18:36); Christ's second coming and his judgment will be accompanied by divine manifestations in the form of cosmic disturbances (Mark

13:24-25; Rev. 6:12-17; Heb. 12:26-27). All these statements only preserve different aspects of the transcendentally preeminent relationship of the Christ-event to the sphere of the present world and thereby emphasizes the sovereign lordship of God in the soteriological and eschatological event, as well as in the event of creation. But none of these statements say how this eschatological event of worldwide dimensions will come about, in the sense of how it will affect the existence of the present world of creation. They fall silent before what no tongue can utter. Whether what is new will be preceded by the destruction of the existing world, or whether the great turn of events will take place through the renewal and transformation of creation in surpassing form—this question is left open.

If we except the controversial passage Hebrews 1:10-12 (in which the statement about the eschatological renewal of the world which has become "old like a garment" may simply have the function of stressing by force of contrast "the immortality and constancy of the divine *kyrios* Christ,"[84] there are only two New Testament writings that are exceptions in offering precise information about the lack of continuity between the old and the new, and in which the end of the world divides God's new world from the present one.

One of these passages is in 2 Peter. This is probably the latest of all the New Testament writings.[85] Chapter 3:5-7, 10, 11-13 several times expresses the expectation of an end of the world through fire, in connection with the Last Judgment. Ideas taken from Qumran, Hellenism, and hellenistic Judaism are drawn on here.[86] This view may appear strange to us in its combination of the elements of water and fire with the active Word of God, and in its parallelism between the Flood (the end of the world through water) and the Last Judgment (the end of heaven and earth in their present form through fire), which will be followed by the promised new heaven and new earth in which righteousness dwells (3:13). But leaving that on one side, we should note how the passage functions in the Epistle as a whole. A closer investigation of the text shows[87] that these statements about the end of the world belong within the framework of the author's intention to fortify the church as it waits for Christ's *parousia,* since it was greatly disturbed by the ever-increasing delay of the Second Coming. And support was needful in the face of opponents who put forward the view that everything would simply go on as it had always done since creation, without anything new happening (3:3-4).[88] In opposition to this view, the writer affirms Christ's *parousia* and the conduct of Christians that is in accord with it (3:11ff; cf. v 3) by pointing to the future judgment, to which he lends argumentative support through statements about universal fire. The question of the continuity or discontinuity between the world of creation and the new world is therefore not the aim of these assertions. Their function is to underline the admonitions about the *parousia*. They are not in themselves the subject of theological reflection.

The other writing is the Book of Revelation,[89] where from chapter 17 onward the seer proclaims the course of events at the end. These events include the final destruction of Rome, which represents the earthly power persecuting the church (chaps. 17–18); the destruction of Satan, in the representatives of his power on earth (chap. 19), through his thousand-years' imprisonment and final annihilation (chap. 20); and the destruction of the power of death (chap. 20)—all this leading on to the vision of the undiminished world of salvation prepared for believers (chaps. 21–22). This visionary view of end-time events undoubtedly also includes the notion of the end of heaven and earth, i.e., of the existing world (21:1; in 20:11 on the other hand, metaphors of judgment),[90] especially since the expected descent of the New Jerusalem from heaven presupposes the end of the existing earth, together with the earthly Jerusalem (cf. 21:2).[91] Yet we must again ask: What is the seer's intention in making these statements? Linking up with apocalyptic traditions, especially the prophecies in Trito-Isaiah (esp. Isa. 65) and Ezekiel (esp. 40ff), and like them, he wants to bring out the fact that the final salvation of believers springs from the free and unrestricted initiative of God; that it definitely and finally excludes everything that resists or opposes it, and everything evil; that it is part of the continuous fulfillment of God's promises; and that a world of salvation will be set up in which all life's adversities and losses (so much a part of man's experience in the present world) will have passed away. That is why the New Jerusalem is pictured as the bride of Christ and the place of God's direct presence, a place which therefore needs no temple; where there are neither tears nor death nor suffering nor crying nor the pain of an existing world whose burdens have been laid on it by man; where there is neither sun nor moon, or day or night, because God and Christ are its light; where the gates are continually open because the city is unthreatened; where the water of life and the tree of life provide for the redeemed, who look upon the face of God.

This, therefore, is not simply speculation without foundation. The metaphors hold fast what was always the fundamental biblical conviction: that the unscathed and undiminished world on which all the living depend is not within the power of the living themselves. It is fore-given by God, bestowed as a gift, and it exists in man's bond with him. The Revelation grasps this fundamental conviction under the pressure of experience of reality in the actual existing world. That is to say, it grasps it within the viewpoint of the Christ-event as the object of expectation. And in this way it preserves for future salvation what Genesis 1 and 2 had proclaimed as the foundation of the existing world in the event of divine, unrestricted creativity.

II. Thematic Aspects

If we look back at the New Testament findings as we have shown them, we are faced with a result which at first sight hardly provides any direct support for our contemporary attempts to master the crisis of the natural world and environment. The essential cohesion of the natural world and environment and everything in it, including human life, is never explicit as an independent theme. The New Testament, unlike the Old, offers no thematically distinct statements about creation, let alone extensive passages on the subject, covering the elemental world of life in its totality. The reason for this is a simple one, but an understanding of it is blocked by a modern, secular outlook on life. The New Testament is thematically concentrated on its testimony to the new activity of God in the coming of Jesus Christ; and this coming of Christ opens up a sphere of meaningful and fulfilled life which is not confined to the existing natural world, but aims to go beyond it in God's future world. It is this perspective which determines the New Testament's message; and all the statements made about the phenomena of the natural world as we see it are auxiliary to this.

But this is not all; for, on the other hand, for Jesus and his New Testament witnesses this new divine coming is not something isolated. Nor does it come about in some imaginary sphere. It takes place in God's incarnation and in the work of the church in the midst of the present world. It does not deny that world, and it by no means overlooks the sphere in which the living have always existed. But it accepts this and includes it, as God's world of creation, in the comprehensive whole of divine activity which reveals its goal in the coming of Christ. As we have seen, the New Testament message leaves us in no doubt that, in Christ, the God to whom the Old Testament testifies enters his world of creation. Accordingly in the New Testament his coming is not merely perceived by reference to the Old, but also within the framework which the Old Testament itself opens up: the framework of the world's comprehensive dimension of meaning as a whole, both in time and space. So far the sphere of the natural world and environment as we see it in the New Testament is not simply eliminated, practically speaking, or reduced in functional statements bearing on another life in another world. Therefore, the New Testament (in its relation to the Old) also includes definitions of significance which apply to the existing natural world and environment and everything living in it, even if these are not expounded and expressly formulated with an eye to any specific problem of concern to our modern world.

But in the New Testament as well as in the Old we shall, of

course, only perceive the significance of biblical statements for our present challenges if these challenges are seen on the level of the fundamental questions that we raised at the beginning when we were considering the cause of the problem—man. That is to say, we shall only perceive this significance if the essential cohesion of the natural world and environment with everything living, including man, is not accepted unquestioningly and without reflection; and if, on the other hand, we do not try to preserve it by making running repairs here and there, because we are so appalled at its deficiencies and the crises that threaten its existence. The meaning of the New Testament statements only emerges when this total cohesion is seen as the foundation and presupposition for the meaningful event of life, when it is in conformity with genuine experience, and when guiding fundamental attitudes, basic convictions, goals, models, values, and norms for individual and social behavior in the natural sphere correspond to it. This fundamental level is of essential importance for our attitude to the environment. It is only on this level, which determines the meaning of our own existence and the existence of other things—its impediments, its fulfillment, and its future—that the viewpoints and definitions to which the New Testament also testifies emerge in their illuminating and guiding significance for the elemental threats of our time, which are summed up under the heading of the world and the environment.

As we have frequently stressed, a thorough theological exposition of the New Testament testimony, to achieve the valid form of Christian truth and life for our contemporary environmental problem, is inevitably beyond the scope of what can be said here. But we shall work toward it in the following thematic sections, where we shall try to find out what light the New Testament findings shed on our present problem; and also how its statements are related to our Old Testament findings. The center of the New Testament proclamation is the Christ-event, the coming of God into the world; and it is there that we must accordingly begin. In the following sections we shall then consider the New Testament's conclusions, which emerge as definitions of significance for the existing natural

world and environment, for its future, and for the bearings of
Christians living in it.

1. Jesus Christ as God's Entry into the Natural World and Environment

a. Jesus Christ as God's revelation of himself in the midst of the world

Whatever words and ideas are used in the New Testament
for what can only be expressed in metaphorical terms—the
foundation of the New Testament testimony is the conviction
that *God* came into the world in the *man* Jesus of Nazareth, in
his ministry and in what happened to him. By perceiving and
showing this new divine self-revelation in the man Jesus, the
New Testament preserves the essential and fundamental fact of
the biblical experience of God; for according to this experience
God is not an extrapolation in the framework of a given world
reality, but its transcendent and free foundation, which is
proclaimed in what is incalculable and indefinable, and as such
reveals the reality of the world. And in Jesus of Nazareth this
reality is the supreme event: the event through which God
himself enters directly into the reality of the world in the
ministry and fate of this person; enters its political and social
dimensions, and into the experience of individual existence;
but he also enters the elemental foundations of the natural
world. Here the New Testament unreservedly shares the Old
Testament's view that it is impossible for man—simply by
himself, in what he experiences, thinks, and does—to see and
find the true meaning of the world's reality in all these
dimensions. He needs to take the meaning that God confers as
his center. Only, these divine definitions of meaning are now
exclusively revealed in the way the God to whom the Old
Testament testifies reveals himself in his relation to the world in
Jesus' ministry and fate.

For the New Testament, the meaning of Old Testament
statements about creation, the meaning for Israel of the
experiences and promises of salvation history, the meaning of

Wisdom and Law as behavior conforming to God's commandments—all these things are now tested against this advent of
God. And the meaning of the dichotomy which people felt
between God's creative activity and his activity for Israel and
the nations in the political and social sphere of salvation
history—the contrast between creative activity and individual
destiny—the contrast between conduct that looks toward God
and what actually happens to people in life—all that is also
tested against this. In short, the meaning of all the problems
where the activity of God in the natural world and environment
come under consideration, at least from the Exile onward, are
now tested against the coming of God in Christ; we have
continually discovered, in going through the New Testament
findings, that Jesus and his New Testament witnesses
undoubtedly pick up the problems and attitudes which
determine the perception of God that we found in the late Old
Testament writings.

And yet the coming of God in Christ is not simply a
homogeneous continuation of the theological movements of the
later Old Testament tradition. For the New Testament, Jesus is
not just one more teacher of Wisdom or one more prophet of the
end-time or yet another apocalyptic herald of esoteric
revelation or another "teacher of righteousness,"[1] who has
joined the prophets as valid interpreter of the Old Testament
testimonies and as an expert on God's plan for the world. In
Jesus *God* has become *man,* and so Jesus of Nazareth is God's
fundamental revelation of himself in the world, a revelation that
determines everything now and in the future. He is this
revelation in the totality of his human existence, in what he says
and does, as well as in what happens to him in the world of men
and women, where he suffered, was put to death, and rose
again. That is why the coming of God in Christ also has
consequences for the biblical tradition as a whole, because it
bursts the confines of that tradition through its new and—in this
respect—transformed perspective, directed toward all sectors
of the actual world in which we live, in the political and social
sphere just as much as in the elemental guarantees of the
natural world and environment.

b. The transformed outlook on the world

The meaning and validity of the Old Testament prophecies of a new future divine world (Matt. 11:5; 2 Cor. 1:20) are now shown in the light of God's revelation of himself in Christ. The differentiations between Israel and the other nations which belonged to salvation history are now relativized for the benefit of Jesus' followers—the church made up of Jews and Gentiles—as the Gospels, Paul, and the Epistles to the Ephesians and the Hebrews expound theologically; and this is shown in the light of God's unrestricted gift to all men, in the conduct of Jesus. The will of God in the Law, as Jesus shows it, is tested in the light of God's coming in Jesus; and his rejection and crucifixion is, as Paul expounds, the end of the Law as path of salvation for men and women. God's coming in Jesus reveals the meaning of the admonitions, precepts, and insights of Wisdom, as we can see from the frequent use of Wisdom sayings in the Synoptic proclamation of Jesus.[2]

Not least, for the New Testament *the meaning of natural life in an elemental, natural world* is to be tested in the light of God's coming in Jesus; tested in its divine givenness, in its actual situation, and in its future, from now on opened up by God. To perceive in experience, thought, and act the nature, meaning, and future of the natural world and environment and all the life in it, including one's own, now means seeing the world in the framework of God the creator's revelation of himself in Jesus Christ. It means becoming aware of the experiences to which this divine self-revelation leads us and of what stands the test of these experiences. It means finding the actual form actions and decisions have to take in life if they are to conform to this new event. The statements which the New Testament makes about creation have clearly shown us this essential relation, in the context of Jesus' ministry in the Synoptic Gospels, as well as in the theological conclusions drawn in the Acts of the Apostles, and above all in Paul and his developed use of creation terminology (which is reminiscent of Deut.-Isa.). We also find it in John, in the connection between Jesus as mediator of creation and his redemptive work, and in Colossians and Hebrews, as well as in the final visions of the Revelation. The theological link between creation and the kingdom of God, between the doctrine of creation and eschatology, therefore plays an important part, down to the doctrinal discussions of the present day (see e.g., W. Pannenberg, Jürgen Moltmann, and K. Stock[3]).

In these statements the New Testament testimony certainly links up with the late Israelite viewpoint: a world created by God but distorted by man into a state of injustice and imperfection, a world which it is puzzlingly difficult to reconcile with God's ruling power, but where there is nonetheless the promise of a new divine world. The new coming of God in the man Jesus of Nazareth, however, transforms this outlook. Now it is no longer the Law and the esoteric, apocalyptic teachings of Wisdom that try to bring man's actions and behavior within their grasp, so as to withstand the puzzle of God's rule in the present world, the disharmony between the "once" of salvation history and the "then" which only belongs to the future. Now the God who turns directly toward everyone stands in the midst of the world, as man. The one who suffers from the world and burst it apart, judging it and giving it new bearings, reveals God in the midst of the world. He appears before all eyes and opens up a way to all who follow the Jesus who has turned toward us in his saving acts, a way which will also be extended to bring in the whole of God's world of creation.

This transformed New Testament view of the world is no longer nourished by the divine tradition; it is nourished by the future—the future of the kingdom of God, which dawns in Jesus' ministry, is affirmed in his resurrection, and is opened up as liberation for all men in what he says and in his suffering and death. Jesus expectantly proclaimed this divine kingdom as the world's goal. He promised it to his followers, and his ministry was the token of its fulfillment,[4] as he created righteousness and expounded the riddles of God's providence.[5] Though they often employ different concepts, ideas, and aspects, all the New Testament witnesses proclaim this kingdom as the new divine world opened up and guaranteed to believers in Jesus' ministry and fate. In this world God will grant salvation, life, and righteousness in all-embracing scope in his perfect and undiminished kingdom. And—as in Yahweh's bestowal of life, which is the foundation of the Old Testament viewpoint—he will do this before any act on the part of man; without any intervention on man's part (not even by believers, as regards the universal realization of the Kingdom and the time of its coming); and apart from any possibility of steady development within the world, again not even through believers.

For the New Testament witnesses, therefore, the world (as the divine activity that confers significance) is concentrated in its total spatial and temporal perspective on a continuous event; and this event is marked by two initial appointments on God's part. These are fundamental, and, as we have already seen comparably in the Yahwist's history, their quality extends to the primal period. On the one hand, we have God's creative activity for all men, which insures life and the world of the living, and which goes on existing even when man cuts himself off from that creative activity, or when Israel frees itself from what Yahweh has savingly bestowed on it. On the other hand, on the ground of this continuing world of creation, we have the same God's all-embracing saving activity in Jesus Christ. This saving activity is again directed toward all men, quite apart from their specific ethnic, political, and social forms of life, and quite independent of their culpable orientation toward themselves and the world. It seeks believing trust as the acceptance of this divine gift and—in the present world of creation culpably distorted by man and in a history of Israel marked by judgment—it throws open a future of salvation in which God's creative activity for the world and God's saving activity for the chosen people belonging to the church of Jews and Gentiles will find realization in a new divine world. And both movements or decrees of this divine event include the elemental world of man and nonhuman life.

c. Faith as perception of the transformed outlook on the world

This new event, then, has universal scope and reaches as far as the elemental world of life, which belongs to nonhuman life as well. But it is noticeable that in the ministry of Jesus and in his proclamation in the gospel, the event is concentrated on people. It is to people that it is proclaimed and to people that it is appropriated. Accordingly, faith is the New Testament concept mainly used to describe the acceptance and corresponding perception of this event in experience, thought, and act.

Why is this new turning of God toward the world directed primarily to people in the New Testament? It is because the transformation of a world of creation distorted by people begins with the believing acceptance of the gospel by people; even though God brings this about for the salvation of the nonhuman world of creation too, as Romans 8 shows particularly. By directing the saving event mainly toward people, before all other created things, the New Testament is reflecting what the Old had already grasped when it saw man as having a particular position and responsibility for the whole world of creation.

This has consequences for man's attitude with regard to the world. For in the natural world in which he lives, be it the political world or the world of nature, man is now primarily pointed toward God's inclination toward him in the man Jesus, with the whole perspective which that opens up. In this way the New Testament, just as much as the Old, contradicts every attempt to measure the importance of what it says about the natural world and environment by the yardstick of pluralistic sensibility about the ecology in the present, or by our widespread desires or fears. The New Testament seeks faith, and itself provides the yardstick. It calls men and women to adopt the perspective that is opened up here and to see the subject of the world and the environment in the light of the God who has been proclaimed in Christ and who has been tested by experience. From him we can acquire guidance for meaningful experience, understanding, and action in the natural world; from him we can receive what we do not know of ourselves; from him we can accept scrutiny, bearings, and criticism with regard to our ecological sins of omission and our ecological desires and strivings. But though the New Testament for its part provides the yardstick, it still makes it clear that the believer's orientation toward the Christ-event must primarily and fundamentally have the following aim: to look toward Christ and God's future world, not toward the survival of our natural world; to look for the salvation of "eternal life," and not for the guarantee and equipment of natural life; to fix our eyes on existence in the kingdom of God, and not on improvements in the world of politics; to seek the fellowship of believers, not social position, security, social improvements, or a leveling of social status.

Does the coming of God in Jesus of Nazareth mean then for men and women separation from the world, in the final analysis, unworldliness? Does it mean that the actual form life takes and its actual living conditions have merely a relative value? The New Testament answer is a decisive yes and an equally decisive no! The following aspects of the subject will show how this is true of the elemental sector—the natural world.

2. The Natural World and Environment in the Light of Christ's Coming

The New Testament message enjoins man to take his bearings exclusively from God, as he has now revealed himself in the Christ-event, and to make his center the future of an unscathed and just world opened up by God and by God alone. The coming into being of this world remains solely the act of God, in the sense that it is only God who can fully realize it. This is an expression of the fundamental experience to which Yahweh lays claim and which is to be found in the testimony of the Old Testament, in the passages about creation and in the eschatological prophecies: the experience that the equipment for living enjoyed by man and all living things in his world, and which is relevant for life's meaning, is not at the disposal of the living thing itself. These things are always God's gifts, ordained and given together with life, or denied, or to be expected.

But in the New Testament this exclusive orientation toward the Christ-event and the future kingdom of God, which already dawns in it, is never followed by the conclusion that man is thereby removed from his existing world, the world in which he moves and to which the natural world and environment and all living things in it also belong. The New Testament never concludes that the world can only be seen now as a devalued, hostile, or neutral sphere, without importance for the realization of significance, so that indifferent, libertine, or ascetic contempt of the world would be the appropriate expression for the overcoming of the world by the redeemed. Not only did Jesus in his ministry keep men and women firmly in their existing world in the face of the dawning kingdom, because that is the sphere where God can be encountered in the realization of significance, in hope for that kingdom.[6] The New Testament Epistles are evidence that on many occasions the early church also had vigorously to oppose similar tendencies toward contempt of the world and the self, and toward an independent and high-handed anticipation of the divine future.[7]

On the contrary, for the New Testament the orientation toward God in the Christ-event opens up a view of the existing world (and therefore of the natural world and environment as well) in which man and the world are bound together. This view may be summed up under three headings: first, the natural world and the environment as the sphere of God's creative activity and of the manifestations of the nearness of his salvation in Christ; second, the natural world as the sphere where man's self-centeredness rules; and third, the natural world as the living space for faith. Let us now consider these three headings.

a. The natural world as the sphere of God's creative activity and the nearness of his salvation

For the New Testament the coming of God in Jesus does not mean the breaking in by the divine into a hitherto godless and God-remote world. It means the approach of the Father who has created this world (according to the Synoptic Gospels); the coming of the Son into God's created world (according to Paul); the coming of Christ, the mediator of creation, into the world he has created (according to the Gospel of John, Colossians, and Hebrews). Because this coming takes place in the form of God's incarnation in the midst of the world, it is the

most extreme form of acceptance of the existing world as a world
that has always been sustained by God's acts, and toward which
his creative activity and Christ's saving activity both point.
Indeed the nearness of the God who inclines toward the world
in order to save it—a nearness which becomes plain once man
takes his bearings from the man Jesus—and his manifestations
of the kingdom of God in the midst of the world—is directly
opposed to any tendency to turn divine activity in the world into
a riddle (as in Eccles., Eth. Enoch, and 4 Ezra). And it is equally
contrary to the consequent central position given to the Law in
a world where significance will only be conceded at some future
point—a viewpoint of late Israel in which the creation
statements are put to argumentative theological use. The
ministry of Jesus was a sign of the realization of conferred
righteousness, and the meaning and fulfillment of the promises
to Israel. But the nearness of God manifested in Jesus also
opens up his direct creative activity once more in the
elemental, given conditions of the natural world and environment of the living. When we were looking at the New
Testament writings, we saw with what directness Jesus and the
Synoptic Gospels point man to the elemental experience of the
givenness of natural life and the equipment for living, and how
they stress the dependency of all living things. Likewise, for
Acts and for Paul, in their linking with the hellenistic-Jewish
tradition, people can be addressed, in the wake of the gospel's
proclamation, on the fore-giving and fore-given foundation of
the elemental world of life. In contrast to the dominance of the
Law's regulations (Matt. 5:21ff; 12:12ff),[8] but also in contrast to
a life centered on the natural or human sciences, with their laws
and structures, in which perception is totally objectified, the
New Testament again shows encounter and participation in the
event of life as being the all-embracing, meaningful framework
of relationship for experience, thought, and act;[9] and it brings
this to fruition in the existential way in which the love of Jesus
and his witnesses approaches the world.

But why does the New Testament, in the framework of the
proclamation of the gospel, also point the person it addresses to
the elemental reality of his existence? Why does it point him to

his existing world as a world of creation guaranteed by God? Certainly here, as in all the New Testament's statements about the divine creation of the world, the connection is being preserved between God's activity in the world to which the Old Testament testifies, and his new coming in Christ. The New Testament upholds the unity and identity of God in his different activities for the world, while the existence of the living thing is still understood as divine gift, which is not at the living's own disposal. But the connection between the statements about creation and the gospel in the three groups of texts we have considered is closer still. The fact that man can be addressed on the subject of God's creative activity in his existing world is part of the proclamation of the gospel itself, because the significance of the creation-event—and with it the natural world and environment—for the event of salvation is obvious.

When in his proclamation Jesus points to the experience of the elemental gift of life conferred by the fatherly goodness of the Creator—a gift not at the disposal of the living thing itself—he does so because this is evidence that we should not hanker to acquire our own self-created meaning for life, or security for the future, but should make our center the fulfillment of life's meaning which God now brings close to us and promises us in Jesus.

In Acts, man's own elemental experience of life and the world of life points to an ordained divine foundation, and this provides the starting point for the proclamation of the gospel to non-Jews: the impulse to preach the one God of Israel, who transcends the world and who now gives himself in Christ for the salvation of all.

For Paul, on the other hand, this pointer toward that experience of God by way of the natural world of life, which is also open to, and knowable by, people who are not Jews, reveals the actual perversion of this experience in the conduct of life. It is toward this that God's justifying activity in Christ's cross is directed, in reconciliation and out of grace.

In each case, therefore, attention is drawn to the existing world of life as the divine creation fore-given to existence, in

order to show that the God who now comes close to us in his
saving acts in Christ is the reality of experience which was always
fore-ordered and given with life, thus making man, who is
dependent on God, open for the divine gift in Jesus. The fact of
being alive and the fact of being invited to the future of salvation
(which comes close to us in the meaning of life) are related to one
another in the one event of God's gift to the world.

A further reason for the theologically positive evaluation of
the existing natural world of life, as a world guaranteed by God
the creator, must be added. It is connected with God's
incarnation and is such a matter of course for the New
Testament that it is not independently treated at all. In
guaranteeing an elemental world for the living—until the
turning point of the end-time—God provides the imperishable
foundation for the fact that in this world Jesus can by word and
deed (and in what happened to him) set up the sign of what is
now and is to come. This guarantee makes it possible for there
to be people to whom the gospel can be preached, and for
Christ to set up signs of the coming God, who has appeared in
him as liberator of the world for creation and as the actual form
that "new creation" itself takes. And not least, the fact that
contemplation and experience are possible in a world
guaranteed by God presupposes the possibility of expressing
God's coming in Christ in metaphorical language, deriving
from that world, without blurring the abiding difference
between God and the world. [10] To sum up all these aspects: for
the New Testament the natural world and environment and
everything living in it as the world of creation belong, not to the
sphere of existence that has been overcome and emptied of
meaning and so is a matter of indifference; under its different
facets, it is actually one of the necessary and divinely
guaranteed presuppositions for the gospel, until the day when
God brings about his kingdom in all its fullness.

This brings us to an important conclusion.
We have already stressed that it is not possible for the
Christian church to make contemporary challenges (such as

today's environmental and survival crisis) the determining canon of Christian action, just because the present generation—whatever their background—believe that it is essential or opportune to meet that challenge; nor is it possible for the church then to seek for suitable legitimations for its actions from a biblical tradition which extends over more than a thousand years—in our case the Old Testament texts which deal with the Creation. Moreover, an eco-biblicism of this kind, conforming to the present, would be only seemingly biblical. For Christians it would really be the surrender of their obligatory primary orientation toward the center of the Christian message, which lies in the New Testament witness. It would mean subjecting that to a mere consensus of present opinion, however humane, social, and desirable it may be. Biblical legitimations here would be at most the means of making people who are guided by Christian tradition also assume responsibility.

We have seen from our New Testament findings that it would also be a serious misunderstanding of biblical precepts if we were hastily to classify our present survival crisis as a sign of the prophesied end-time, the date of whose coming, according to the New Testament, is reserved for God alone and cannot be known by Christians, let alone be hurried on by them. And it would be equally inadmissible to see this crisis as the phenomenon of a passing world which does not need to affect Christians, because they are solely centered on Christ and God's coming kingdom.

On the contrary, the New Testament has shown us that, according to its testimony too, the elemental, existing natural world and environment is God's creative work for all the living, as long as God allows it to continue. And as such it is the necessary presupposition, providing forms for proclamation of the gospel in word and deed in the midst of this present world. That means that it is not contrary to the intention of the gospel when we draw on the Old Testament creation texts in order to arrive at a Christian perception of the natural world and environment, since these texts have no exact counterpart in the New, where they are already presupposed. Indeed to do so is in line with the gospel and its worldwide dissemination and in line with Christian orientation toward God in Christ and his future kingdom. We can say even more. In a period when the endangering of the world and environment (which belongs to all the living) is a threat to survival, the active form of Christian existence enjoined by the New Testament is to help to preserve the elemental sphere of the natural world and environment at its most serviceable for the lives of all the living. It must be kept as something where the good things created by God can be experienced in the event of his gift of life and the equipment for living—a gift which is a process, not achievable by man and not at his disposal, but which can yet undoubtedly be destroyed by him. So Christians are enjoined to preserve these things for the coming divine salvation which has been opened up by Christ and which, according to Romans 8, is to include nonhuman creation too.

In this way the New Testament empowers Christians, in the special challenges of our time, to bring the Old Testament creation texts to bear on our present problems, and to extract particular clues or indications from them, as we have tried to do in the Old Testament section, since these keep their validity in the framework of the New Testament viewpoint as well. For these texts points us to an elemental view of the natural world and environment as God's creative event which guarantees life, a view which overrides the fateful division between man and nature, and overcomes the catastrophic preeminence of this division. They point to a cognitive perception of the natural world and environment which includes the utilization of nature through scientific knowledge and economic exploitation by self-centered man and his methods and mechanisms, and which limits these things along the lines laid down by the processes of life as a whole, in the context of all the living. They point out that life is the solely orienting fundamental experience in the perception of the natural world and environment which testifies to God the creator as the transcendent foundation of all dependent life—though it is an experience that has been widely supplanted. They point to God, the creator who transcends the world, who lays down the fore-ordered and overriding meaning, norms, and values which guarantee life and insure the continuance of the world of creation for the benefit of all the living. In this way it gives bearings that determine human actions, as these affect the natural world and environment, but it limits man's autonomous exploitation of the world, which is in effect destructive. The New Testament empowers us to such an acceptance of the Old Testament creation texts in forming our theological opinions and deciding the guidelines for the Christian action laid upon us under the particular conditions of our present. Our actions must certainly be determined by our theological view of the natural world and environment— though this is not as yet inherent in such form in the Old Testament creation texts, since it only develops out of the Christ-event. The two following sections will demonstrate this.

b. The natural world as the sphere where man's self-centeredness is paramount

The Yahwist's primeval history and the Priestly Writing as well distinguish between the event of creation and the actual reality of the world, right down to the realm of nature. Israel's Wisdom maintained the distinction between creation and the world. From the exilic period onward the divine activity in creation and the existing world which realizes or effects righteousness became the dominating theological problem in Israel's perception of Yahweh. But in the New Testament the deep cleft between the existing world as the event of creation and—still on the basis of creation—as the event formed by man became utterly and radically obvious, because of the rejection, expulsion, and putting to death of the incarnate God. Jesus already tells us that man is wicked (Matt. 7:11; 12:34; cf. 12:45; Mark 8:38; 9:19). In the Gospel of John and in Paul the result of this is a double perspective of the existing world which distinguishes between "creation" and "the world" or "this world"—a double perspective which is actually terminologically fixed. This world as manifested in Jesus' crucifixion, gives the existing world its character as the "happening" of man's autocratic self-realization in forming his world politically, socially, personally, and—just as much—in the natural sector.

In this way the existing world of creation is marked by the suppression, disregard, or replacement of God by man, who makes himself the center and considers his own interests, goals, and securities in a completely autonomous way. All this gives the present world its character and diminishes it.

This "happening," which determines the world, the New Testament sees as the actual setting up of a sphere where the power of sin is paramount—sin which suppresses God, sin which man continually takes on himself through what he does and to which he has himself simultaneously and inescapably fallen victim; for in this happening man has always perverted the special position for which he was created in the world of creation, has put himself in the place of God the creator, and really takes his bearings from created things, from extrapolations of what he himself determines meaning to be (Rom. 1:26). When in this connection the New Testament talks about the power of sin and about demons and Satan as the powers dominating the world, it does not mean intermediate beings which limit God's activity and have a negative influence on the fate of men and women. These things are the summing-up of the power of man's autonomous determination of meaning, directed against God, which on the one hand is nourished by man himself, and at the same time has him in its toils.

Accordingly, the world in this New Testament sense is largely the world of man and, as this negative event, everything toward which human acts and aspirations are directed in man's attempts to isolate himself from God. This includes man's depreciation of elemental human life—we may think of Jesus' promise of the forgiveness of *sins* when he is asked for *healing*. It also includes the created natural world and environment, which man drags into this world-event determined by him himself. Paul expressly emphasizes this in Romans 8:20, seeing nonhuman creation, not as the mere instrument of human living, but, like the Old Testament, as something created with independent significance and value over against man, as part of God's creative event.

Of course Paul did not visualize today's survival crisis in the natural world and environment, any more than the New

Testament saw a form of "this world" in which the event of autonomous, human perception of the world is driven toward the actual destruction of the created, fore-given natural foundations for life enjoyed by the living. But according to what the New Testament tells us, there can be no doubt that in the face of the cross of Christ this situation, which is the primary challenge for us today, is also the manifestation of the vortex of human sin, with all its power, in which man is now expelling God from even the elemental spheres where the life of the living is constantly guaranteed, for the sake of a self-imposed and self-centered determination of significance. These acts of men and women do not come about simply because of scientific knowledge as such, or because of the transformation of the world by the processes of labor as such, or through the utilization of the world by technology, economics, or industry as such. They come from what is behind these things: the unbridled striving to build or to preserve now, for ourselves, a self-imposed, continually more demanding world, by exploiting the (still) given natural equipment for living, and by disregarding the constant and enduring will of the Creator and his meaningful decrees, which aim to guarantee life in the *whole* world of creation, in the future as well.

This situation of ours is frequently analyzed today, and its origin is recognized as being due to men and women. According to the New Testament, the cross of Jesus Christ unmasks it as the manifestation of sin, as our human way of pushing God out, as the consistent form of the present world as "man's world." The cross of Jesus Christ shows that man is not the cause of this situation of ours just because he has a special formative position in the natural world, which makes him superior to nature. He is its cause because he is in the power of sin through his rejection of God, as the relationship that is shown to him to give bearings, meaning, values, and norms derived from the elemental world of creation as a whole, and to which he, like all other living things, owes his natural life. The cross of Christ also reveals that the world of man cannot free itself by itself and out of its own initiative from this tendency to destroy the elemental world of life, including the foundations of man's own life, which were laid down at creation. Man cannot free himself either by means of particular pragmatic technological measures (essential though these are for the prevention of destruction in any given case), or because he is shocked at the obvious threat to the world of life in its total and continued existence. He cannot do it by himself because the preservation of the interests of the individual—or the group—or nations—as well as general orientation toward one's own particular increased feeling for the value of living, whether it is desired, or already acquired, or suggested, do not (in spite of common sense and insights born out of fear) lead to any common action in which men and women step beyond themselves and what they do to look toward God (Rom. 1:20ff). The testimony of the New Testament is unanimous, hard, and uncompromising on this point. Men and women cannot of themselves step beyond the power of their own sin.

We may counter this with secular hopes born of more confidence in men and women. For example, we may hope to succeed in expanding the concept of "the common good" to cover everyone, the people living now and those still to be born, indeed the whole of the natural world and the life in it. Or we may hope to achieve a general acknowledgment of basic values and basic rights in elemental life as well as in the sphere of state-sponsored action, to be a general level of accepted norms, where the catastrophic clash of interests would be controlled and people would arrive by their own initiative at guidelines based on the interests of the whole, not merely those of the individual. Such attempts are not to be despised, according to the New Testament, any more than state action (Rom. 13[11]); it should be supported. But the New Testament does not encourage any illusions about the real effect. To control evil by regulating particular interests in favor of the common good is not to abolish sin; and in a world of suffering and inferior living that cannot be eradicated, the common good is not salvation. Even the problem of the necessary worldwide and long-term realization of the efforts we have mentioned would still have to be faced; and this would in itself again cancel out the intention of the whole, because it would involve the threat of employing worldwide dictatorial controls as instrument.[12]

Here again the New Testament writings are quite unanimous. The sphere of sin's power, and with it everything that makes human life dependent on this world, inwardly and outwardly, can only be overcome in believing acceptance of Jesus Christ and in the orientation and identification of personal life which he brings about, in place of man's autonomous self-realization. They can only be overcome in the believing recognition of guilt and the acceptance of Jesus' forgiveness of sins, his definition of the meaning of life, and his opening up, in each particular, individual believer, the divine future for all, which has now come close to us.

Jesus and the New Testament witnesses never give way to the illusion that everyone will accept Jesus Christ in faith. Consequently, they never fall victims to the illusion that this human world could be transformed once more into an unscathed world of creation through the proclamation of the gospel, let alone through human efforts. In the framework of the world of men and women, the event of creation remains diminished, damaged, suppressed, and threatened; and the natural world and environment of the believer does not escape from this ambivalence.

c. The natural world as the space in which faith lives

The New Testament considers that believers are by no means removed from their existing world when, through faith, their sole center becomes God's revelation of himself in Christ and the imminent kingdom of God. On the contrary, they are pointed back to the world as the sphere in which faith has to prove itself. But the experience of the world of the living changes in the light of this newly revealed viewpoint, and this change also affects the natural world and environment and the believer's participation in its elemental life.

If the manifested Christ-event is accepted as being God's bestowal of salvation, which gives life its identity and includes it in the event of conferred fulfillment of meaning in the kingdom of God—an event which points to the future—then the form of the existing world we see, down to the natural, elemental sphere, is viewed in the context of faith's recognition of sin. It is viewed in this way because it is the expression of man's mistaken view of himself, which is self-centered and opposed to God. The believer is no longer molded and determined by this self-centeredness. He has been liberated from it. But on the basis of a world perverted in this way, the sustaining, nondisposable, long-suffering, life-conferring divine creative event emerges through faith's perception of what God is like. For the believer, in spite of all the world distortion, the whole natural world and environment, in its entire life-promoting structure and its continuance, is once more revealed in the event in which the God who is close to us in Christ guarantees the most elemental and fundamental thing of all—life—and provides for it in his fatherly goodness. This is not only true of the natural world as a whole; it applies especially to the fact of the believer's being-alive, and to the lives of others and to their equipment for living. It is true not only of the believer, but of all men and women. And it not only applies to humans; it is equally true of everything that is alive, and of their independent right to live—the birds and the lilies (Matt. 6) and all created things (Rom. 8). As the living space in which faith lives, the natural world and environment ceases to be the world provided for man's autonomous self-realization. It emerges once more, on the basis of its existence and continuance, as the sphere of God's creative activity, as the nondisposable, loving offer of life through God, who now in Christ turns toward the salvation that is approaching.

Because of his orientation toward God as he now reveals himself in Christ, the believer certainly does not see the event of creation in the natural world and environment as a self-contained divine edict of significance related to the elemental value of natural life, its duration and its equipment that gives joy to the living. In this way he diverges from the Old Testament creation texts which we looked at earlier. He rather ranges himself beside Old Testament prophecy and apocalyptic, perceiving the natural world as pointing to a goal, as an event directed toward the imminent divine future. It is this event that provides the yardstick for a meaningful "eternal life," life not called in question by any imperfections or by death. This is shown especially in the statements about life which we met on the lips of Jesus in the first three Gospels, and which we came across in the Gospel of John and in Paul (see pp. 216ff and 220ff).

Accordingly, the believer sees his natural world and environment as an event of creation in a number of different ways. (1) It is the divine event which God will bring about in his future salvation (and which will draw in nonhuman creation too; cf. Rom. 8)—even though that future salvation is conceived of in various ways in the New Testament, since it can only be expressed in metaphorical terms. (2) It is the guarantee of the elemental foundations for living enjoyed by everything toward which the saving event is directed. (3) It is the presupposition for the gospel, which is directed toward all men. (4) It is the sphere in which—with the coming of Jesus and in the presence of the divine Spirit[13]—God's salvation is already manifested in the existing world in the form of signs.

Because God's saving event in Christ is directed toward the existing world in its character of divine creation, this elemental creation perspective also enters into the form in which salvation already exists in the midst of the world as we see it. It may be found, on the one hand, in Jesus' pointing to the immediate presence of the Creator and what this means for the behavior of created beings, as well as in the re-found liberty to move about in the natural world and environment as the world of creation, free from what determines man's own world. But on the other hand, we may find it equally in the signs that are themselves the manifestations of salvation, and which point with primal and historical directness and universality within the world itself toward its character as creation. We see these manifestations when Jesus turns to all men simply as human beings, cutting right through all differentiations between the devout and the undevout, the rich, the poor, and the outcasts, and between Jews and Romans. We see them in the way Jesus and his witnesses act toward the sick, the handicapped, and those who have died prematurely. We see them in the irrelevance of ethnic, state, class, and social differentiations between people in Christ's church (e.g., Gal. 3:28; 6:15). We see them in the loving service performed by Christians toward one another and toward everyone, which includes attempts to relieve and diminish life's imperfections in the human field, incorporating these attempts as "signs" belonging to the form salvation takes in our existing world. And in view of the salvation given to man, we see these manifestations of salvation not least in the field of our own experience, of our own, natural life. Track has recently shown this on the level of Christian experience;[14] and it also applies to the sphere of life's outward relationships, as we see in the ethics of Jesus[15] and the admonitions of the New Testament Epistles, with their rigorous directness, which resists any legalistic straightjacket.[16]

According to what we have already said, there can be no doubt that this form taken by salvation in the existing world (which Paul already calls the "new creation" and which has dawned for believers in Christ) also includes active intervention for the preservation of the creation event, both because that event aims at the salvation of man and for the sake of nonhuman creation. But this is only one aspect of the way in which the natural world and environment presents itself to the believer.

For the believer is not just put into his existing world as the world of creation; according to the New Testament, during his whole earthly existence he is also part of this world. And "this world" means a world marked by the power of human self-centeredness and sin, where God is pushed out. It is a world characterized, right down to the natural sphere itself, by frailty, imperfection on the elemental level, weakness, transience, and death; for these are the signs of God's judgment on men and women—judgment into which even Jesus was "delivered up" (Rom. 4:25; 8:32). Even nonhuman creation is not excepted, since it too is subject to nothingness because of man's sin, without any act of will of its own (Rom. 8:20). Even if Christ frees the believer from this world as a power that determines his endeavors, his identity, his goal, and his definition of significance, he is still exposed all the same to the counterattack of this world against God, against Christ, and against the gospel. The New Testament shows this impressively in many passages, in what it has to say about persecution and suffering. Though the believer belongs all his life to the existing world, he also belongs to the natural world and environment, i.e., not to a primal world of creation that has been everywhere liberated, but to a world that everywhere bears the burdens imposed by man and his suppression of God. In this world his natural life and his elemental equipment for living is threatened, endangered, and persecuted, like the life of everything else; and this is so in the midst of natural world and environment where nonhuman creation is subject to the same destiny of suffering and, like believers, "groans in travail" (Rom. 8:22-23). Link has recently impressively shown[17] that this experience of suffering is only endured in the way the New Testament intends when we break through the objectifying and rational knowledge of the world in a critical way and absorb our knowledge into the same existential, time-related, total perception—a perception "proved upon the pulses"—which recognizes the natural world too as being a creative event. He writes:

> Meanwhile—in view of the global results of scientific civilization—we are today beginning to see that the suffering caused by man is not confined to crises in the individual life but includes the possible breakdown of the world itself. It boomerangs, striking back at the causes themselves, and threatening the very roots of the conditions, even of objective perception, thereby calling in question the presupposition of the whole technological world which gives our present life its character: the presupposition that objective relationships exist in the world. Suffering reveals a fundamental crisis of rationality. It defeats the enlightened confidence that we can guarantee the future of the earth through the methods of objectification practiced in science, economics, and politics. Thus, just because it involves a crisis that burst apart the reliability of an objectively "given" world, perception through suffering is today becoming "for the first time the unavoidable potential of the only future of human conditions that is still open to us."[18]

Yet in making Christ its center, faith does not see the suffering form of the natural world and environment and everything in it as calling God the creator in question; it is simply the measure of man's distorting perversion of creation. It is not perceived as something that casts doubt on God's saving will, which, on the contrary, opens up a new, all-embracing world of creation in the future. It is not perceived as something that makes the Christian's responsibility for creation senseless; on the contrary, he is enjoined to exert an active influence to preserve the evidences of creation in the natural world, in spite of all its distortion, and to participate in all attempts to alleviate the suffering of the world of creation and to diminish it in every individual case. But the believer knows that according to the New Testament this suffering form of the natural world and of his own life as a whole cannot be overcome through endeavor and progress of whatever kind. For the cross of Christ shows us that it is connected with the marks of autocratic man's power in the existing world, and this cannot be overcome by endeavor and progress either. It shares with man himself a common indissoluble history in which life lives at the cost of other life and autonomous definitions of life are enforced at the cost of another life's development. For the believer, the suffering which characterizes the existing world is the result of man's assertion of himself against God, while the insurmountable suffering of his own elemental life is the form taken by his participation in the saving rejection, suffering, and death of Christ.[19] For because God is not merely concealed in the suffering of the world (as in the Old Testament) but takes this suffering on himself in Christ—the suffering caused by man in his autocratic thinking, experience, and actions—the believer, being incorporated in this suffering, is also pointed to the divine reality of the world, even though this is distorted by suffering. He is pointed to its character as creation and its future in the kingdom of God, which the risen Christ guarantees.[20]

Through participation in God's suffering in Christ, outlook on the natural world and environment changes for the believer, in experience, knowledge, and action. He perceives that that suffering which constitutes the character of his own life, in its frailty as well as in the hostility to faith, does not call his life and that life's meaning in question. He perceives it in patience and hope as being the living sign of his acceptance into Christ's salvation. He is thereby *free* to perceive the suffering which constitutes other human life, and free to help bear its burden in sympathetic love, to weep with those who weep as well as to rejoice with those who rejoice (Rom. 12:15; cf. 1 Cor. 12:26). In considering the grave impairments of the life of nonhuman creation, he does not have to accept—as if they were something independent of moral values—the inevitable results of autocratic man's knowledge and exploitation of nature, which seem to be the only things that count. But he can apprehend this situation—which is insurmountable as a whole—as what the cross of Christ critically shows to be the distortion of the Creator's will—as its suffering, which, like the suffering of believers, is the suffering of creation and is suffering "in hope" (Rom. 8:20). [21]

3. The Future of the Natural World and Environment in the Light of Christ's Coming

In this section we shall be considering the New Testament's eschatological statements, which talk about the end of the present world, about time, and about the future significance of man and the world of creation. We have therefore to look at the end of the fulfillment of man and all living things in the world of creation, which the New Testament writings see as included in God's coming in Christ; for these writings are of one mind about the thing itself, although they use varying metaphors and concepts to express it. The subject is therefore not the mere empirical temporality of the world; for the view of these New Testament statements are directed rather toward the realization of quality and meaning, which is uninterrupted and includes the future, and which God aims at in what he does for the living in the world. But the subject is no longer the guarantee of God's creative event which aims at permanence, continuance, and hence future and the significance that includes. For in the New Testament— following the Old Testament's prophetic and apocalyptic thought—this continuance of the creation-event is given a qualitatively new horizon and a limit through God's coming in

Christ. It now becomes the time limit which God grants his world of creation between Christ's coming and the realization of salvation, which is to include the world. What do the New Testament's eschatological statements have to say about the future perfect realization of significance of the natural world and environment and all the living things in it?

If we define "future" in the sense of the expectation that human endeavors, progress, insights, solidarity, and technology will ultimately succeed in creating a whole, good, just, and meaningful world, down to the sphere of the natural world and its equipment for living, then the New Testament position is quite clear and unequivocal. In this sense the natural world and environment utilized by man, and indeed human life itself, has no prospect and future at all. On the contrary, this world will pass away through these very forces. The New Testament does not arrive at this view because the restricted knowledge available to the ancient world meant that it knew little about man and his potentialities. On the contrary, it knew him all too well. For the cross of Christ reveals the madness at the heart of man. He devises a perfect world and tries to achieve it with a self-centeredness that vastly overestimates what he can do; and then comes crashing down in destruction of the living, in loss of meaning, in the struggle between ideas, interests, and methods, and in violence—open, or concealed in many guises. In the biblical view this madness of man's has always set its stamp on the world constructed by human beings. It perverts God's goodly world of creation, turning it into a world of suffering; it brutalizes man with its autocratic urge for self-determination in the relations between man and man, and between man and the nonhuman world; and it is the rejection of God that finds its most acute expression when the God who inclines to us in Jesus was put to death on the cross.

If God is to remain the God who, as creator transcending the world, guarantees to the living everything that is not at its own disposal and who, as giver of life, also establishes fulfillment of meaning in an unscathed and just world of life for all the living; then, for the believer, the New Testament is only

being logical when it says that the unscathed and just world of
God's cannot exist as long as this madness of man's is at work in
all its manifestations and materializations, even down to the
natural world. It is then quite logical—to look at the matter in a
different way—for the New Testament to see this mad world
and everything that is marked by it as proceeding, not toward
final perfection, but toward its end, when it will be judged and
annihilated by God. And it is equally logical when the New
Testament expresses this in statements about the Last
Judgment, about the passing of this world, and even in the
statements about the downfall of the existing world that we find
in the Revelation.

If, on the other hand, we define the future of the natural
world and the living in it in the sense that God (who has
created and continually guarantees that natural world and
environment for a meaningful life united with him) will not
become man's victim, but will bring whatever he does and
intends in a just and unscathed world to a definite goal—then
the world of creation and the living things in it certainly have a
meaningful future in perfection. This again is the clear
testimony of the New Testament. In the face of a world
condemned to death, God has opened this future for the
world of creation through his coming in the man Jesus of
Nazareth. He has opened it to all men who accept him and,
with them, to the whole world of creation. It is a future which
the New Testament tries to express in different ways, using
terms like "the Kingdom of God," "eternal life," "glory,"
"immortality," and including the detailed, metaphorically
described events in the Revelation.

According to the testimony of the New Testament, this
future certainly does not mean the world's restoration to the
undiminished event of creation; it is not a repetition of the
event of creation, nor its improvement, and certainly not a state
which, since the coming of Christ, can be continually
developed from what already exists, with the help of believers
and by means of particular political orders, forms of society, or
social conditions. This future is a new event of definitive
finality, which completely realizes what God's creation planned

from the beginning. It fulfills what we are told in Genesis 1:31: "And God saw everything that he had made, and behold, it was very good." Indeed the disclosure of the future of salvation in Christ makes obvious for the first time what creation really is. It is not a sending forth of the living being out onto the path of failure; he is speeded on the way to his salvation.

Like the creation-event from the beginning and like the Christ-event, the setting up of this future divine world is God's act alone and, as such, is simply in opposition to the self-entanglement of man's autocratic molding of the world, with its blasphemous confusion between God and man, the Creator and the created. In the New Testament sense, the kingdom of God has therefore to be distinguished from the grandiose but infantile utopias of perfection, which multiply the things that are desirable without considering human reality, just as it must be distinguished from realistic, projected aims at the improvement of actual, given political and social conditions, necessary though these are. According to the New Testament, a transposition of the kingdom of God into prefigurations of this kind, and thereby the transposition of God into man's better potentialities, would be merely a renewed manifestation of the madness of our human rejection of God.[22] According to the testimony of the New Testament, the realization of the whole and just world of the kingdom of God is reserved for God's action and is therefore removed from the disposal of man, both with regard to the initiative and power that brings it about and also the time of its consummated reality and fulfillment. If this were not so it would not be the kingdom of *God*. The decisive, essential, and valid thing in the eschatological statements of the New Testament that we are discussing here is not that they are supernatural, miraculous fantasies from a world beyond, but the facts that are in accordance with experience: the realization that, like creation from the beginning, the kingdom of God, the new creation, immortality, and glory are granted by God and only by him, and are outside any significance that man can confer.

If the meaningful future of the world of creation, opened up in Christ, warranted by his resurrection and proclaimed since that event, is entirely reserved for God's own activity, it only seems, in consequence, to lose its importance for our perception of the existing natural world and environment in the time God still allows it to have—time whose duration is unknown to us. What does this importance consist of?

It consists of the basic perspective determining our view of the existing natural world. For the future of the world of creation opened up in the Christ-event shows the existing world to be a fallen one, which has still its temporal existence but no significant future arising from its own initiative. It shows autocratic man as the cause of this destruction of the meaning of elemental life in his natural world and environment. It makes it evident that human endeavors to form the natural world and environment into a world that is just and perfect according to man's own standards are simply madness. It is a madness which unmasks the sinner who pushes God out and has as future only death, transience, and loss of significance. It thereby reveals a sober view of the natural world as we see it, and preserves us from ecological illusions, as well as from frustration over the gap between utopia and reality.

On the other hand, it is just as strongly opposed to all resignation and despair about the world; for it makes it equally clear that in Christ God turns to man, his life, and all created things with the offer of meaning, salvation, and righteousness in a perfect, final world. God now points men and women through Christ to this future event, which is already beginning, thereby *liberating* them from having all by themselves to give their worldly existence contentment and meaning, even though it is existence in illusion, anxiety, fear, madness, and violence. It shows man that the elemental fact of being alive with his equipment for living, given to him with life and not at his own disposal, is embedded in the continual creative activity of God, who grants life to every living thing in the natural world and environment, provides for it, and is the guarantee for the continued existence of the living, a guarantee which in itself determines values and creates obligation. It allows him to see that the creative event, as the ground of all specific life and of all natural equipment for living, is the bestowal of God's fatherly goodness, in joy over existence and the beauty of the world; but that it has the aim of leading man, and with him all created things, into the divine future of perfect life, which has been opened up through Christ. It allows him to realize that the blessedness of being alive in a well-equipped world of life and of being-alive in the natural world is not in itself an ultimate value that fulfills life's meaning. And it also shows him that his imperfect, arduous life in a world full of pain, and all being-alive in a world marked by suffering, do not—even in view of death— mean a final question mark that destroys life's meaning.

It shows him that in looking toward God in Christ and his coming kingdom—an outlook that calls forth faith and trust—even the survival crisis of the natural world and environment in our time, which was our starting point, is not simply a manifestation of terror that means the end of all significance. It is the manifestation of human madness and the suffering that characterizes the world. But the future of creation predestined by the Creator is above even this.

The failure of the world does, however, not allow the situation to be a matter of indifference for the believer. It encourages his suffering and compassion in patience and hope for the God who has come close to us in Christ. And it activates his thinking, his love, his imagination, his willingness for renunciation and sacrifice, and his involvement. It makes him ready to do what is necessary, soberly and steadily, and—even in a secular world with secular views of action—to work to preserve God's world of creation from man as long as the Creator himself still gives it time. In this way the believer wards off the resignation that would seem to be an obvious reaction to the reflection that the survival crisis of the natural world and environment can be slowed up by individual counter-measures but cannot be overcome altogether, since it is entangled in such a complicated way in economic, social, and political power-processes. And control of the crisis is all the more impossible because initiatives that are right in part and in the short term can become problematical in the context of the whole and in the long-term view. Christian action is not centered on, or motivated by, fear. Its center is the connection between the divine future and the view of the world as creation. Consequently it is free for the untiring performance of token acts. It is free to draw attention to viewpoints that keep alive responsibility for the natural world and environment as the world of creation.

Action in hope for this future is not action as a form of consolation. In opposing such a notion H. H. Schmid points to the "concrete form of eschatological thinking in Jesus' life, death, and resurrection." He goes on:

> This deeply expressed experience of the connection and yet difference between the unscathed world and actual reality, the kingdom of God and the "profane" world, could again save us today from over-hasty ideological thinking and its results— whether these results take the form of violence, frustration, or resignation, or all of them together; while the faith to which it testifies creates the basis for an existence in the light of the promise of peace and righteousness, in hope for the goal of peace and righteousness. "Gospel" would then be the synonym neither for "changing the world" nor for "unworldliness"; it would mean laying the foundation for a possible world and a possible human existence under the ultimate definition of salvation: taking the world seriously, but just because of that not overvaluing it; closely related to it but, just because of that, making a fundamental distinction between God and the world; seeing the world as God's creation but, just because of that, preserving the eschatological proviso.[23]

But in considering what the New Testament has to say about Christian action in the light of the future of salvation, we have already made the transition to the subject of our next and final section.

4. The Preservation of the Natural World and Environment as the Goal of Faith

What this heading suggests cannot be found anywhere in the New Testament, or at least not in this form. But let us pick up what has emerged up to now in the course of our consideration of the New Testament texts and the theses we picked out (pp. 216ff and 237ff).

In the New Testament it is a frequently expressed idea, and indeed a matter of course, that God's creative activity takes place in the natural world and environment, as it has done from time immemorial, and as it will continue to do until God brings his new world, opened up in Christ, to a full and ultimate consummation. The New Testament also brings out man's special position and the dependency of the natural world on him, in the sense that it is man himself who, by pushing God out, has wrested his own existence as created being, together with the whole world of creation, into a perversion and suffering which overlays and contradicts God's continuing creative event, violating it and making it meaningless, whereas God's activity aims at fulfillment of significance and continuance in a bond with the Creator.

But, as we have already stressed, the New Testament does not yet envisage the situation in which the madness of man endangers the elemental cohesion and continuance of all the living to such a degree that the whole creative event in the natural world and environment is itself threatened in its fundamental reality, duration, and continuance, and ceases to be the object of responsive perception. Consequently, the proclamation of the gospel does not include any theological clarification in this respect. It offers no injunctions about behavior, no definitions of norms, and no admonitions about the actions we are to take.

But this silence is not a silence of principle. The New Testament implicitly includes among the goals of Christian action the goal of preserving the natural world and environment as the creative event of God's elemental bestowal of life. Accordingly, in tracing the New Testament facts in the light of the present day, we frequently come upon ones with consequences for Christian action; for, as the New Testament sees it, the creative event is God's presupposition and foundation for the saving event now opened up in Christ. But then Christian action aimed at preserving the natural world and environment is also a necessary way of implementing faith, a necessary act in the proclamation of the Gospel of Jesus Christ.

Acts of this kind are a proclamation of the saving inclination of God toward everything he has created, for as long as he allows the time limit to be prolonged and the period of faith to last.

It is the task of faith to work for the preservation of the natural world as the world of creation. This belongs to the service of the gospel and the proclamation of the salvation revealed in Christ. To this extent, for the life lived in faith and its bond with Christ, the same provisions continue to apply which, with a view to our present situation, we were able to extract from the creation texts in our Old Testament section, with regard to their view of *man*, who is bound to Yahweh the creator and of the way he shapes the natural world and environment. But of course they only apply in the light of the new perspectives which God's coming in Christ has opened up.

The reason these new perspectives are so important is that it is only God's acts in Christ and the kingdom of God revealed in him which show for the first time what God's creative activity really is. For it is no longer an event restricted in its significance to the existing sphere and to the span of natural life; it is directed to the future kingdom of God in a new divine world. Consequently, the preservation of the world of creation is no longer an action that has a significance of its own (and in this the New Testament differs from the Old). It is rather itself an action pointing toward a goal, which has its direction, its meaning, and its value in its indication of the hope for the world which God will realize—a hope for which Christ is our warrant.

This means that the preservation of the world of creation as a goal of faith is a partial aim during the era of faith; and according to the New Testament this aim is to be seen as part of a much more comprehensive event. Consequently, preservation of the world of creation as a task of faith is basically different from the attempt to understand and preach the mastery of our modern survival crisis as the presupposition for an achievable, unscathed future world, humanly speaking. According to what the New Testament implies, preservation of the world of creation as a task of faith is free from the illusion that Christian initiatives could accelerate the transformation of the existing world into a whole and just world, at least on the elemental, natural level. The world of creation the believer lives in is a world dominated by the madness of man's rejection of God. According to the New Testament, this madness will only lose its force when God judges and annihilates it in the consummation of his kingdom—which will be at a time and with a power that is reserved for him alone. Therefore, the preservation of the world of creation as the task of faith is also free from the illusion of being able to overcome the imperfection and suffering which characterize the natural world and all the life in it by means of Christian lordship over the world; this lordship, incidentally, was already rejected by Jesus (Matt. 4:8ff[24]). The suffering which characterizes the natural world is in the New Testament the manifestation and result of the madness that has made man snatch to himself his own life as created being and the whole of creation. What faith *can* do, by the power of God in Christ, to preserve the world of creation is to perform untiringly token acts as signs, manifestations of the future salvation in the sphere of the natural world, which testify that God has opened his new world for all created things; crystallizations which give concrete form in life to the unity of God, the creator and redeemer, and to the unity of the divine activity directed toward the world. *Untiringly* to perform token acts as *signs*—this is the single, concrete form, free of illusion, of both the perspective on the eschatological proviso and the unrestricted sober activity for the preservation of the world of creation as the form of action taken by Christian existence.

We have already talked about the signs of this kind that are the manifestations of salvation. In what follows we shall consider their specific ecological implications.

One of these signs, according to the New Testament, is already the believer's fearless acknowledgment of powerlessness, even if this acknowledgment subjects him to isolation and scorn. An acknowledgement of powerlessness frees the whole subject of the ecology from the illusion that our aims are achievable in some utopian and autocratic way by human effort alone. It shows man to be the cause of the ecological problem because of his flight from God. What the world is, what man is, and what the failure of both is—all this is revealed in the Christ-event. The preservation of the world of creation as the realization of faith is in word and deed a process within the framework of the proclamation of the gospel.

The New Testament implies that what definitely belongs above all to these signs is that true validity and primacy should be conceded to the elemental, fundamental value of natural life, both human and nonhuman, for this is in accordance with the Creator's acts. What must also be conceded is the dependency of both human and nonhuman creation on the equipment for living provided by the natural world and environment. This must be so because it promotes life and the preservation of life in all the relevant spheres today—in science and scholarship, especially the natural sciences and medicine, in technology and industry, in the processes of political, social, and economic life, as well as in the personal behavior of the individual. That is to say, what are important are the signs of an active perception, free of illusion, that man is made in the image of God (a concept perverted by autocratic man) with the essential accompanying orientation toward Creator and creation; and a perception too of the *dominium terrae*. But in the new context of the Christ-event both these perceptions must be shown their meaning, as creation intended it, in Jesus' ministry; the limits imposed on them must be shown in Jesus' suffering and his cross; and their goal must be shown in the divine future of Jesus' resurrection. Christian perception of man's special position is therefore free from the titanic overvaluation of human potentialities, and free to act with sober common sense and planning, waiving all overbearing knowledge and action. It is therefore free also from ties with ideal, utopian models of an unscathed world conceived by man, and is free too, in line with the creation-event, for "signs" given by improving existing conditions, doing what is necessary, acting humanely in the circumstances man has created, and restricting what is harmful for the sake of the present and future common good. For the new interpretation of the *dominium terrae* in the context of the New Testament testimony (though incidentally the New Testament never cites this Old Testament definition), the reader should turn to the discussion that is being carried on in the publications of J. B. Cobb,[25] K. Scholder,[26] G. Altner,[27] and, most recently, O. Jensen.[28]

According to the New Testament, therefore, the validity and primacy of the fundamental value of natural and elemental life are certainly not signs which faith has to set up because the elemental fact of being-alive, and with it the natural world and environment, still have a significant value of their own, according to faith's viewpoint. Their purpose is to insure that an elemental personal experience of human life in the context of an event which is directed toward all the living, which includes and gives value to man and nature equally, may be preserved for all, may be experienced by all, and to insure that all may be addressed and appealed to in the light of the creative goodness of God, which is efficacious here and is bestowed on all things and which serves the proclamation of the salvation which God will bestow on his creation.

This includes perceiving the divine creative quality and goal of salvation in nonhuman creation too, thereby actively preserving creation from man's autonomous claims. It is not by chance that the present discussion about the problems of survival should point to the phenomenon of life as a criterion of value that is related to experience, or that it should take up Albert Schweitzer's famous, anti-Cartesian dictum, which urges "reverence for life."[29] According to the New Testament, it is an act of faith to alleviate or diminish the suffering of all created beings, as far as we can, and to show that our incapacity to abolish suffering altogether does not mean destruction of life's significance, but that it represents the suffering character of a life created for God's salvation.

This includes showing and conferring signs, as acts of faith, signs in which life's needs are satisfied and life can develop, in the place of autocratic self-assertion. It means showing signs in quality of living.[30] It means showing signs of the significance that is experienced and of joy and happiness as indication of the eternal fulfillment of meaning which God desires to prepare for all the living. But it also means ceasing to measure life's needs against the restless demands of autocratic men and women, each struggling to find significance all by himself. Instead it means turning toward God's revelation of life's meaning in Christ and the resulting definition of what man really needs in the way of life's essential goods. That is to say, it means, in the fulfillment of Christian existence, setting up the sign of a transformed style of living (cf. e.g., what Paul's Letters have to say about what ought to determine action). This also involves renunciation and readiness to sacrifice for the sake of the equipment in the elemental world of others, the lack of which stands in the way of experiencing God's creative goodness, which is the presupposition and foundation of salvation. To make the event of creation experienceable by people, in spite of its perversion by man, is already a dimension of social action in the Old Testament, and it is no less so according to the implications of the New.

To preserve the natural world and environment as goal of faith in action is therefore love of our neighbor in a form related to our experience of God the creator. This experience must be given expression in appropriate acts of love on the part of the believer. In our present situation especially, this love of our neighbor is certainly not restricted to the elemental life of men and women in their natural, given world. Although the New Testament has nothing to say about nonliving nature, and very little about the animal world, except on the visual level of the parables and metaphors (e.g., Matt. 18:12ff; John 10; cf. Mark 1:13?), neighborly love, since it also means "co-creatureliness" on the part of man, certainly also includes nonhuman life.[31] For according to the New Testament, the world of creation is not only for man but, together with him, is prepared for God's future salvation.

The New Testament and the biblical message as a whole seeks believers, and this is also true in the survival crisis of the natural world and environment in a pluralistic, secular era. But today common necessity and a common alarm are inevitably uniting many people in the task of preserving the natural world and environment for the protection of life; and these people are impelled by the most widely differing motives, expectations, and aims. Following up the intention of biblical views about the subject world and environment, believers, in active cooperation and coresponsibility, will not withdraw from such attempts to discover forward-looking viewpoints and plans and to find scientific and technological possibilities of controlling the survival crisis. They will not withdraw from efforts of this kind, even if they come from non-Christian and secular quarters, for the sake of exposing basic human viewpoints and in order to support elemental perspectives of action centered on life itself. They will support any attempts that do not serve to drive out God or to help autocratic man, who destroys nature, to seize power, but which work toward the goal of preserving the natural world and environment for life.[32] Christians have neither to drive God forward to his eschatological turning point, nor do they have to accelerate creation's fearful rush toward the abyss. On the contrary, in accordance with the New Testament, they will for their part contribute to the keeping of God's event of creation present in the midst of the inescapable damage that has already been inflicted on, and suffered by, life, and they will help to struggle against the destruction of the world of creation, as long as God grants this world a further time limit.

In this framework specific actions and attitudes certainly cannot consist of an illusory, wholesale depreciation of the modifications of nature carried out by science and technology; or (theologically speaking) of an equally illusory preservation of everything natural; even less can they be guided by the maxim about tilling and keeping which applied to a paradise that is now closed to us. Like the Old Testament, the New aims primarily at *man* in his *basic attitude* and *responsibility toward the God who makes himself known to us*. Whether and in what way, in accordance with biblical statements, we have to relate to "the orders of creation" is the subject of vehement theological discussion, as Link's remarks have recently illustrated.[33]

Cooperation and coresponsibility in the preservation of the natural world on the part of believers will, however, be an expression of the proclamation of the gospel. For it is that which gives this preservation its ultimate significance, as the proclaiming, overriding, critical element of that "very good" toward which the collective goals of action of many people tend.[34] Christians will work for the preservation of the world of creation. They will work for it in lives which succeed in being models and which set up the "signs" of creation—their own individual lives as well as the lives of "small groups."[35] They will work for it in their dealings with the natural world by reminding people of God, their creator and the creator of all life. They will work for it by confirming and supporting the fore-given, basic values, perspectives, and directions for perception and cognition which this includes; by showing critically what the world is and what man is—as the cause of his endangered world—in the light of the Christ-event; and by holding out to men and women the salvation which God in his grace wants to give all created things, in order to complete and perfect his creation.

Final Remarks

Under the heading world and environment we have tried to deal with two different tasks at the same time. We have tried to show the biblical findings exegetically, setting them in their own period and showing their particular character; and at the same time we have confronted them with the challenges of our time, challenges which the Bible was not faced with in current form. In order to do this we had to choose the unusual, and for that very reason difficult, method of following up, in the light of our present, statements that belong a long way back in history. At the same time, the tension this involves can be necessary and fruitful. It can release impulses for experience, perception, knowledge, and action in the face of a task with which the Christian proclamation and Christian life are faced all over the world today: the task of testifying effectually to the truth of the biblical God and of living that truth convincingly even in the crisis of the natural world and elemental life which is burdening our time. We shall not reiterate these impulses here. As far as the Old Testament is concerned, I have tried to give examples elsewhere.[1] If we think in terms of the whole Bible, Old and

New Testaments alike, these impulses run through everything that we have said up to now, though of course we have made no claim to completeness.

Above all, it cannot be our intention now, in closing, to cut these impulses down to practical and applicable formulas that we would know how to cope with. As we stressed at the beginning, we want our present book to be taken as a contribution to a working process, with the aim of ascertaining what the theological position is and what a responsible attitude toward the present really means. The radius of this is of course wider than an encounter between the Bible and the present, and goes far beyond what is open to any single individual. New questions, or new developments of old questions, will teach us to discover new things in the biblical findings too. Other detailed problems will bring out other insights, not to mention the task of forming valid theological judgments about our present challenges, or the problem of discovering directions for Christian action, the practical forms it may take, and the considerations and decisions involved, all of which can only be approached theologically after we have ascertained what the Bible has to say, which is what we have tried to do here. For this further process the reader should turn to the work on which we have frequently drawn: the books and essays by Klaus Müller, J. B. Cobb, G. Altner, C. Link, and O. Jensen; the essays in the volume *Umweltstrategie*[2] and in the periodical *Evangelische Theologie* 1974 and 1977; and the volume edited by K. M. Meyer-Abich, which was prepared by the *Arbeitskreis Praktische Theologie der Natur in der Evang. Akademie Hofgeismar*. We must above all mention the great, wide-ranging viewpoints, set against the background of Christian responsibility, which C. F. von Weizsäcker shows us in his writings, the latest of which are *Wege in der Gefahr*[3] and *Der Garten des Menschlichen. Beiträge zur geschichtlichen Anthropologie*, 1977 (which appeared too late for me to make use of in the present book). Our relation to the present and the specific form to be taken by theological statements must be tested against all this work.

Our encounter on the subject of the world and the

environment will not have failed in its task if it encourages theology to seek for biblical clarification in modern questions about the natural world and environment, and on this biblical foundation to inquire about the form Christian truth and life must take in the face of the survival crisis of our time. Our encounter will not have failed in its task if it has been able to lead people of our day, with all their needs and anxieties, to the Bible, as the center from which our lives must take their bearings, where God testifies to himself as creator and redeemer—as truth and meaning, as joy and secret, as goal and future for all the living.

Notes

The first figure in each case represents the number under which the full reference can be found in the bibliography. The second figure is the page number of the book in question:

e.g. 21.15 = G. Bornkamm, *Paul*, p. 15.

Introduction, pp. 15-56

1. 87.73ff; 90.249ff
2. 91.184
3. 129.165-66; 152,1ff; 63.I,830; II,242-43
4. 78.I,204ff; 78,III,882ff; 27.222ff,249ff,361ff; 372ff; 139.I,13ff; 82.153ff,256ff
5. 58.196,136
6. 58.196
7. 31.119
8. 31.111ff
9. 31.111
10. 31.112ff
11. 31.128
12. 59.147
13. 31.112ff
14. 90.326ff
15. 162-277-80; 13.§1A.B;§10D
16. 99.69
17. 108.38
18. 108.34ff; 110.25-78
19. 110.28ff;108.38ff
20. 108.42ff,54-55, 58; 41.7
21. 180.255
22. 180
23. 108–10
24. 3–9
25. 41
26. 133.65ff,112ff
27. 41.7
28. 41.10; 138; 181
28a. 41.7
29. 41.10
30. 41.10
31. 110.30 *et passim;* 108.45ff
32. 110.53
33. 108–10
34. 4; 5; 7
35. 86a–90
36. 108.45ff; 87.74ff; 90.313ff
37. 108.59
38. 108.47ff

39. 4; 5; 7
40. 87.78ff; 90.e.g.,320ff
41. 110.181ff,266ff; 108.51ff; 109
42. 110.181ff; 108.45ff,59ff
43. 87.77ff; 90.313ff
44. 87.78
45. 105.14
46. 105.14; cf. 9.76-77
47. 90.321
48. 87.89,96,99; 33.33ff; 105.15
49. 87.77
50. 162.298,n.50
51. 108.53
52. 108.53-54
53. 108.53
54. 108.60
55. 148.7ff; 7.93ff
56. 90.261-62
57. 90.319ff
58. 7.154ff; 168.462
59. 84.56ff
60. 168.462-63
61. 110.181ff; 108.45ff,59ff
62. 87.77ff; 90.313ff
63. 87.76
64. 30.81; 168.462
65. 133.95ff,112ff; 105.8ff
66. 7.182ff
67. 133.122ff
68. 30.47
69. 110.75-76,156,164ff,470ff;
     108.61ff; 109.333ff,351ff
70. 174
71. 4; 5; 7
72. 105; 106
73. 30
74. 148
75. 3–9
76. 84; 85
77. 86a–90
78. 64
79. 168
80. 171
81. 112
82. 105
83. 33
84. 62
85. 87; 90
86. 8.2
87. 179.38ff

88. 110.164ff;108.61ff
89. 105
90. 7
91. 84; 85
92. 87.79ff,103ff; 90
93. 122.382-83
94. 162.278-79
95. 162.278-79,n.3,279 n.4
96. 162.279-80; 13
97. 110.189ff,379ff; 109.335
98. 4
99. 87

I. Natural Living Conditions in Ancient Israel, pp. 58-64

1. 115.5-37; 113.15-24; 61.6-21
2. 132.1984ff
3. 113.18; 46.356ff
4. 60.12-13; 46.1-2
5. 46.33-34
6. 113.16
7. 113.16
8. 46.150ff
9. 46.42ff,147ff,219ff,356ff
10. 46.134ff
11. 113.187ff;52.82ff
12. 113.228; 57.101-2
13. 46.135
14. 125.122
15. 42.49ff; 38.78ff; 36; 83;
     102.23ff

II. Some Observations About the Texts, pp. 64-113

1. 113.198ff; 129.62ff; 157.525ff
2. 74.84ff
3. 159.66ff; 162.282-83
4. 132.2113-14
5. 124.220
6. 114.149-50
7. 159.126
8. 157; 159
9. 159; 157
10. 35
11. 84.42-43
12. 157; 159
13. 159.15-16
14. 159

15. 159.34ff
16. 157
17. 90.122
18. 157.551ff
19. 156.13-51
20. cf.161
21. cf. 163
22. 156.9
23. 156.13ff
24. 156.14ff
25. 159.74-75
26. 165.80ff,221ff; 141.153ff;
　　162.285-86
27. 4.48
28. 105.15
29. 141
30. 47.66
31. 74.106ff
32. 162.286ff
33. 92
34. 162.282-83
35. 162.286-87
36. 132.2113-14
37. 160.145-46
38. 160
39. 124; 183
40. 211
41. 160.89ff
42. 162.287
43. 160
44. 160-231-32, 239
45. 160.223ff
46. 63.II,556ff; 23a.II,273ff; 153;
　　160.150ff
47. 160.136-37, 151-52
48. 160.152
49. 160.152-53
50. 160.221
51. 15.439
52. 160.156
53. 190.45ff
54. 160.131,183
55. 160.136
56. 162.286ff

III. Thematic Aspects,
pp. 113-227

1. 143.§§10-13; 156.13ff
2. 165; 161

3. 2.I,125
4. 141.31ff
5. 142; 143.67ff
6. 49.119ff; 143.139ff
7. 141.51
8. 129.309ff; 63.I,234ff;
　　23a.I,432ff
9. 2.III,348ff,373ff
10. 23a.529-30
11. 132.1986
12. For evidence in ancient orien-
　　tal texts cf. 35; 83; 183; 147; 17;
　　143; 144; 165; 49
13. 76.13ff
14. 162.282, n.9
15. 165; 141.38ff
16. 141.37ff
17. 152.177ff
18. 141
19. 90.98ff
20. 90.103
21. 156.15ff
22. 155
23. 141.39-40
24. 1
25. 51.221
26. 18.59-64,143-48,288-91
27. 179.96-172
28. 160.175
29. 171.111
30. 67.110,116
31. 90.256
32. 67.110ff,117ff
33. 129.165-66,439-40,460ff;
　　130.357ff; 126.311ff; 127.255-
　　56; 131.189ff,378ff; 128.119ff
34. 183.89ff,798ff; 184.8ff,29ff
35. 141
36. 134.139
37. 5.42
38. 43.489
39. 129.165,439-40; 131.202,382-
　　83
40. 129.165,439; 130.360
41. 90.275ff
42. 127.257
43. 152.1ff; 63.I,229ff,II,966ff;
　　76.21ff; 23a.I,423ff; 160.182
44. 63.I,830
45. 131.298; cf.70.223; 90.105

46. 131.298
47. 160.223ff
48. 179.128
49. 131.75ff
50. 164
51. 131
52. 141.17-18
53. 183.89ff,798ff; 184.29ff; 182.96ff; cf. 162.282-83
54. 183.802; 159.66ff; 90.101
55. 67.124ff
56. 86a.595
57. 160.57,188ff
58. 141
59. 156.13-51
60. 131.189ff,205ff,208ff
61. 131
62. 183.24ff,798ff
63. 126.317; 131.389
64. 131.298
65. 162.288-89,293-94
66. 90.335
67. E.g., see 76.47-48
68. 76.21ff,29ff
69. 171.102
70. 171.102-3
71. 171.104ff
72. 120.47ff,58ff
73. 44
74. 152
75. 76
76. 76.47
77. 49a.205ff,210ff
78. 90.269,317-18ff
79. 90.256
80. 90.279; cf. 325
81. 90.322
82. 90.325-26
83. 90.270
84. 90.269
85. 126.311ff; 127.255ff; 128.119ff
86. 131
87. 131.75ff
88. cf. 90.96ff,268ff
89. 130.361; 90.129ff,280
90. 90.268ff, esp. 270
91. 131.75ff
92. 131.298
93. 131.67-68

94. 131.68
95. 120.33ff; 109.313ff; 110.316ff; 4.60ff; 85.22; 89.34; 90.20-6, 279
96. 90.308
97. 131.211ff; 90. e.g., 104ff
98. 126.317-18; 131.389
99. 117.20
100. 131.131ff
101. 131.145ff
102. 131.131ff
103. 131.131ff
104. 110
105. 108; 109
106. 90
107. 87
108. 4; 5; 7
109. 171.112ff
110. 87.74ff; 90.258
111. 96.15
112. 109.330ff; cf. 110.141ff
113. 87.78,97ff; 90.258-59
114. 109.305
115. 108.54
116. 72.122; cf. 90.104; 170.6
117. 170.6
118. 90.105
119. 131.400
120. 90.285
121. 131.94
122. In his 1974 lecture "Die Klage über das Erfahrungsdefizit in der Theologie als Frage nach ihrer Sache" (printed in his collection of essays *Wort und Glaube* III, 1975, pp. 3-28) and in his "Der Lebensbezug des Glaubens" (*Evang. Kommentare* 9, Stuttgart, 1976, pp. 517-22).
123. 5.105ff
124. 162.293
125. 131.205ff
126. 50
127. 90.261
128. 90.206,337; 86.60,64
129. 86.77
130. 141
131. 90.211
132. 143.67ff; 142

133. 143.74 ff
134. 126.313
135. 85; 90.94 ff
136. 93.101
137. 90.99-100
138. 14.103 ff,258 ff
139. 141
140. 141.32 ff
141. 126.311 ff; 130.360 ff
142. 90.213-14,276-77,282; 86
143. 131.204
144. 131.145
145. 129.439
146. 129.440
147. 126.318
148. 90-211-12
149. 148; 7.11 ff,93 ff
150. 159.85-86
151. 133
152. 145
153. 84
154. 160.152
155. 7; 3
156. 66
157. 186
158. 84
159. 3; cf. 64.144 ff
160. 168.462
161. 5.81 ff
162. 156
163. 113.229 ff,233 ff;
     52.103 ff,107 ff
164. 113.253 ff,261 ff;
     52.113 ff,117 ff
165. 113.286 ff,304 ff;52.126 ff
166. 113.312 ff; 51.144 ff
167. 113.322 ff; 51.146 ff
168. 113.343 ff,352 ff;
     52.151 ff,158 ff
169. 113.360 ff; 52.68 ff
170. 58.8 ff; 57.25-27
171. 34
172. For evidence cf. 24.359-60
173. 176; 146
174. 24.320 ff,331 ff
175. 176.181 ff; 131.190 ff
176. 131.292 ff; 26
177. 131.309 ff; 58.284 ff; 101; 107
178. 176
179. 118.296 ff,314 ff; but also

     176.9 ff
180. 161
181. 162-286 ff
182. 141.54 ff
183. 96; 97
184. 173.381 ff
185. 80.151 ff
186. 155.288-89; 60
187. 155.292-93; 60
188. 90.106-7
189. 63.I,527 ff; 23a.II,774 ff
190. 172.51 ff
191. 141; 164
192. 126.225 ff; 129.399 ff,414 ff;
     131.251 ff
193. For evidence cf. 24.269 ff;
     173.235 ff; 158.254 ff
194. 77
195. 131.267 ff,306 ff
196. 131.291; but also 75.61 ff
197. cf. 131.190 ff
198. 131.292 ff,306 ff; 75.64 ff
199. 131.304
200. 58.210 ff; 57.167-68; 26
201. 131.309 ff; 101; 107; 57.168 ff;
     97.288 ff
202. 158.205; 57.168 ff
203. 131.193-94,222 ff,316 ff; also
     176.289 ff; 57.168 ff
204. 57.170
205. 126.330
206. 96; 97
207. 96
208. 25.27 ff; 158.177 ff *et passim;*
     55.19 ff
209. 97.293-94
210. 154
211. 154
212. On these ideas cf. 24.244-45,
     218 ff; 173.381 ff; 166.10 ff;
     172.61 ff; 11
213. 97
214. 97
215. 96
216. 100; 97.302

B. The Natural World and Environment in the New Testament, pp. 229-231

1. 71.486 ff

2. 71.456

I. Some General Guidance About Textual Findings, pp. 232-258

1. 57.16ff; 95.107; 99.66
2. 53; 21.27ff
3. 99.67
4. 99.65ff
5. 141.159
6. 139.I,27ff; 20.108ff
7. 139.I,27ff; 20.108ff
8. 39.135-36
9. 189.82ff
10. 100; 188
11. On Matt. 6.25ff cf. 90.184-85, 197ff,302ff
12. 111.436-37
13. 98; 111.436
14. 20.120ff; 23.155ff
15. 20.62ff *et passim;* 90.286ff
16. 96.36ff; 97.304-5
17. 82.39
18. 20.58ff,82ff; 82.29ff
19. 23.13ff; 172.143-66
20. 81.§10
21. 82.249-50
22. 82.247ff
23. 27.361ff,372ff; 139.I,49ff; 82.256ff
24. 82.260-61
25. 82.253
26. 82.262
27. 82.269ff
28. 81.§9
29. 21
30. 82.121ff
31. 19.9ff; 22.93ff,119ff; 90.84ff
32. 21.131ff; 82.130ff
33. 21.131ff; 82.162ff
34. 21.145-65; 82.165-83
35. 21.151ff; 82.178ff
36. 21.225ff; 82.203ff
37. 21.184ff; 82.184ff
38. 150.128ff
39. 21.216ff
40. 21.222ff
41. 150; 21.212ff
42. 21.212

43. 21.214
44. 21.172ff
45. 73.116-17
46. 73
47. 167; 166
48. 21
49. 54
50. 150.127-28
51. 150.129
52. 150.130
53. 166; for another view cf. Vögtle 172
54. 54.249-50
55. 54.250
56. 53.250
57. 53.250
58. 73
59. 10
60. 123
61. 116
62. 116.143
63. 116.139-40
64. 116.263; 73.254-55
65. 116.263; 73.225; 48.140-41
66. 73.226
67. 116.266ff,268
68. 116.271ff
69. 116.265-66
70. 73
71. 167; 166
72. cf. 90.226ff
73. 140
74. 21.156; 135
75. 151.19ff
76. 28
77. 151.50ff,184ff,192ff
78. 151.100ff
79. 151.63
80. 151.148-49; on 84.46
81. 56; 176.181ff
82. 119.406ff
83. 172.232ff
84. 172.94ff
85. 81.§30
86. 78.VI,927ff; 172.133
87. 172.122ff
88. 172.132
89. 81.§34; 94
90. 172.112ff
91. 172.118

Abbreviations

Used in the bibliography. The place of publication of periodicals *only* is given, since the place of publication of series appears after individual titles.

ATD   *Das Alte Testament Deutsch*
BBB   *Bonner biblische Beiträge*
BEvTh   *Beiträge zur evangelische Theologie*, Munich
BK   *Biblischer Kommentar*
BSt   *Biblische Studien*
BWANT   *Beiträge zur Wissenschaft von Alten und Neuen Testaments*
BZAW   *Beiheft zur Zeitschrift für die altestamentliche Wissenschaft*

DtPfBl	*Deutsches Pfarrersblatt*
dtv	*Deutscher Taschenbuch Verlag*
epd	*Evangelischer Pressedienst*
EvTh	*Evangelische Theologie*, Munich
FRLANT	*Forschungen zur Religion und Literatur des Alten und Neuen Testaments*
HAT	*Handbuch zum Alten Testament*
HNT	*Handbuch zum Neuen Testament*
KAT	*Kommentar zum Alten Testament*
KuD	*Kerygma und Dogma*, Göttingen
NTD	*Das Neue Testament Deutsch*
StZt	*Stimmen der Zeit*, Freiburg
THAT	*Theologisches Handwörterbuch zum Alten Testament*
ThB	*Theologische Bücherei*
ThEh	*Theologische Existenz heute*, Munich
ThSt	*Theologische Studien*, Zürich
ThZ	*Theologische Zeitschrift*, Basel
TThZ	*Trierer Theologische Zeitschrift*, Trier
TU	*Texte und Untersuchungen zur Geschichte der altchristlichen Literatur*
VF	*Verkündigung und Forschung*, Munich
VTS	*Supplements to Vetus Testamentum*, Leyden
WMANT	*Wissenschaftliche Monographien zum Alten und Neuen Testaments*, Neukirchen-Vluyn
WUNT	*Wissenschaftliche Untersuchungen zum Neuen Testament*
ZAW	*Zeitschrift für die altestamentliche Wissenschaft*, Berlin
ZThK	*Zeitschrift für Theologie und Kirche*, Tübingen

Bibliography

The following books are necessarily only a selection of those which might be cited on this far-reaching subject. They are either works that are easily available and designed for the general reader, or special studies that have a direct bearing on the present book's argument.

Biblical quotations in the text are taken from the Revised Standard Version. For late Israelite sources, see the translations in Charles, *Apocrypha and Pseudepigrapha of the Old Testament*, cited under 29 below.

1. Albertz, R., *Weltschöpfung und Menschenschöpfung*, Calwer Theologische Monographien A 3, Stuttgart, 1974.

2. Alt, A., *Kleine Schriften zur Geschichte des Volkes Israel*, I-III, Munich, 1953/59.

3. Altner, G., "Ist die Ausbeutung der Natur im christlichen Denken begründet?" *Umweltstrategie*[cf. 40 below], pp. 33-47.

4. ———. "Biologie und Schöpfung—die Erfahrung des Lebendigen durch die moderne Biologie," epd-Dokumentation Nr. 31/75, Frankfurt, 1975, pp. 39-56.

5. ———. *Zwischen Natur und Menschengeschichte. Anthropologische, biologische, ethische Perspektiven für eine neue Schöpfungstheologie*, Munich, 1975.

6. ———. "Ökologie und die Sonderstellung des Menschen," *Überlebensfragen* 2, ed. A. M. K. Müller, *et al.*, Stuttgart, 1974, pp. 127-35.

7. ———. *Schöpfung am Abgrund*, Neukirchen-Vluyn, 1974.

8. ———. "Vorwort zum Themaheft 'Zur Theologie der Natur,'" EvTh 37, 1977, pp. 1-2.

9. ———. "Die Trennung der Liebenden—Variationen über den Ursprung des Lebens," EvTh 37, 1977, pp. 69-83.

10. Balz, H. R., *Heilsvertrauen und Welterfahrung. Strukturen der paulinischen Eschatologie nach Römer 8. 18-39*, Munich, 1971.

11. Barth, C., *Diesseits und Jenseits im Glauben des späten Israel*, Stuttgarter Bibel-Studien 72, Stuttgart, 1974.

12. ———. *Die Errettung vom Tode in den individuellen Klage- und Dankliedern des Alten Testaments*, Zollikon, 1947.

13. Barth, H., and Steck, O. H., *Exegese des Alten Testaments. Leitfaden der Methodik*, Neukirchen, [8]1978.

14. Barth, K., *Die Kirchliche Dogmatik* III/1, Zollikon, 1957, [4]1970. Eng. tr., *Church Dogmatics* (The Doctrine of Creation), Edinburgh, 1969, by J. W. Edwards, O. Bussey, and H. Knight.

15. Baumgartner, W., *Hebräisches und Aramäisches Lexikon zum Alten Testament*, I-II, Leyden, 1967/74.
16. Becker, J., *Auferstehung der Toten im Urchristentum*, Stuttgarter Bibel-Studien 82, Stuttgart, 1976.
17. Beyerlin, W., ed., *Religionsgeschichtliches Textbuch zum Alten Testament*, ATD Erg. Reihe 1, Göttingen, 1975.
18. Bloch, E., *Atheismus im Christentum. Zur Religion des Exodus und des Reichs*, Frankfurt, 1968. Eng. tr., *Atheism in Christianity*, New York, 1972, by J. T. Swann.
19. Bornkamm, G., *Das Ende des Gesetzes. Paulus-Studien*, Munich, 1952, [5]1966. Eng. tr.. *Early Christian Experience*, London, New York, 1969, by P. L. Hammer (tr. is a selection from *Das Ende des Gesetzes* and *Studien zu Antike* [cf. 22 below].
20. ———. *Jesus von Nazareth*, Stuttgart, 1956, [10]1975. Eng. tr., *Jesus of Nazareth*, London, New York, 1960, by I. and T. McLuskey, with J. M. Robinson.
21. ———. *Paulus*, Stuttgart, 1969, [3]1976. Eng. tr., *Paul*, New York, London, 1971, by D. M. G. Stalker.
22. ———. *Studien zu Antike und Urchristentum*, Munich, 1959, [3]1970. Eng. tr., *Early Christian Experience*, London, New York, 1969, by P. L. Hammer (tr. is a selection from *Das Ende des Gesetzes* [cf. 19 above] and *Studien zu Antike*).
23. Bornkamm, G., Barth, G., and Held, H. J., *Überlieferung und Auslegung im Matthäusevangelium*, WMANT 1, Neukirchen-Vluyn, 1960, [7]1975. Eng. tr., *Tradition and Interpretation in Matthew*, London, Philadelphia, 1963, by P. Scott.
23a. Botterweck, G. J., and Ringgren, H. (ed.), *Theologisches Wörterbuch zum Alten Testament*, Stuttgart, vol. I, 1973; vol. II, 1977 (ThWAT).
24. Bousset, W., and Gressmann, H., *Die Religion des Judentums im spät-hellenistischen Zeitalter*, HNT 21, Tübingen, 1903, [3]1926 (rev. Gressmann), [4]1966.
25. Brandenburger, E., *Adam und Christus. Exegetisch-eligionsgeschichtliche Untersuchung zu Röm. 5. 12-21 (1 Kor. 15)*, WMANT 7, Neukirchen-Vluyn, 1962.
26. Braun, R., *Kohelet und die frühhellenistische Popularphilosophie*, BZAW 130, Berlin, New York, 1973.

27. Bultmann, R., *Theologie des Neuen Testaments*, Tübingen, 1952, ⁷1977. Eng. tr., *Theology of the New Testament*, London, New York, 1952, by K. Grobel.
28. Burger, C., *Schöpfung und Versöhnung. Studien zum liturgischen Gut im Kolosser—und Epheserbrief*, WMANT 46, Neukirchen-Vluyn, 1975.
29. Charles, R. H., *Apocrypha und Pseudipigrapha of the Old Testament in English*, I-II, Oxford, 1963.
30. Cobb, J. B., *Is It Too Late?* Beverly Hills, 1972.
31. Dahmen, F. W., "Das ökologische System," *Umweltstrategie* [cf. 40 below], pp. 111-36.
32. Delling, G. and Schmidt, W. H., *Wörterbuch zur Bibel*, Hamburg, 1971.
33. Dembowski, H., "Ansatz und Umrisse einer Theologie der Natur," EvTh 37, 1977, pp. 33-49.
34. Diepold, P., *Israels Land*, BWANT 95, Stuttgart, 1972.
35. Dietrich, W., " 'Wo ist dein Bruder?' Zu Tradition und Intention von Genesis 4," *Beiträge zur Alttestamentliche Theologie (Festschrift W. Zimmerli)*, ed. H. Donner *et al.*, Gottingen, 1977, pp. 94-111.
36. van Dijk, J., "Sumerische Religion," *Handbuch der Religionsgeschichte*, ed. J. P. Asmussen, and J. Laessoe, I, Göttingen, 1971, pp. 431-96.
37. Dürr, L., *Die Wertung des Lebens im Alten Testament und im antiken Orient*, Kirchhain, 1926.
38. Edzard, D. O., "Die Frühdynastische Zeit," *Fischer-Weltgeschichte. Die Altorientalischen Reiche* I, Frankfurt, 1965, pp. 57-90.
39. Egger, K., "Landwirtschaft und Überlebenskrise," *Überlebensfragen* 2 [cf. 6 above], pp. 100-126.
40. Eichholz, G., *Auslegung der Bergpredigt*, BSt 46, Neukirchen-Vluyn, 1965.
41. Engelhardt, H. D., ed., *Umweltstrategie. Materialien und Analysen zu einer Umweltethik der Industriegesellschaft*, Gütersloh, 1975; intro. (pp. 7-12) by H. D. Engelhardt, K. E. Wenke, H. Westmüller, and H. Zillessen.
42. Falkenstein, A., "Die Ur- und Frühgeschichte des Alten Vorderasien," *Fischer Weltgeschichte. Die Altorientalischen Reiche* I, Frankfurt, 1965, pp. 13-56.
43. Fohrer, G., *Das Buch Hiob*, KAT XVI, Gütersloh, 1963.

44. Frankfort, H. and H. A., Wilson, J. A., and Jacobsen, T., *The Intellectual Adventure of Ancient Man*, Chicago, 1946.

45. Friedrich, G., *Utopie und Reich Gottes, Zur Motivation politischen Verhaltens*, Göttingen, 1974.

46. Galling, K., ed., *Biblisches Reallexikon*, HAT 1, Tübingen, 1937, ²1977.

47. Gemser, B., *Sprüche Salomos*, HAT 16, Tübingen, 1937, ²1963.

48. Gerstenberger, E. and Schrage, W., *Leiden*, Stuttgart, 1977. Eng. tr., Nashville, 1979, by J. Steely.

49. Gese, H., "Die Religionen Altsyriens," *Die Religionen der Menschheit*, vol. 10, 2, Stuttgart, Berlin, Cologne, Mainz, 1970, pp. 3-232.

49a. ———. *Zur Biblischen Theologie. Alttestamentliche Vorträge*, BEvTh 78, Munich, 1977.

50. Goeke, H., *Die Anthropologie der individuellen Klagelieder*, Bibel und Leben 14, Dusseldorf, 1973, pp. 13-29, 112-37.

51. Gollwitzer, H., *Krummes Holz-aufrechter Gang. Zur Frage nach dem Sinn des Lebens*, Munich, 1970, ⁷1976.

52. Gunneweg, A. H. J., *Geschichte Israels bis Bar Kochba*, Stuttgart, Berlin, Cologne, Mainz, 1972, ²1976.

53. Hahn, F., *Das Verständnis der Mission im Neuen Testament*, WMANT 13, Neukirchen-Vluyn, 1963. Eng. tr., *Mission in the New Testament*, London, New York, 1952, by K. Grobel.

54. " 'Siehe, jetzt ist der Tag des Heils.' Neuschöpfung und Versöhnung nach 2 Korinther 5.14-6.2," EvTh 33, 1973, pp. 244-53.

55. Harnisch, W., *Verhängnis und Veheissung der Geschichte. Untersuchungen zum Zeit- und Geschichtsverständnis im 4 Buch Esra und in der syr. Baruchapokalypse*, FRLANT 97, Göttingen, 1969.

56. Hegermann, H., *Die Vorstellung vom Schöpfungsmittler im hellenistischen Judentum und Urchristentum*, TU 82, Berlin, 1961.

57. Hengel, M., *Juden, Griechen und Barbaren. Aspekte der Hellenisierung des Judentums in vorchristlicher Zeit*, Stuttgarter Bibel-Studien 76, Stuttgart, 1976.

58. ———. *Judentum und Hellenismus. Studien zu ihrer Begegnung unter besonderer Berücksichtigung Palästinas bis zur Mitte des 2. Jahrhundert v. Chr.*, WUNT 10,

Tübingen, 1969, ²1973. Eng. tr., *Judaism and Hellenism*, London, Philadelphia, 1974, by J. Bowden.

59. *Herder Lexikon Umwelt*, Freiburg, ³1976.

60. Hermisson, H. J., "Diskussionsworte bei Deuterojesaja," EvTh 31, 1971, pp. 665-80.

61. Hilgemann, W., and Kettermann, G., *dtv-Perthes-Weltatlas*, I: *Naher Osten*, Munich, Darmstadt, 1973.

62. Hübner, J., "Schöpfungsglaube und Theologie der Natur," EvTh 37, 1977, pp. 49-68.

63. Jenni, E., ed., *Theologisches Handwörterbuch zum Alten Testament*, vol. I, Munich, 1971, vol. II, Munich 1976 (THAT).

64. Jensen O., *Unter dem Zwang des Wachstums. Ökologie und Religion*, Munich, 1977.

65. Jeremias, G., *Der Lehrer der Gerechtigkeit, Studien zur Umwelt des Neuen Testaments* 2, Göttingen, 1963.

66. Jobling, D. K., "*And have dominion . . .*" *The Interpretation of OT Texts concerning man's rule over the creation from 200 B.C. to the time of the Council of Nicea*, dissertation, Union Theol. Seminary, New York, 1971.

67. Joest, W., *Gott will zum Menschen kommen. Gesammelte Aufsätze*, Göttingen, 1977.

68. Jüngel, E., *Gott Als Geheimnis der Welt*, Tübingen, 1977, ²1977.

69. ———. *Paulus und Jesus*, Tübingen, 1962, ⁴1972.

70. ———. *Unterwegs zur Sache. Theologische Bemerkungen*, BEvTh 61, Munich, 1972.

71. ———. "Gelegentliche Thesen zum Problem der natürlichen Theologie," EvTh 37, 1977, pp. 485-88.

72. ———. "Metaphorische Wahrheit. Erwägungen zur theologischen Relevanz der Metapher als Beitrag zur Hermeneutik einer narrativen Theologie," *Metapher*, ed. P. Ricoeur and E. Jüngel, EvTh Sonderheft, Munich, 1974, pp. 71-122.

73. Käsemann, E., *An die Römer*, HNT 8a, Tübingen, 1973, ³1974. Eng. tr., *Commentary on Romans*, Grand Rapids, 1978.

74. Kaiser, O., *Einleitung in das Alte Testament*, Gütersloh, 1969, ³1975. Eng. tr., *Introduction to the Old Testament*, Minneapolis, 1975, by J. Sturdy.

75. Kaiser, O., and Lohse, E., *Tod und Leben*, Stuttgart, 1977.

76. Keel, O., *Die Welt der altorientalischen Bildsymbolik und das Alte Testament,* Zürich, Neukirchen, 1972, ²1977.

77. Kellermann, U., "Überwindung des Todesgeschicks in der altestamentlichen Frömmigkeit vor und neben dem Auferstehungsglauben," ZThK 73, 1976, pp. 259-82.

78. Kittel, G., and Friedrich, G., ed., *Theologisches Wörterbuch zum Neuen Testament,* vols. I-IX, Stuttgart, 1933-73.

79. Koch, T., Selbstregulation des Politischen? Von der Notwendigkeit kollektiver Handlungsziele, StZt 194, 1976, pp. 105-16.

80. Kraus, H. J., *Biblisch-theologische Aufsätze,* Neukirchen-Vluyn, 1972.

81. Kümmel, W. G., *Einleitung in das Neue Testament,* Leipzig 1921, 17th ed., Heidelberg, 1973 (up to 14th ed. under Feine, Paul).

82. ———. *Die Theologie des Neuen Testaments nach seinen Hauptzeugen. Jesus, Paulus, Johannes,* NTD Erg. Reihe 3, Göttingen, 1969, ³1976. Eng. tr., *The Theology of the New Testament According to Its Major Witnesses: Jesus—Paul—John,* Nashville, 1973, by J. E. Steely.

83. Laessoe, J., "Babylonische und assyrische Religion," *Handbuch der Religionsgeschichte* [cf. 35, above], pp. 497-525.

84. Liedke, G., "Von der Ausbeutung zur Kooperation. Theologisch-philosophische Überlegungen zum Problem des Umweltschutzes," in E. von Weizsäcker, *Humanökologie und Umweltschutz, Studien zur Friedensforschung* 8, Stuttgart, Munich, 1972, pp. 36-65.

85. ———. "Schöpfung und Erfahrung. Zum interdisziplinären Beitrag der neueren Arbeit am Alten Testament," epd-Dokumentation Nr. 31/75, Frankfurt, 1975, pp. 8-24.

86. Link, C., "Das Bilderverbot als Kriterium theologischen Redens von Gott," ZThK 74, 1977, pp. 58-85.

86a. ———. "Die Erfahrung der Schöpfung. Zum Gespräch zwischen Theologie und Naturwissenschaft," Evangelische Kommentare 8, Stuttgart, 1975, pp. 593-96.

87. ———. "Die Erfahrung der Welt als Schöpfung," *Anthropologie als Thema psychosomatischer Medizin und Theologie,* ed. M. von Rad, Stuttgart, Berlin, Cologne, Mainz, 1974, pp. 73-121.

88. ———. "Gott-verborgen in der Welt," *Naturwissenschaft*

und Theologie, ed. H. Aichelin and G. Liedke, Neukirchen-
Vluyn, 1974, 1975, pp. 168-77.

89. ———. "Schöpfung und Erfahrung. Zum Gespräch
zwischen Theologie und Naturwissenschaft," epd-
Dokumentation Nr. 31/75, Frankfurt, 1975, pp. 25-38.

90. ———. *Die Welt als Gleichnis. Studien zum Problem der
natürlichen Theologie,* BEvTh 73, 1976.

91. Löwith, K., *Meaning in History,* Chicago, 1949, ⁶1973.

92. Lohfink, N., "Die Priesterschrift und die Geschichte,"
Congress Volume Göttingen 1977, VTS 29, 1978, pp. 189-225.

93. ———. *Das Siegeslied am Schilfmeer,* Frankfurt, 1965.

94. Lohse, E., *Die Offenbarung des Johannes,* NTD 11,
Göttingen, 1924, ¹¹1976.

95. ———. *Umwelt des Neuen Testaments,* NTD, Erg. Reihe 1,
Göttingen, 1971, ²1974. Eng. Tr., *The New Testament
Environment,* Nashville, 1976, by J. E. Steely.

96. Luck U., *Welterfahrung und Glaube als Grundproblem
biblischer Theologie,* ThEh 191, Munich, 1976.

97. ———. "Das Weltverständnis in der jüdischen Apokalyptik,
dargestellt am äthiopischen Henoch und am 4 Esra," ZThK
73, 1976, pp. 283-305.

98. D. Lührmann, "Liebet eure Feinde (Lk 6.27-36/Mt
5.39-48)," ZThK 69, 1972, pp. 412-38.

99. ———. "Wo man nicht mehr Sklave oder Freier ist.
Überlegungen zur Struktur frühchristlicher Gemeinden,"
WuD NF 13, 1975, pp. 53-83.

100. ———. "Der Verweis auf die Erfahrung und die Frage nach
der Gerechtigkeit," *Jesus Christus in Historie und Theologie. Festschrift H. Conzelmann,* ed. G. Strecker, Tübingen,
1975, pp. 185-96.

101. Marböck, J., *Weisheit im Wandel,* 888 37, Bohn, 1971.

102. Mead, M. and Fairservis, W., "Kulturelle Verhaltensweisen
und die Umwelt des Menschen," *Umweltstrategie* [cf. 40
above], pp. 15-32.

103. Merk, O., *Handeln aus Glauben. Die Motivierung der
paulinischen Ethik,* Marburg, 1968.

104. Metzger, M., *Grundriss der Geschichte Israels,* Neukirchen-Vluyn, 1963, ⁴1977.

105. Meyer-Abich, K. M., "Zum Begriff einer Praktischen
Theologie der Natur," EvTh 37, 1977, pp. 3-20.

106. ———."Das Harren der Natur. Eine Praktische Theologie

der Natur als Aufgabe," *Evangelische Kommentare* 8, Stuttgart, 1975, pp. 487-89.

107. Middendorp, T., *Die Stellung Jesu ben Siras zwischen Judentum und Hellenismus*, Leyden, Brill, 1973.

108. Müller, A. M. K., "Der Mensch an der Zeitmauer des Überlebens," *Überlebensfragen* 2 [cf. 6 above], 1974, pp. 34-66.

109. ———. "Naturgesetz, Wirklichkeit, Zeitlichkeit," *Offene Systeme* I, ed. E. von Weizsäcker, Stuttgart, 1974, pp. 303-57.

110. ———. *Die Präparierte Zeit*, Stuttgart, 1972, ²1973.

111. Müller, U. B., "Vision und Botschaft. Erwägungen zur prophetischen Struktur der Verkündigung Jesu," ZThK 74, 1977, pp. 416-48.

112. Noller, G., "Die ökologische Herausforderung an die Theologie," EvTh 34, 1974, pp. 586-601.

113. Noth, M., *Geschichte Israels*, Göttingen, 1950, ⁷1969. Eng. tr., *History of Israel*, London, 1958, by S. Goodman; ²1960, tr., rev. P. R. Ackroyd.

114. ———. *Das vierte Buch Mose (Numeri)*, ATD 7, Göttingen, 1966, ²1973. Eng. tr., *Numbers. A Commentary*, London, 1968, by J. D. Martin.

115. ———. *Die Welt des Alten Testaments*, Berlin, 1940, ⁴1962. Eng. tr., *The Old Testament World*, London, 1966, by V. I. Gruhn.

116. Osten-Sacken, P. von der, *Römer 8 als Beispiel paulinischer Soteriologie*, FRLANT 112, Göttingen, 1975.

117. Pannenberg, W., *Glaube und Wirklichkeit. Kleine Beiträge zum christlichen Denken*, Munich, 1975. Eng. tr., *Faith and Reality*, Philadelphia, 1977, by J. Maxwell.

118. ———. *Grundfragen Systematischer Theologie*, Göttingen, 1967, ²1971. Eng. tr., *Basic Questions in Theology*, London, Philadelphia, 1970, by G. H. Kehm.

119. ———. *Grundzüge der Christologie*, Gütersloh, 1964, ⁵1976. Eng. tr., *Jesus—God and Man*, London, Philadelphia, 1968, ²1977, by L. L. Wilkins and D. A. Priebe.

120. ———. "Kontingenz und Naturgesetz," in A. M. K. Müller and W. Pannenberg, *Erwägungen zu einer Theologie der Natur*, Gütersloh, 1970, pp. 33-80.

121. ———. *Theology and the Kingdom of God*, Philadelphia, 1969.

154. Steck, O. H., "Die Aufnahme von Genesis 1 in Jubiläen 2 und 4. Esra 6," *Journal for the Study of Judaism* 8, Leyden, 1977, pp. 154-82.

155. ————. "Deuterojesaja als theologischer Denker," KuD 15, 1969, pp. 280-93.

156. ————. *Friedensvorstellungen im alten Jerusalem. Psalmen—Jesaja—Deuterojesaja*, ThSt (B) 111, Zürich, 1972.

157. ————. "Genesis 12:1-3 und die Urgeschichte des Yahwisten," *Probleme biblischer Theologie. Festschrift G. von Rad*, ed. H. W. Wolff, Munich, 1971.

158. ————. *Israel und das gewaltsame Geschick der Propheten*, WMANT 23, Neukirchen-Vluyn, 1967.

159. ————. *Die Paradieserzählung. Eine Auslegung von Genesis 2:4b–3:24*, BSt 60, Neukirchen-Vluyn, 1970.

160. ————. *Der Schöpfungsbericht der Priesterschrift*, FRLANT 115, Göttingen, 1975.

161. ————. "Strömungen theologischer Tradition im Alten Israel," *Zu Tradition und Theologie im Alten Testament*, Biblisch-Theologische Studien 2, Neukirchen-Vluyn, 1978.

162. ————. "Zwanzig Thesen als altestamentlicher Beitrag zum Thema: 'Die jüdisch-christliche Lehre von der Schöpfung in Beziehung zu Wissenschaft und Technik,' " KuD 23, 1977, pp. 277-99.

163. ————. "Der Wein unter den Schöpfungsgaben. Überlegungen zu Psalm 104," TThZ 87, 1978, pp. 173-91.

164. Stock, K., "Creatio nova—creatio ex nihilo. Bemerkungen zum Problem einer eschatologischen Schöpfungslehre," EvTh 36, 1976, pp. 202-16.

165. Stolz, F., *Strukturen und Figuren im Kult von Jerusalem*, BZAW 118, Berlin, 1970.

166. Stuhlmacher, P., "Erwägungen zum ontologischen Charakter der καινη κτισις bei Paulus," EvTh 27, 1967, pp. 1-35.

167. ————. *Gottes Gerechtigkeit bei Paulus*, FRLANT, Göttingen, 1965, ²1966.

168. Teutsch, G. M., "Mitgeschöpf oder Ausbeuter? Eine Frage nach der chrislichen Bestimmung des Menschen in der Natur," DtPfrBl 77, 1977, pp. 461-63.

169. Thielicke, H., *Der Christ im Ernstfall. Das kleine Buch der Hoffnung*, Freiburg, 1977.

170. Track, J., "Erfahrung Gottes—Versuch einer Annäherung," KuD 22, 1976, pp. 1-21.
171. ————. "Naturwissenschaften und Theologie. Erwägungen zu einem interdisziplinären Dialog," KuD 21, 1975, pp. 99-119.
172. Vögtle, A., *Das Neue Testament und die Zukunft des Kosmos*, Düsseldorf, 1970.
173. Volz, P., *Die Eschatologie der jüdischen Gemeinde im neutestamentliche Zeitalter*, Tübingen, 1934.
174. Wahlert, G. von, "Biologie als Dienst am Menschen. Ansätze für eine anthropologische Grundlegung der Humanökologie—eine Problemanzeige," *Studien zur Friedensforschung* 8 [see 84 above], pp. 66-79.
175. Walther, C., "Die Welt des Menschen verantworten. Bemerkungen zum Theorie-Praxis-Problem in der Theologie," *Humane Gesellschaft. Beiträge zu ihrer sozialen Gestaltung*, ed. T. Rendtorff and A. Rich, Zürich, 1970, pp. 75-90.
176. Weiss, H. -F., *Untersuchungen zur Kosmologie des hellenistischen und palästinischen Judentums*, TU 97, Berlin, 1966.
177. Weizsäcker, C. F. von, *Die Einheit der Natur. Studien*, Munich, 1971, dtv 4155, Munich, 1974.
178. ————. *Die Geschichte der Natur*, Stuttgart, 1948, ²1954.
179. ————. *Die Tragweite der Wissenschaft*, vol. 1: *Schöpfung und Weltentstehung. Die Geschichte zweier Begriffe*, Stuttgart, 1964, ⁵1976.
180. ————. *Wege in der Gefahr. Eine Studie über Wirtschaft, Gesellschaft und Kriegsverhütung*, Munich, Vienna, 1976.
181. Wenke, K. E., "Wirtschaftswachstum und Umweltkrise," *Umweltstrategie* [cf. 40 above], pp. 61-107.
182. Westermann, C., *Forschung am Alten Testament*, vol. II, ed. R. Albertz and E. Ruprecht, ThB 55, Munich, 1974.
183. ————. *Genesis 1-11*, BK I/1, Darmstadt, 1972, ²1976.
184. ————. *Schöpfung, Themen der Theologie*, vol. 12, Stuttgart, 1971. Eng. tr., *Creation*, Philadelphia, 1974, by J. J. Scullion.
185. Wilckens, U., *Das Neue Testament übersetzt und Kommentiert*, Hamburg, 1970, ⁴1974.
186. Yegerlehner, D. A., "*Be fruitful and multiply and fill the*

earth." *A history of the interpretation of Gen. 1:28 and related texts in selected periods,* dissertation, Boston, 1975.

187. Zahrnt, H., "Religiöse Aspekte gegenwärtiger Welt- und Lebenserfahrung," ZThK 71, 1974, pp. 94-122.

188. Zeller, D., "Weisheitliche Überlieferung in der Predigt Jesu," *Religiöse Grunderfahrungen. Quellen und Gestalten,* ed. W. Strolz, Freiburg, 1977, pp. 94-111.

189. ———. *Die weisheitlichen Mahnsprüche bei den Synoptikern, Forschung zur Bibel* 17, Stuttgart, 1977.

190. Zimmerli, W., *Die Weltlichkeit des Alten Testaments,* Göttingen, 1971. Eng. tr., *The Old Testament and the World,* Atlanta, 1976, by J. J. Scullion.

K. Lehmann's important essay, "Kreatürlichkeit des Menschen als Veranwortung für die Erde," *Internationale Katholische Zeitschrift "Communio,"* 7, 1978, pp. 38-54, appeared after the manuscript of the present book had been completed. I should like to dra͞   ͤnd essay͞